SR-71
REVEALED
THE INSIDE STORY

Best wishes!

Rich Graham

Richard H. Graham

ZENITH
PRESS

First published in 1996 by Zenith Press, an imprint of MBI Publishing Company, 400 First Avenue North, Suite 300, Minneapolis, MN 55401 USA

Zenith Press titles are also available at discounts in bulk quantity for industrial or sales-promotional use. For details write to Special Sales Manager at MBI Publishing Company, 400 First Avenue North, Suite 300, Minneapolis, MN 55401 USA.

To find out more about our books, join us online at www.zenithpress.com.

Library of Congress Cataloging-in-Publication Data
Graham, Richard H.
      SR-71 revealed : the untold story/ Richard H. Graham.
            p. cm.
      Includes index.
      ISBN-13: 978-0-7603-0122-7
      1. SR-71 (Jet reconnaissance plane)—History. I. Title.
UG1242.R4G73   1996
358.4'583'0973—dc20   96-7242

On the front cover: Kadena Air Base, Okinawa, Japan, August of 1983, Les Dyer and Denny Whalen wait for light signals to take the runway. Having the ocean so close to the field allowed our supersonic decel to be a continuous descent from 80,000 feet to landing. Often, the main gear struts were so hot after landing you couldn't touch them in the hangar. *Les Dyer*

On the back cover: The author, Colonel Richard H. Graham, USAF (Ret)

Printed in the United States of America

CONTENTS

FOREWORD

When I arrived at Beale Air Force Base in August 1974, I had no idea how this assignment would impact my life. What I did know was that I was going to have the opportunity to fly the highest-flying, fastest jet aircraft in the world and join a team whose mission had visibility at the highest levels of our government. At that time I could not begin to appreciate the advanced technology that Kelly Johnson and the Skunk Works had blended together to provide the performance capabilities that would allow two men to fly at over three times the speed of sound and above 80,000 feet, in areas of the world that we euphemistically called "denied areas."

Likewise, there was no way I could anticipate the close bonds that existed within the SR-71 crew force and how several of those intrepid aviators would become lifelong friends, participants in a great adventure, and members of a fraternity unlike any that I had known existed. One of those was Joseph T. "JT" Vida. He would become my best friend, in fact more like a brother. As a formed crew in the SR-71, we shared many of the experiences that the reader will find in this book. It is a fitting tribute that this book is dedicated to his memory. JT's heart was broken when the SR-71 aircraft was retired, well before its time, and he would be very excited that Rich Graham had decided to tell the "Habu" story.

Rich Graham is eminently well qualified to author a book on the subject of the SR-71 program. He has the insight of a pilot who has flown the aircraft in all the areas of the world that the "Habu" ranged. He has occupied leadership positions in the program, ensuring that the SR-71 and the 9th Strategic Reconnaissance Wing remained the premier operational organization in the Air Force while under what could be only be described as intense "friendly fire." His toils in the halls of the Pentagon give his descriptions of the budget battles concerning the demise of the SR-71 the credibility of one who has been there.

This is Rich's story. It is about striving to maintain a tradition and reputation built by those who had gone before in "the program." It is about a truly unique group of aviators and support personnel who had an opportunity to fly and work on the finest aircraft the world has ever seen and, at the same time, participate in the most challenging missions our national leadership directed. These missions were to have significant ramifications around the globe.

When I left the SR-71 crew force, with 966 hours in the "Habu," the high-time pilot on active duty, several people asked me if I was sorry to leave before reaching the 1,000 hour mark, a milestone that only one pilot before me had reached. My answer was simply, "I'm glad to have gotten 966." Rich Graham and JT Vida understood that. JT ended his SR-71 career with almost 1,400 hours, the most flying time in the aircraft of all crew members. I know he would agree with me, and it is my hope the reader will understand, when I say we were very lucky to be Habus.

Colonel Tom Alison, USAF (Ret)
Curator, National Air and Space Museum
Smithsonian Institution
Washington, D.C.

ACKNOWLEDGMENTS

Years ago I began recording my fond memories as an SR-71 crew member, never anticipating they would one day be turned into a book. I sat at my computer day and night, reminiscing while I documented our lives as Habus. Many of the stories brought a smile to my face while the latter days of the SR-71 program stirred up somber and sad emotions. Over the years I was encouraged by many other Habus to write this book.

I would like to acknowledge the efforts of many friends and Habus whose contributions to this book enriched each page. It's their stories, tales, and folklore that give this book life and make it very unique. Many of them read early editions of my manuscript and provided me with feedback, insuring a highly accurate accounting. I am deeply indebted to the following Habus: Tom Alison, Pat Bledsoe, Bill Burke, Buz Carpenter, Al Cirino, Rod Dyckman, Les Dyer, Steve Grzebiniak, Pat Halloran, Roger Jacks, Joe Kinego, Phil Loignon, John Manzi, Joe Mathews, Barry MacKean, Jay Murphy, Bill Orcutt, Curt Osterheld, Terry Pappas, Geno Quist, Randy Shelhorse, Lee Shelton, Bernie Smith, Mike Smith, Doug Soifer, Frank Stampf, and B.C. Thomas. Without their first hand accounting as SR-71 crew members, the book would be dull and lifeless.

I have to specially thank my former RSO, Don Emmons, for helping me remember some of the experiences I had almost forgotten. He kept me straight while we flew the SR-71, and kept me on course while writing this book. When I asked Tom Alison if he would honor the book with a foreword he didn't hesitate for a second, and I owe him a debt of gratitude. Some of the more technical aspects of the SR-71's recording systems were explained to me by former "Tech Rep", Tom Brown, helping me present them simplistically to the reader. Mr. A. J. "Arnie" Gunderson of Pratt and Whitney, better known as "Mr. J-58" among the crews, was instrumental in helping me with specifics of the SR-71's engine. Beale's one and only expert in pressure suit operations and high altitude physiology, Mr. Tom Bowen, aided me considerably in his area of expertise.

For reference material, aviation writer Paul Crickmore, was invaluable for letting me use his well researched and documented data. I have to give a special thanks to Bob Gillon, a good friend and ex-Marine fighter pilot, for his candid critique of my manuscript. His unbiased comments gave me a new focus and direction for writing this book.

After the book was written, I began searching for appropriate pictures, a formidable task itself. Surprisingly, very few Habus took pictures of the aircraft while they were in the program. There were so many excellent photographs of the SR-71 taken by professional photographers that we as crew members never took time to take our own pictures. I am deeply indebted to Gary Jones, who provided me with an unlimited number of photographs he had taken of the SR-71 and crews at RAF Mildenhall. Great appreciation to Lockheed's Denny Lombard, who gave me access to the Skunk Works' entire photographic collection of the Blackbird family of aircraft.

No book would be complete without thanking the one person who knows the book as well as I do, my wife Pat. She has read six complete versions of the book and labored through every one of them with her detailed editing and literary advice. My editor, Michael Haenggi, deserves a special thanks for keeping the book on track and the thankless job of editing the manuscript. Finally, I have to thank Lt. Col. Joseph T. "JT" Vida, one of our most highly respected and dedicated SR-71 crew members, for giving me the drive and Habu spirit to complete the book.

PREFACE

This book is written about the SR-71 and the crews who flew it. The same story could have been written about any number of SR-71 crews who once dreamed of flying this aircraft, finally finding themselves presented with the opportunity to be part of this elite fraternity of aviators. As civilians, early Blackbird crew members were chosen and recruited by the CIA for their special talents. Later, Air Force crew members traveled from as far away as Germany and England, at their own expense, to personally deliver their application package for entry into the SR-71 program. They wanted to be part of a select and highly unique, specialized group of aviators flying the highest performing aircraft the world has ever known.

They all aspired to fly vital SR-71 reconnaissance missions that had no distinguishing differences between their peacetime and wartime roles. As an instrument of peace they wanted to fly an aircraft that sorted out the differences between what others say and what they do. They wanted the personal gratification of flying crucial intelligence gathering missions for their country, rather than flying routine training missions for a future conflict. They welcomed the tremendous responsibility of gathering worldwide intelligence, used by the President of the United States and the National Command Authorities (NCA) in making decisive military and political decisions. Habus eagerly anticipated flying the world's most sensitive reconnaissance missions levied by our government.

As modern warfare and regional conflicts changed from the jungles of Vietnam to the rapid conclusion of Desert Storm, increasing demands by Theater Commanders created new intelligence capabilities. Today, commanders have the ability to look at a picture of the entire battlefield with real-time intelligence, allowing them to make vital decisions affecting the outcome of a conflict. Unfortunately for the SR-71, during the late 1970s and early 80s, the Air Force's senior leadership, as well as the intelligence community, became enchanted with overhead satellite reconnaissance. Their shortsightedness failed to keep the SR-71 modernized with state-of-the-art capabilities and thus paved the way to its demise.

When the Blackbird first arrived on the island, Okinawan residents pointed to the aircraft flying around the island and shouted, "Habu, Habu!" It reminded them of the indigenous snake on Okinawa, called the Habu. The snake was generally not aggressive, but when backed into a corner it could inflict a painful and sometimes deadly bite. Thus, the SR-71 became affectionately nicknamed "Habu"(pronounced "Haw-boo") by those who flew it and those closely associated with the program. Along with the aircraft being nicknamed "Habu," SR-71 crews were likewise called "Habus." Although the SR-71 was never officially nicknamed by the Air Force, it was popularly known among worldwide aviation circles as the "Blackbird." When the U-2s arrived at Beale in July of 1976, they didn't like calling the aircraft by its proper nickname, so they came up with their own name, referring to the SR-71 in a disparaging manner as "The Sled." We never had a competitor before and accepted this as part of typical squadron rivalries that went on within Air Force units.

Other aircrews will never understand the deep feelings of pride, camaraderie, and kinship experienced among Habus. They worked and played hard, as a close knit team, with only one goal in mind—to enjoy flying this beautiful Blackbird for as long as possible. Their lives were entwined in mission secrecy, temporary duty (TDY) to worldwide locations, and flying an aircraft held in awe throughout aviation circles. With the help of highly dedicated maintenance personnel and hundreds of patriotic civilians working on the aircraft, the SR-71 remained a success story for well over 21 years.

The SR-71 has been called "The seeker of truth, that is without peer or equal." The fact that the aircraft had no equal made it truly "unique" within the Air Force, causing it to gather critics along the way. Some were merely envious of the aircraft we flew while others were resentful of our lifestyle, believing we were pampered compared to other flying units in the Air Force. The spectrum of critics ranged from those who labeled SR-71 crews "Prima Donnas," to those who actively sought to dismantle the entire SR-71 program.

The book is written through the eyes and perspective of many Habus who were willing to share their thoughts, emotions, and stories. Without their special contribution, this book would be one of many others written on the SR-71. From small details, personal accounts, Habu legends and traditions, and behind-the-scene activities, the reader gains a greater appreciation of just how "unique" the Blackbird program really was. The majority of this book I wrote from personal experience, as well as from notes and papers compiled over my 15 year association with the SR-71 program. I was fortunate enough to have a broad range of military assignments within the SR-71 community and the Pentagon, giving me access to the senior leadership of the Air Force. Since retirement, I've had the time to put my thoughts, emotions, and memories into words.

Practically every Habu had a tour in Vietnam and was a product of that era. For that reason, many of the stories and tales freely related in this book have to be put into perspective of that time. Many things that were once considered as acceptable behavior during the Vietnam era are not tolerated in today's military environment. At one time, a driving while intoxicated conviction had no major impact on your military career—today it would be ruinous. Even as late as 1976, many stateside military installations, like Nellis AFB, Nevada, had "strippers" performing in their Officers Clubs every Friday night, and "Happy Hours" to encourage drinking and socializing among senior and junior officers. As times changed, so have the military's sensitivities and awareness to social issues of the day. Today's military is much more attuned to being "politically correct."

INTRODUCTION

Very few Air Force crews were fortunate enough to be chosen for the SR-71 program. Chapter 1 sets the stage for the beginning of my SR-71 career. Details of how SR-71 crews were selected for their flying skills and physical condition unfolds throughout Chapter 1. Over the years, Habus developed a close and special relationship with Lockheed and other Technical Representatives ("Tech Reps"), who helped the Air Force maintain the highly sophisticated SR-71 and its unique intelligence sensors. Chapter 2 talks about what these avid civilian supporters meant to our program. The SR-71 simulator program was the most intense and nerve racking training in the entire Air Force. Even the most experienced Habus left their egos behind every time they stepped into the "box." For every SR-71 flight that took place, there was another back-up crew, called the "mobile" crew to take care of all the flight details and make sure each mission ran smoothly. Chapter 2 discusses the mobile crew's important duties performed before and during every SR-71 flight. To fly safely in the harsh, low-pressure environment of 80,000 feet, where outside temperatures reached -60°C and leading edges of the aircraft rose to 300°C from skin friction alone, crews were required to wear a full pressure suit. Chapter 3 gives the reader a first hand accounting of what the pressure suit is all about and how it feels to be cocooned in one for hours on end. Fuel thirsty SR-71s could not perform their missions without air refueling, and Chapter 4 explains just how important it was to have our own special tankers to perform that vital task—the KC-135Q model tankers.

Chapter 5 delves briefly into the SR-71's roots—the A-12 and YF-12 family of aircraft. In Chapter 6, the technical features of the aircraft are discussed from an SR-71 crew member's point of view. I've tried to keep the chapter as simple as possible, and at the same time give the reader an appreciation of the aircraft's complexity—no small task! The peculiarities of our one and only SR-71 trainer aircraft, the "B" model, are covered in Chapter 7. The SR-71 flew two types of missions on a daily basis: training missions at Beale AFB in California and our worldwide intelligence gathering missions, called "operational" sorties. All of our operational sorties were flown under rules of the Peacetime Aerial Reconnaissance Program (called PARPRO), specifically established for aerial reconnaissance during peacetime. The aircraft and crews were also "on the books" for a third reconnaissance mission in the event of a nuclear attack on the Soviet Union. All three of these missions are examined in Chapter 8.

Home for the SR-71s and their crews was Beale AFB, located just outside the twin cities of Marysville and Yuba City, Calif. However, the majority of our operational missions were flown from other locations around the globe, called Detachments, or "Dets" for short. The first SR-71 operational sortie flew out of Kadena AB in Okinawa, Japan, in 1968, where they continually flew until the program was terminated in 1989. Habus worked hard and played hard. Chapter 9 describes the Det flying environment on Okinawa and how Habus lived during their six week tours of duty on the island. In the mid-1970s we expanded our global reach and added RAF Mildenhall, in England, for flying operational missions. Chapter 10 takes the reader to RAF Mildenhall, where SR-71s were soon roaming the skies over Europe gathering vital intelligence. In Chapter 11, an operational sortie is flown in detail from one of the Dets, giving the reader a cockpit perspective and vivid impression of the demands placed on flying the SR-71 at Mach 3. All the Habus were assigned to the 1st Strategic Reconnaissance Squadron (1st SRS) at Beale AFB. The squadron's traditions and rich heritage are covered in Chapter 12.

Chapter's 13 and 14 were the most difficult to write because of the deep emotion they evoke. They were dark days for Habus everywhere and emotions ran high as the program came to an end. My four year tour in the Pentagon gave me deeper insights to the program's demise, and Chapter 13 explores these perceptions. Both Chapters examine the final days of the SR-71 program, discuss why it was terminated, who were the friends and enemies of the program, and why I believe a need for the SR-71 still exists today.

After I returned to Beale in June of 1986, rumors were beginning to circulate about the possible retirement of the SR-71 fleet. From a 9th Wing Commander's perspective, Chapter 14 covers the tremendous amount of turmoil and uncertainty that took place between 1987 and 1989 as the SR-71 program came to an end. The political decisions to terminate the SR-71 program, and those I believe primarily responsible, are further discussed in Chapter 14. The last squadron commander talks candidly about the final days of the squadron and how he preserved a small piece of our Habu legacy, traditions, and history. The three SR-71s given to NASA for use as high altitude, high speed test beds are discussed in Chapter 14.

In Chapter 15 Congress adds $100 million to the 1995 defense budget to bring back three SR-71s. In 1990, Senator Byrd and other influential members of congress were told a successor to the SR-71 was being developed and that was why it was being retired. They subsequently found out there is no successor to the SR-71 and that the aircraft is needed to fill an intelligence void. Chapter 15 documents the return of the SR-71s. Through our Blackbird Reunions, held every two years, the Habu spirit will live forever, regardless of the outcome of the SR-71's return. Lastly, a tribute is paid to one of our most highly respected Habus, "JT" Vida, and to whom this book is dedicated.

CHAPTER ONE

STARTING IT ALL

M y fascination with the SR-71 first began when President Johnson announced the presence of Lockheed's YF-12 on 29 February 1964. On 24 July 1964 he made a further announcement confirming the existence of an aircraft about to be named the SR-71. The first public photographs of the SR-71 revealed a sleek, sinister looking black aircraft that was sure to become the envy of every Air Force aviator. To a raw recruit just entering pilot training, the idea of flying that plane became one's wildest fantasy. After my five year tour as an IP in T-37's at Craig AFB in Selma, Alabama, I set off on an assignment to Vietnam in June of 1970.

My "pipeline" to Vietnam was by way of an F-4 upgrade assignment to Davis-Monthan AFB in Tucson, Arizona. It was there during my training I flew with a GIB (F-4 terminology for "Guy-In-Back"), Col. Keith Branham (Ret), who was a former RSO in the SR-71. The back-seater in the SR-71 was an Air Force navigator called the Reconnaissance Systems Operator, shortened to RSO. Ironically, Keith and I received the same follow-on assignment, and in March of 1971 we reported in to the 555th Tactical Fighter Squadron ("Triple Nickel"), Udorn Royal Thai AFB, Thailand.

We were teamed up as roommates in our squadron "Hooch." Keith never talked much about the SR-71, and I resisted prying into what I knew was a Top Secret aircraft and mission. It wasn't until I was in the SR-71 program that I learned Keith and Bob Spencer flew the third SR-71 to Okinawa in March of 1968 for the original deployment. Even as I got to know Keith and learn more about the aircraft over the year, the SR-71 still seemed an impossible dream. My next assignment was to F-4Ds on the Japanese island of Okinawa, the furthermost island of the Southern Ryukyu chain extending from Japan.

My first direct association with the SR-71 was in June of 1972 while assigned to the 18th Tactical Fighter Wing, 44th Tactical Fighter

Squadron, Kadena AB, Okinawa, Japan. All the SR-71s were located on the opposite side of the flight line from where we flew our F-4s. At that time it was the only permanent location SR-71s were flying out of, other than their "home," Beale AFB, California. I continued to see SR-71s in the skies over Kadena and knew flying a machine like that must be a thrilling experience. Lady luck was on my side and opportunity knocked. In October of 1973, the boss of our Standardization/Evaluation (Stan/Eval) shop, Lt. Col. Bob Bellis, was ready to go to lunch and invited me along. He mentioned that he had to stop by the Kadena passenger terminal to say good-bye to an Air Force buddy leaving for the states.

I went inside the terminal with him, and he introduced me to his friend, Lt. Col. Jim Shelton, who happened to be the current SR-71 Squadron Commander back at Beale. After the two chatted for a while, Lt. Col. Shelton asked me if I ever thought about applying for the SR-71 program. After some discussion I began to realize the small cadre of SR-71 pilots came from various flying backgrounds in the Air Force, and that I had as good a shot at getting into the program as anyone else. I knew the odds were slim but went away excited by the mere thought of flying the SR-71.

Applying and Waiting

The very next day I headed over to the base personnel shop to see what the requirements were and how to formally apply to the SR-71 program. All my fighter pilot friends thought I was crazy. First of all, I would be going into a command that fighter pilots detested—the Strategic Air Command (SAC, pronounced "sack"). They surmised I would be stuck in SAC for the rest of my career and never be able to get back in the fighter business again. They also knew SR-71 pilots didn't fly very often, and in fact, they predicted the SR-71 program was about to close down. After several weeks of gathering the required documents, I mailed my application package to Beale in September 1973. I didn't hear a word until two months later, and then it was from the SR-71 Commander on Kadena, Col. Tom Estes. The unit was called OLKA (Operating Location Kadena) and later changed to Detachment 1 (Det 1) in August of 1974. He wanted me to come over to his office for an interview with him and meet some of the SR-71 crews.

The interview must have gone well because afterwards Colonel Estes arranged for me to return to Beale on one of their KC-135Q tankers for a week-long evaluation, interviews, and a physical exam. After the initial interview, the crews invited me over to their Bachelors Officer's Quarters (BOQ) for a drink later that evening. Little did I know at the time, this was as much a part of the interview process as were the formal proceedings at Beale. I met the SR-71 crew going back on the tanker with me; Capt. "Buck" Adams and Maj. Bill Machoreck. During the 14-hour flight across the Pacific Ocean, I received plenty of advice on the interview process.

I had my two T-38 evaluation flights with Lt. Col. Jim Sullivan who was Chief of the SR-71 Stan/Eval Section. The week of evaluations seemed to go well enough, but I wasn't sure of anything. I returned to Kadena on the next tanker and waited impatiently for the outcome. I was finally notified in April 1974 by Colonel Estes that I was accepted into the SR-71 training program and to shortly expect formal orders assigning me to Beale. When I got off the phone I remember jumping in the air in disbelief and pure joy!

The Selection Process

As an applicant, the SR-71 selection process seemed mystical to me. However, from the "inside" it was a very methodical screening process designed to choose the best crews with the aptitude to fly extremely sensitive reconnaissance missions. Once the applicant put his "package" together, with all of his Officer Efficiency Reports (OER's), Stan/Eval check rides, endorsements, recommendations, biography, flying time history, etc., it was sent to the 9th Wing's Crew Selection Office, in charge of screening and maintaining the records. Some applicants, like Capt. Bob Coats (now Lt. Col. Ret), personally delivered their application from as far away as Germany.

The application process allowed SR-71 crews to look over each applicant's file and make comments as to their suitability. There was no doubt that a first-hand endorsement from an another Habu helped an applicant's chances of getting selected for the interview and physical. After that they were on their own.

A Selection Board convened whenever the squadron commander determined a new crew member (or crew members) would be needed. It typically met at least once every six months to select one or more crew positions needing to be filled about seven to nine months down the road. It usually took that long to select the individual, report to Beale for their week of evaluations, obtain the medical results, convene the Selection Board for a final decision, and issue orders for them to start training. Whenever the SR-71 crew force was getting thin quickly, selectees could be handled more expeditiously through all the hurdles.

The Selection Board typically comprised the Deputy Commander for Operations, 1st SRS Squadron Commander and Operations Officer, the Chief of the SR-71 Stan/Eval Branch, SR-71 Simulator Instructors, and other SR-71 pilots and RSOs having inputs. The pilot and RSO applicant folders were placed in separate piles which contained anywhere from five to ten applications for each position. Board members sat around the table and all the folders were passed out. Each folder was reviewed in detail by all board members and notes taken on every applicant.

After everyone had gone through all the folders, each applicant was discussed by the entire board. It was as fair and unbiased as a selection process could be. We selected what we thought were the "best of the best." Over the years of selecting SR-71 crews, I came away with one observation—the more recommendations an applicant had from General Officers, the *less* likely were his chances of getting into the SR-71 program. We wanted endorsements from officers who had a first-hand knowledge of the applicants abilities and airmanship skills—not how good he looked or how well he could push papers. Flying skills rather than politics were the name of the game!

Our basic hiring philosophy was to invite out the crews we thought we would like to hire, and then look to see if there was any reason *not* to hire them. In the end, the Selection Board chose a pilot and/or RSO to bring to Beale for a week of evaluation and interviews. During the week, the applicant was scheduled for personal interviews with the 1st SRS Squadron Commander, 9th SRW Deputy Commander for Operations, and finally, with the 9th SRW Commander. In actuality, the applicant was being interviewed and "evaluated" by everyone associated with the SR-71 program during his entire week at Beale. The "uniqueness" of this squadron required a strong bond between crew members.

Sometimes, even the "informal" interview had dire consequences for an aspiring candidate. I recall one applicant who was at "Happy Hour" in the Beale O'club on the final night of his evaluation process. He criticized the SR-71 crews at the bar that night about their appearance and how he thought their hair was too long for Air Force standards! He might have been right, but needless to say, he didn't make it into the program. Another applicant got drunk at the Officers Club and acted so obnoxious, he wasn't hired either. Most applicants were forewarned by a Habu friend, or intuitively knew they were being evaluated the entire time, and acted accordingly. Our crew force was so small, we had to be able to get along with each other and "police" ourselves. Former SR-71 pilot, Lt. Col. Les Dyer (Ret), recalls his "informal" interview.

In late 1980 I was serving an exchange tour with the RAF at Valley in north Wales flying the British Aerospace Hawk aircraft. Pondering my upcoming assignment for the summer of 1981, I decided to apply for the SR-71 program in hopes of cracking that very small cadre of operational pilots. I was selected for an interview in February 1981 and set out on the very long journey back to the U.S. for the week-long process.

I first arranged to be dropped off at RAF Mildenhall by one of my "mates" from the RAF squadron. To my good fortune, then Lt. Col. Rich Graham, squadron commander of the 1st SRS, was deployed to RAF Mildenhall with the SR-71, along with Majors Nevin Cunningham and Gene Quist. My good fortune continued while I sat out a few days waiting for KC-135 transport back to Beale. Geno (a buddy from our USAF Academy days) arranged for me to be interviewed by Lt. Col. Graham in the informal surroundings of the RAF Mildenhall Officer's Club. A few "adult beverages" in the club that evening made it a less stressful situation than the upcoming interviews with the 9th SRW brass when I finally arrived at Beale. Unknown to me at the time, before I arrived at Beale, Lt. Col. Graham had already sent word back to his superiors that I passed his interview with flying colors.

Once again good luck prevailed, and the week of T-38 evaluation flights, SR-71 simulator missions, personal interviews, and medical evaluations went well enough for me to be selected to join the squadron in July of 1981. That week was a pivotal point in my career and led to four and a half years of flying the world's finest aircraft and association with the greatest aviators of that time.

Later on, when I became part of the interview process, my primary objective was to find out *why* they wanted to apply for the SR-71 training program. After posing a few probing question to the applicant, it usually became obvious to me when he was using the high visibility, SR-71 program as a "springboard" to help launch his Air Force career to greater heights. I had little patience for this type of aircrew mentality, and in a heartbeat, gave him a "Do Not Recommend" rating. We were looking for candidates that had something to contribute to the SR-71 program—not what they could get out of it! The formal interview was also a good time to let each applicant know about the extensive TDY commitment SR-71 crews incurred. If the applicant was married, now was the time to be sure he understood that he wouldn't be seeing much of his family and find out how he felt about it. After each formal interview a comment sheet was filled out on the applicant, as well as a recommendation to hire, or not to hire.

Each pilot applicant received a minimum of two evaluation flights in the T-38 with either the Squadron Commander or an SR-71 pilot qualified as an Instructor Pilot (IP) in the T-38. We were evaluating the applicant's general airmanship skills and his ability to stay ahead of the aircraft, a skill crucial to flying the SR-71 at 2,200 mph. A T-38 flying evaluation form was filled out on each candidate, becoming part of his final selection board records.

Since the SR-71 simulator was such a vital part of the training program, we gave the applicant an SR-71 simulator evaluation to see if he was capable of handling the most basic tasks without falling flat on his face. We knew from his application package how well he performed in aircraft he had flown, but we needed to see how he would cope under the stress of flying the SR-71. He received a short, but intense briefing from the instructor on the cockpit layout and content of the mission to be conducted during the evaluation. The instructor would intentionally task saturate the prospective pilot or RSO, evaluating his capability to perform under stress in a completely foreign environment. For some candidates the SR-71 simulator was overwhelming while others took things in stride. A simulator evaluation form was filled out on each applicant.

One of the unspoken reasons that kept many good Air Force aircrews from applying to the SR-71 program was the extensive physical examination. Originally, applicants had to take the equivalent of an astronaut's physical at the Brooks Aerospace medical facility in San Antonio, Texas. In some instances, physical problems were found that permanently grounded several pilots. Believe me, if you ever want to stop an Air Force pilot from doing something, just tell him it "might" permanently ground him from ever flying again. Once word got around about the physical exams for the SR-71 program permanently grounding applicants, aircrews became very reluctant to apply either because they had something wrong with them that only they knew about, or they were afraid something might be discovered during the physical exam. In either instance, many good aviators were unwilling to take such a gamble.

During the early-70s, the SR-71 physical exam was moderated to an expanded annual Air Force aircrew physical given at Beale. It required an extra day at the Travis AFB, California, hospital doing various tests that the Beale hospital was not equipped to handle. It included treadmill testing of the heart, an electroencephalogram (EEG) test of the brain, lung capacity test, glucose tolerance testing, extensive blood tests, full sinus X-rays, and a one hour interview with the "shrink."

During my interview the "shrink" asked a lot of basic questions about family, my Air Force background, and why I wanted to fly the SR-71. All of his probing was designed to put the applicant at ease and listen to him talk about things close and familiar to him while he was trying to determine if the applicant would be a sound and stable SR-71 crew member. Our program demanded level-headed crews that knew how to apply and follow very specific rules. It was important to weed out anyone who just might try something stupid or "off the wall" flying highly sensitive reconnaissance missions in unfriendly airspace. Under normal circumstances, there is very little room for improvising at Mach 3!

The final selection was often informal and proceeded quickly since we were then only discussing one or two prospective aircrews at the most. As expected, most of the discussions revolved around how well the applicant performed on his T-38 flights, simulator missions, interviews, and physical exam. Occasionally, some General Officer forced us to interview "their" favorite candidate, in which case, we became very suspicious and particular about how well he could fly an airplane. Few made it into our ranks.

If the applicant was not accepted for SR-71 training, a very polite letter was sent to him from the 1st SRS Commander restating that our program is very, very competitive and to be chosen for the interview process is an honor in itself. Once the Selection Board voted "yes" on an applicant, he received a phone call from the Squadron Commander welcoming him into the program and established the timing for his training to begin. It was also a good time to let him know he faced a grueling 10-month training program that had *no* guarantees with it—there were still many hurdles to cross.

CHAPTER TWO

MY EARLY SQUADRON DAYS

I recall the day in June of 1974 I reported to the 1st SRS Squadron Commander, Lt. Col. Jim Shelton. After chatting for a while he hit me like a "ton of bricks" by asking if I wanted to go to Air Command and Staff College right away and then come back into the SR-71 program after my year of school. I thought for about two seconds and said that if I had any choice I would rather start SR-71 training now and go to school four years later. Like most Habus, I believed in the axiom, "A bird-in-the-hand is worth two-in-the-bush," or in this case, "A black-plane-in-the-sky was better than a-large-gray-desk!"

Lieutenant Colonel Shelton said he would have to talk to his superiors and let me know. I couldn't believe I was this close to the airplane and now it might be slipping right out of my reach. I could never trust the Air Force personnel system to bring me back to Beale after school. What if the SR-71 program suddenly found themselves with an excess of pilots? Where would that leave me? Fortunately, common sense prevailed, and I was told several days later I would start training sometime in October. Talk about one relieved pilot! I was told my RSO was a B-52D Radar Navigator, Capt. Don Emmons, coming from Dyess AFB, Texas.

Most aircrews arrived for SR-71 training with an Air Force Top Secret (TS) security clearance. However, the SR-71 program was compartmentalized and demanded a Special Access Required (SAR) security clearance, a rare classification, reserved only for highly sensitive military programs. The unclassified SAR name for the SR-71 program was called "SENIOR CROWN." The SENIOR CROWN security clearance was issued at Beale for all personnel who had a "need to know" about the SR-71 program and included practically everyone who worked at Beale—from maintenance folks to the clerk typist in the squadron.

The SR-71 aircraft's Operating Manual (called the "Dash-1") and checklist were classified "SECRET NOFORN." That security designation meant that the manuals were classified SECRET and had a "No Foreign" government dissemination caveat. Once you were briefed into the SENIOR

CROWN access program, aircrews signed for, and were issued their flying manuals at the squadron. To control all the classified documents issued to Habus, an entire wall of the squadron administration room was lined with security safes. This was a Habu's first introduction to an increasing maze of combination locks, cipher codes, and secrets he would have to memorize in order to fly a mission.

Whenever a Habu was flying, he was personally responsible for keeping his SECRET NOFORN aircraft checklist secure. Often, to prepare for the next day's mission, Habus took their checklist home to study but kept it in their possession at all times. One Habu was not so fortunate. On his way home, he stopped at the local McDonald's restaurant to eat. Not wanting to leave his checklist in the car he took it inside to study while he ate his dinner in private. Unfortunately, when he left McDonald's he also left his checklist behind. It was found by another customer who recognized it as a classified military document and turned it into the security police on Beale. A security investigation looked into the incident and determined there was no compromise of classified information.

The "Orange Bag"

The one uniform I couldn't wait to wear was the distinctive SR-71 flight suit and associated patches—the "orange bag" as we called it. To an Air Force aviator, the flight suit represented what he stood for in his world of military flying. Organizational patches worn on the flight suit dressed it up and gave the aircrew an identification to his unit and aircraft he flew. Every military aviator in the world takes note of other flight suits to see if they can determine what aircraft they fly from its patches. I often saw the SR-71 crews on Okinawa and knew their distinctive orange flight suits were worn proudly. There was nothing mystical about the color, but once those patches were put on, the flight suit took on a whole different meaning—belonging to a "unique" Air Force organization, flying the fastest, sleekest, most sinister looking aircraft in the world!

The "orange bag" had the round 1st SRS patch on the right chest, a blue name tag and wings on the left chest, the "3+" patch on the right sleeve, and the treasured "HABU" patch on the left sleeve. *Only* SR-71 crews who flew operational missions could wear the prized "HABU" patch on their flight suits. A classic tale of just how prized Habu patches were began on a trip to Barksdale AFB, Louisiana. We were there for their annual open house and flew the SR-71 in for static display all weekend. After all the aircraft arrived, the base hosted a free cocktail party at the Officers' Club for the Air Force Thunderbirds and all the aircrews participating in the open house. After several hours at the club, Don and I left the party along with the Habu crew that flew the airplane in. Each crew was given a courtesy car from a local dealership to use for the weekend. We were following them when they got pulled over by the base Security Police. Knowing the crew had been drinking, Don and I pulled in behind the police car to see if we could help.

Fortunately, the security cop recognized the orange flight suits and patches as belonging to SR-71 crews. He was about to give the driver a sobriety test when I noticed his keen interest in the SR-71 patches, so we began talking to him about the airshow. As it turned out, he was an aviation enthusiast and collected patches. He asked if it was possible to get a "HABU" and "MACH 3" patch for his collection. We spotted a chance for mutual benefits! I told him he could have the patches right now if Don and I could drive the other crew back to our hotel. He agreed! I ripped the Velcro patches off my flight suit and handed them over. He was happy, and so were we!

One day in the late 70s, Det 1 Commander Lt. Col. Bob Cunningham called all six crews in to work and told us we were not allowed to wear orange flight suits anymore. He said it was for security reasons, but we knew better. Along with wearing the distinctive flight suit came the added burden of always standing out. The real reason was, a General Officer on base had seen a Habu in his orange flight suit doing something he didn't approve of and called Lt. Col. Cunningham about the incident. Bob also had a 15th Air Force inspection team arriving shortly and didn't want any problems, particularly with orange flight suits running around, so he ordered us not to wear them.

It just so happened that the inspection team he was concerned about was lead by Col. Ken Collins (Ret), a former A-12 pilot, SR-71 pilot, and 1st SRS Commander. On the first night we invited Colonel Collins to our BOQ for a few drinks and to reminisce about the "old days." As the evening progressed we proceeded to tell him about the new rule of no orange flight suits on Okinawa and how strong our feelings were to continue wearing them. At 2 A.M. Colonel Collins called Lieutenant Colonel Cunningham at home from our BOQ room and told him to, "get over here immediately," he had something he wanted to discuss. Bob arrived promptly, and after a drink or two, we discussed the issue logically. The next day "orange bags" were back in style!

You can not imagine how much the "orange bag" was detested by the senior leadership in SAC. Every few years they got a new Commander-in-Chief (CINCSAC, pronounced "sink-sack") or another General Officer who wanted to make all the aircrews look the same, like clones. In 1981 SAC announced they would no longer stock orange flight suits in their supply system, and the U-2 and SR-71 crews had to change over to the standard olive-drab flight suit. In the end, the U-2 and SR-71 squadrons got together and had a formal "wake" to retire the wearing of the "orange bag." The orange flight suit still hangs in the U-2 squadron bar at Beale AFB today, commemorating the occasion.

T-38s

At Beale, crews typically flew the SR-71 only about three or four times a month. Even though the SR-71 simulator program was demanding and realistic, actual flying time was still needed to keep our flying skills honed. The T-38 was considered the low-cost alternative to maintaining our flying proficiency. Subsonic, it flew and handled similar to the SR-71 and thus, was chosen to be the companion trainer for SR-71 crews. The first of the T-38s arrived at Beale on 7 July 1965. The checkout in the T-38 took pilots about four to six weeks to complete all phases of flying—contact, instrument, formation, cross-country, and SR-71 "pace chase."

Our local T-38 flying area was a Military Operating Area (MOA) called Whitmore, located about 60 miles NNE of Beale. The airspace was basically pie-shaped and divided into three flying areas, so it could accommodate several aircraft at the same time. In Whitmore we practiced aerobatics, stalls, basic instrument flying, and formation practice between 11,000 and 23,000 feet. It was also the designated area to rendezvous with the SR-71 whenever we practiced "pace chase."

"Pace Chase"

The T-38s were also used as a chase aircraft for the SR-71 whenever it got into trouble and needed to be looked over externally. Flying the T-38 in formation with the SR-71 was called "pace chase." Every time an SR-71 was flying at Beale, a T-38 had to be up flying or "cocked" on the ground, ready for immediate response with a qualified "pace chase" crew member.

For every aspiring Habu, it was awesome to fly "pace chase" beside the aircraft they hoped to fly someday soon. I loved to take the T-38 and slowly maneuver it around the SR-71 to enjoy its grace and beauty from all angles and vantage points. I knew I would never want to leave this program. It offered the best flying a young Captain could ever ask for!

On one occasion I needed the "pace chase" aircraft to look me over. It was right after takeoff, when both Don and I heard a loud "BANG" coming from somewhere in front of the rudder pedals. I was on our climbout speed of 400 knots and thought I might have hit a bird. Looking out over the nose I noticed a large piece of the nose section beneath the aircraft had blown open, still attached, but flapping in the air stream. I couldn't tell the full extent of the damage because the piece was underneath the nose and all I could see was one end of it flapping about. Colonel Joe Kinego (Ret) recalled the radio call Don made back to Beale informing everyone of our problem: "I remember this incident and the funny (then scary) call Don made on the radio, 'The nose is coming off!'".

The T-38 chase rejoined and told us the extent of our damage while we returned to Beale. It was comforting to know everything else was intact. A one-by-two foot metal section of the nose had ripped open while still attached at one end. I always felt fortunate that it happened during daylight. Had it been at night, we might have discounted the possibility of anything being wrong and continued the mission. Talking to Lockheed engineers later, they determined there was a good possibility, if we had gone supersonic, the entire nose section (which is removable) might have imploded from the supersonic shock wave. That scenario would have probably necessitated an ejection for us!

Our Habu "Family"

Our start of training was also the beginning of a close bond with civilians that none of us had previously experienced in the Air Force. The personal relationships that developed between SR-71 aircrews, Lockheed personnel, and other Technical Representatives made our program very "unique." Our Habu family extended from the likes of Kelly Johnson and

Ben Rich, to the Lockheed mechanic turning the wrenches out on the flight line.

Another group of civilians we became close to were the Technical Representatives, employed by their specific companies (Pratt & Whitney, Northrop, Itek, Goodyear, Honeywell, etc.), each having highly sophisticated equipment on the SR-71. For short we called them "Tech Reps." As civilians, they played an important role in maintaining our aircraft and lived wherever the SR-71 was deployed—Okinawa, England, Beale.

"Tech Reps" were *the* experts in their specific fields. If you wanted to know why something happened that wasn't in the book, they would either know the answer or go back to their company that made the system to find the answer. Because of the extreme heating and pressure experienced at Mach 3 speeds, anything unusual occurring in the aircraft manifested itself differently every time the aircraft flew. All the aircraft fluids, electrical systems, and computers reacted to heat and pressures in their own unique manner. This kept the "Tech Reps" busy, trying to find answers and solutions. As crew members, we had a wealth of experts and knowledge available to us.

There was another group of civilians Habus grew fond of. They were the surrounding community leaders from Marysville, Yuba City, Grass Valley, and Nevada City. Local civilian support for Beale AFB and the SR-71 program was tremendous, with most of the community leaders having served in the military at one time. We socialized with them on the golf course, at "Happy Hour" at the Officers' Club, or attending other military functions on base.

Early in my SR-71 career I recall a military function at the Beale Officers' Club that included all the local community leaders. As the evening progressed, everyone migrated downstairs to the large bar and dance floor. I left, as did most of the other Habus, around 1 A.M. and went home to bed. Sometime around 2 A.M. the phone rang, it was Colonel Storrie (now Maj. Gen. Ret), our Wing Commander, saying, "This is a Habu recall, report to the Officers' Club immediately!" Even though I knew it was a prank, I still had a Habu obligation to get dressed and drive to the club. As I pulled up, I could see a commotion in the Officers' Club parking lot. Walking towards the group of Habus I could see a car that was parked differently from all the others—to say the least!

The local sheriff, Jim Grant, had tried to drive his car forward from the upper level parking spot! His car was now precariously balanced on its frame hanging over a four foot wall. We waited until all the Habus arrived, before lifting the front end up. One of the wives believed the phone recall was a merely a ploy on Colonel Storrie's part to get the party going again, so she accompanied her husband to the Officers' Club in her nightgown and hair rollers. Colonel Storrie told us he could have the bar opened again if we all wanted to have a night cap. By now, we were all awake and felt like partying but just didn't have the energy.

The longer Habus remained in the SR-71 program, the closer they got to local legends like Gavin Mandry, General Roger Smith, "Shakey" Johnson, Dave Wheeler, Bob Nicoletti, Carl Estes, Tony Bevaqua, and the secretary to every 9th SRW Commander, Mrs. Mary Ulmer. They were proud of the SR-71 and fully understood its economic contribution to the local community.

The SR-71 Training Program

I met my RSO, Capt. Don Emmons, for the first time in September 1974 during flight line ceremonies for Capt. Buck Adams (now Brig. Gen. Ret) and Maj. Bill Machoreck (now Lt. Col. Ret) . They had just set the London to Los Angeles world speed record in the remarkable time of 3 hours, 47 minutes, 36 seconds (5,645 miles) while returning from the Farnborough Air Show. It was RSO, Capt. Bruce Liebman (now Lt. Col. Ret), who found me in the crowd that day and introduced me to Don, my future flying partner. Little did I know then that the two of us would set an obscure SR-71 record of our own that the rest of the world would never hear about or celebrate over—from that day forward until January 1980 we had the longest continuous time as an SR-71 crew flying together—5 years and 4 months!

SR-71 training lasted around 10 months. The goal was to complete training with 100 hours in the aircraft, after which crews were considered Combat Ready and cleared to fly operational sorties. The 100 hour requirement was established by Habus before my time and remained as a requirement to insure a certain level of proficiency before flying the SR-71 on worldwide operational missions. It wasn't until after achieving 100 hours in the SR-71 that you even began to feel somewhat comfortable and in control. At about the 300-hour point you were on top of the aircraft, and at 500 hours you were in charge and could "hear the airplane talk" to you.

We started our training in mid-October. The SR-71 training program was not a formal Air Force school; it had no designated ground or flight instructors. All the training was accomplished by regular SR-71 crew members. For the first two weeks, aircrews attended a Field Training Detachment (FTD) course, designed to instruct new aircraft mechanics in the "nuts and bolts" of maintaining and repairing the SR-71. For us it provided a solid background and overview of the aircraft's systems.

The SR-71B model was our normal trainer aircraft, tail number 956. There was an SR-71C model (tail number 981) stored at Beale, having the front end fuselage of the engineering mock-up of an SR-71A, and the aft portion from a wrecked YF-12 (tail number 934). The "C" model remained in storage at Beale and was to be used only if the "B" model was going to be grounded for an extended period of time. Maintenance named the "C" model the "Bastard" because of its hybrid origin. They hated to work on the aircraft because it didn't conform to standard SR-71 maintenance procedures and was difficult to troubleshoot and repair. I was fortunate enough to fly the "C" model twice during my training because 956 was undergoing heavy maintenance. It had a reduced fuel capacity and, consequently, accelerated better because of its greater thrust-to-weight ratio. It flew strangely—the needle and ball were never centered because it was in a constant yaw. Subsonic, it handled like all the other SR-71s.

After successfully passing simulator mission number 12 you were ready to start your five training rides in 956 with an instructor pilot (IP). My

IP was Maj. Lee Ransom, a soft spoken instructor, but very knowledgeable in every aspect of the aircraft. Lee taught me the skills necessary to fly the aircraft well and didn't get wrapped up in the "nuts and bolts" of the aircraft. In my military flying career, I've known several pilots who knew the "nuts and bolts" of their aircraft so well that it actually became a detriment on their ability to fly the aircraft well—they just lost focus on flying the airplane.

The SR handled like two different aircraft, depending on whether you were subsonic or supersonic. Subsonic, it flew like a heavy F-4—responsive to stick inputs and light on the controls. Supersonic there was nothing like it! It had a heavy stick feel at Mach 3 in the pitch axis but was very responsive in roll. When the stick was neutral, it seemed as if there was a dead spot in pitch control, making it difficult to fly without over correcting. Hand flying precise turns seemed to be an exercise in futility. Consequently, we seldom hand flew the aircraft at Mach 3.

Habus "flew" the aircraft through the autopilot in the pitch and roll axis by two small control wheels located on the lower right console of the cockpit. Even through the pressure suit gloves you had enough feel in your fingertips to roll the wheels delicately. Most crews found air refueling no problem. The SR-71 was very stable while refueling and only required small changes of power to adequately maneuver the aircraft.

There was no such thing as a subsonic training mission, new crews jumped right into the pool, training at Mach 3 on their first mission. Habus often commented that, "Subsonic time is a waste of time!" After the first flight at Mach 3, crews were given the highly prized Mach 3/SR-71 pin, a Lockheed SR-71 model, a Mach 3 certificate (suitable for framing), and a Mach 3 wallet card signed by C.L."Kelly" Johnson. The Mach 3 pin was attached to your pressure suit by the Wing Commander at a plane-side ceremony with champagne, squadron crews, and family members in attendance. Additional certificates and SR-71 pins were given out at the flying hour milestones of 300, 600, 900, and 1,000 hours in the aircraft.

Habus always joked that you could probably get a free cup of coffee anywhere just by presenting your Mach 3 card. For Don and I, however, the Mach 3 wallet cards proved to be extremely valuable at the Farnborough International Air Show, England, in September of 1976. Having enough days off from work, we drove to the village of Farnborough and found ourselves a bed & breakfast to stay at while attending the airshow. After walking around all the exhibits on the first day, we passed by the Lockheed chalet and asked the security guard if we could possibly go inside because of our association with Lockheed's SR-71. He said, "Let me check" and disappeared inside.

He came back shortly with the Lockheed representative in charge of the chalet, who asked if we could prove our SR-71 affiliation. Immediately, Don and I whipped out our Mach 3 wallet certificates signed by C.L. "Kelly" Johnson. He was visibly impressed and escorted Don and I inside the chalet. It was only two years earlier that the SR-71 set the world speed record between New York and London and landed at the Farnborough Airshow for static display. That historic event was still fresh in aviation circles. He escorted Don and I to the bar for drinks and then showed us to the buffet table.

We chatted with several Lockheed employees, and once the word spread that two SR-71 crew members were there, everyone wanted to meet us. Over the next few days Don and I didn't have to buy any food or drinks and had the best seats in the house to watch the airshow. To this day we still carry our Mach 3 wallet cards, hoping for another free admission!

The majority of our five "B" model rides were devoted to basic Mach 3 flying, air refueling, and plenty of traffic pattern work. About 30-40 minutes at the end of each sortie were devoted to practice landings. The fifth flight was the check ride and the sixth flight your first solo in the "A" model with an experienced RSO in the back seat. New RSO's flew their first sortie in the "A" model with an experienced pilot, and after that the new crew flew together for the first time.

It was somewhere around this point in training that you awoke to find a black SR-71 silhouette spray painted on the entrance to your driveway. It was a Habu tradition on base to have the SR-71's silhouette sprayed, by some mysterious means, on the new crew member's driveway. No one ever questioned who did it, you were just happy it was there, knowing one day you would probably be painting someone else's driveway. Flying the SR-71 was also an expensive proposition. You were expected to buy a drink for everyone in the entire Officers' Club bar after your first and solo flights, and host the "new crew" party for the entire squadron and their wives. Everyone willingly paid for those milestones!

The first three months of student training was largely comprised of the simulator program. After that, it was a combination of flying the SR-71, with simulator missions mixed in to complement the flying. The last three months of training primarily concentrated on flying, with a smattering of practice operational simulator missions. While building toward 100 hours, the student crew flew increasingly complex mission profiles. They started out with straightforward Mach 3 sorties with one air refueling close to Beale and progressed to numerous air refuelings far away. Next, they flew low Mach (2.6 and 2.8) sorties with high bank angle turns (in excess of 30 degrees). Then they moved on to high Mach sorties with high bank turns. Every combination of bank angle and Mach number required an in depth knowledge of the aircraft's operating characteristics. Training finished up with about 15-20 hours of night flying.

Throughout the ten months of training, crews were also flying the T-38 on a regular basis. Every Habu had to attend a Water Survival School at Homestead AFB in Florida and a special classified survival course at Fairchild AFB, Washington, for aircrews flying highly sensitive reconnaissance missions. They were also learning more and more about the electronic and photographic sensors that surrounded their cockpits. They developed close friendships with, and learned from the "Tech Reps" who maintained the multi-million dollar electronic and photographic equipment. They learned how their reconnaissance missions were developed and put together by watching mission planners do their job. Every new Habu was required to visit the Wing Flying Safety Office and read all the classified accident reports on former A-12, YF-12, and SR-71 aircraft. The idea was to make everyone aware of how the various accident scenarios developed and hopefully assist in preventing them from happening in the future.

The Dreaded SR-71 Simulator

The only SR-71 simulator in existence was at Beale. Prior to beginning our simulator training, Don and I attended several briefing and debriefing sessions with other crews to see what transpired. We knew the simulator was the one place where crews either made it into the SR-71 program or failed—it was very demanding and stressful. Most crews received around 120 hours flying simulator missions before ever stepping foot inside an actual SR-71.

All the simulator training missions were well thought-out and included an outline and accompanying lesson plan. Each training mission became increasingly more complex, building on all the previous ones. Their scenarios were developed and refined over the years by Habus who found a better way of presenting and instructing the training. Crews had unrestricted access to the simulator, enabling them to study and prepare for simulator missions at their own pace.

Normally, there were two simulator periods a day. One in the morning starting about 0730 and ending around noon, the other starting about 1300 and ending around 1700. A typical simulator period had the students arriving early, so they could go over any last minute details, and have all the mission materials laid out and ready before the instructors arrived. The mission briefing lasted around an hour. The instructor pilot briefed the overall mission profile and emergencies to be covered during the session. At the end of the briefing, time was allocated for the instructor pilot and RSO to brief their individual student on what to expect in each cockpit.

After the simulator was thoroughly preflighted, a technician stuck his head in the briefing room door to let the IPs know the simulator was up and running. When he said, "Its ready," my heart would start to race. To the student, it was as if he had said, "The guillotine is ready!" There were many days students wished he would open the door and say instead, "It's broken now, and we don't know how long it's going to be before it's fixed." Every time you step into the simulator as a student, you sweat bullets! After the briefing there was usually enough time for a quick cup of coffee, a donut, and trip to the bathroom before jumping into the simulator. We would be in there for about two to two and a half hours although the simulator did have a "freeze" capability in case a student needed to get out sooner.

Most missions typically ended with a major emergency, requiring a rapid descent to subsonic speeds and a landing somewhere other than Beale, so students could practice strange field approaches. Prior to the student crew's first flight in the aircraft, they received a simulator mission wearing the pressure suit. For the first time, they were able to experience the difficulty of maneuvering around the cockpit and flying the aircraft in a pressure suit. It's also the only time we could simulate the total loss of cabin pressure at 80,000 feet, resulting in a rapid decompression and suit inflation, to see how the student pilot and RSO handled the emergency. After each simulator mission, Don and I went over the items we "screwed up" and then prepared for the next one. Most crews in training took the same approach.

The most important skill being taught and evaluated in the simulator was how to cope with SR-71 emergencies and still be able to handle the aircraft safely—all at 33 miles a minute. Crews needed to fly the airplane, keeping it upright until they were subsonic and it began to handle like a regular aircraft. Both normal and emergency procedures required a high degree of crew coordination—pilot and RSO working closely together to identify and solve problems that developed. Crew coordination was the one area that tested the strengths and weaknesses of each crew to their limits. You could watch patience wearing thin, and personalities changing dramatically, as crews were confronted with demanding emergencies that had to be solved and rectified quickly. As good an aviator as every Habu thought he was, you left your ego behind when you stepped into the SR-71 simulator. You could be humbled at any time! Former SR-71 pilot and 1st SRS Commander, Col. Joe Kinego (Ret) talks about his simulator training days.

I remember this training as the most intense training I have ever experienced. Roger, my RSO, and I would spend hours at night together reviewing procedures and "chair flying" the next simulator mission. This made us very close, but more importantly, it instilled the necessary confidence we had in each other. We knew that the other guy was ready for anything!

It may sound easy, but one of the most difficult tasks to teach new pilots, was to be able to accurately describe what problems were occurring in his cockpit so that the RSO could understand, find, and read the correct checklist procedures. Many experienced Habus have misidentified the aircraft's real problem and had the RSO reading a similar, but incorrect, checklist procedure. That's precisely why our RSO's needed an excellent working knowledge of the entire aircraft and its systems. Crew coordination was an area where crews either passed or failed miserably! Former SR-71 pilot Lt. Col. Bernie Smith (Ret) discusses the importance of crew coordination and other factors that made SR-71 crews work as a team.

There is no doubt in my mind that the crew coordination between the pilots and RSOs in the SR program was one of the strongest contributions to its outstanding safety record. In the airline business this is called CRM, or Cockpit Resource Management—the ability of a crew to function and communicate effectively in the cockpit.

The intense simulator program was the cornerstone of establishing crew coordination. Teaching a pilot to communicate the correct information to his RSO so that he could coordinate the right procedure was difficult, but essential. As a simulator instructor taking a new crew through training, I was always amazed watching the crew transform from two separate individuals to one polished team.

Another important factor that contributed to this close bond was the fact that crews spent so much time with each other. They worked and lived together with six-week TDY's several times a year. It seemed we spent more time with each other than with our own families. All this added up to a bond and trust between each other that allowed two separate individuals, sitting in two separate cockpits, with two different roles, to perform like one individual, to accomplish one very demanding job. This bond was a strong factor during an SR-71 emergency Eddie McKim and I had at night on 22 December 1982.

About one and a half hours into the mission while eastbound over Canada, we experienced a left generator failure. We selected Grand Forks AFB as the nearest suitable emergency recovery airfield. During the descent a primary hydraulic system failed, indicating an accessory drive system (ADS) failure. An ADS failure is one the most serious emergencies that can occur on the SR-71. Landing soon became imperative.

We dumped fuel to reduce our landing gross weight as we neared Grand Forks. The weather was deteriorating rapidly. It was now 200 feet overcast, one-half mile visibility, and a slippery runway with an RCR of six and freezing drizzle. During this emergency I flew the ILS approach down to minimums. At minimums, where you should execute a missed approach if the runway environment is not in sight, the visibility was so bad I could not see anything. Since there were no suitable alternates available and since we were low on fuel, the idea of a missed approach was not too exciting. I'll never forget Ed's words as I sat there at minimums staring into an opaque windshield, "I have the strobes insight, you're on center line, keep on coming." With no forward visibility from the back seat, he was looking through his View Sight and had picked up the Sequence Flashing Lights beneath the aircraft. It was this bond, or trust, I had in him that made me pull the throttle to idle and sit there until I felt the runway.

The student simulator training missions were numbered 1 through 11, each one being a major milestone towards the final check ride, simulator number 12. Before each numbered mission the student crew received a practice mission covering the same items as the numbered mission. If they successfully passed the practice mission, they were recommended for the numbered mission. If a crew failed a numbered mission they received extra simulators and additional help preparing them for the recheck. A recheck was usually given by the most experienced SR-71 crew on station to make sure the student crew performed up to accepted standards and to add credibility to their program continuation recommendation in case the student crew did not perform well.

Depending on how bad the students screwed up and what it involved determined the fate of the crew. At this point, they could either receive additional training or be released from the program. I am aware of only three pilots and two RSOs dropping out of the SR-71 program. The pilots were all skilled aviators but just not cut out to be SR-71 pilots. All three individuals went back to flying their former aircraft, one of whom was later killed when his RF-4 aircraft crashed. One of the RSOs who failed was "sponsored" into the SR-71 program by a four-star General Officer. He hadn't flown recently, had minimum flying time, and didn't perform particularly well on the interview, but was issued to us anyway. He was eventually eliminated from the program.

The "Mobile" Crew

Mobile duty consisted of assisting the fliers in their preflight routines, a very responsible position that could determine the success or failure of each mission. The mobile crew was generally a formed crew, but didn't necessarily have to be for training sorties. Our mobile check-out came shortly after our sixth flight in the SR-71. For operational missions the mobile crew also performed as the back-up crew, ready to fly the mission in case the primary fliers couldn't for one reason or another.

In a typical day, the mobile crew arrived at the squadron about half an hour after the fliers to pick up the mobile kit bag (containing various regulations and instructions), the portable FM military two-way radio called a "brick," and car keys for the mobile car. The car was standard military issue, but had red warning lights on top and was equipped with two UHF radios to keep in touch with the fliers. The mobile crew joined up with the fliers in the Physiological Support Division (PSD) kitchen. They ate the required preflight meal of steak and eggs (a high protein/low residue meal) with the fliers and discussed the specific mission to see if there were any particular needs. The mobile crew departed PSD about the same time as the fliers went to suit-up. After a short drive to the aircraft hangar the mobile crew began to preflight the cockpits. The pilot and RSO went through their respective cockpits in detail to ensure everything was working and ready for the fliers.

After the fliers arrived at the aircraft, they remained in the van on cooling air while PSD technicians took the crew's food, water, and checklists up to the cockpits and began a preflight of the ejection seat and oxygen systems. The mobile crew entered the van and briefed the fliers on any last minute changes or things they found wrong on preflight. On a signal from PSD that everything was ready, the fliers exited the van and climbed into their cockpits

It was then back to the mobile car to monitor radios and wait for engine start. Engines started, checks completed, and a flash of the taxi light signaled they were ready to taxi. The mobile car always preceded the aircraft on taxiways and runways for takeoff to preclude the aircraft's powerful engines from sucking up harmful material or taxiing over anything damaging to the tires. The six nitrogen-filled main gear tires used such high pressure (415psi) that taxiing over a nut or bolt could damage a tire sufficiently to require changing. It always amazed me what junk we found lying on taxiways and runways.

Shortly after our mobile checkout, Don and I were leading the SR out on the parallel taxiway at Beale, when suddenly Don yelled out "Stop the car!" He jumped out and ran outside while I radioed the SR to stop taxiing because Don had discovered something on the taxiway. Don was in front of the car picking things up, finding more and more of whatever it was. He gathered it all up, ran back to the car, jumped in, opened up his hand and said, "Look at all these Rich—they look like golden B-B's!" At first glance I thought he had really found something that would surely cripple the SR's, tires and we would be heroes for the day. On closer inspection, as we looked into the palm of his hand, we found he had picked up about a dozen rabbit droppings! Unknown to us at the time, Beale had an abundance of large jack rabbits living around the flightline, and when their droppings baked in the 100°F plus temperatures, they turn a golden color and harden. Instead of heroes of the day we felt like fools of the day. The fliers never asked, and we preferred not to mention our discovery!

If the mission proceeded normally, the mobile crew drove out to the runway to await the arrival of the SR-71 and initiated UHF radio contact when he was about 30 minutes away. If there were any major maintenance problems or requests from the fliers, they gave mobile a radio call to let them work out the details. At Beale, all SR-71 training sorties used the static call sign "Aspen" followed by its numerical designator. "Aspen-39" was reserved for flying the SR-71B trainer so Air Traffic Control and other aircraft flying in the Beale traffic pattern could give priority to its training mission.

After the SR-71 landed and turned off the runway, the mobile crew was there to usher the aircraft back to the hangar. A good mobile crew had a cold beer waiting for the thirsty fliers! After a short chat with the crew about how the mission went, our mobile duties were basically finished.

CHAPTER THREE

Physiological Support Division (PSD) and the Pressure Suit

As a physical environment, space begins at about 125 miles above the earth, but as a physiological environment it begins at about 63,000 feet, where the atmospheric pressure becomes so low that fluids boil at body temperature. The main function of the pressure suit was to save your life at the extreme altitudes, temperatures, and speeds the SR-71 flew. Above 45,000 feet a crew member's Effective Performance Time (EPT) is between nine to twelve seconds without oxygen. EPT is the amount of time an individual is able to perform useful flying duties before going unconscious. Without a suit on at 80,000 feet, *and* the loss of all cabin pressure or an ejection scenario, you would not survive.

Another problem called decompression sickness, or the "bends," can develop anywhere above 18,000 feet and is caused by nitrogen gas bubbles escaping from body tissues and fluids—similar to bubbles forming when opening a bottle of carbonated drink. Varying degrees of pain can result in your joints and chest, either incapacitating or proving fatal to the individual. Frost bite to the skin would occur rapidly at 80,000 feet, where the outside air temperature is around -56°C. The pressure suit prevents or reduces the chances of these problems from occurring.

Most people are amazed to find that the SR-71 didn't have sealed cockpits upon ejection (like the F-111), but individual ejection seats. There have been ejections from the SR-71 at high Mach and high altitude, as well as low airspeed on the runway. The pressure suit and ejection seat combination have served Habus well, with only one known fatality during ejection. The pressure suit became our capsule and protector.

The organization that maintained our pressure suits was the Physiological Support Division, or "PSD" for short. The facility was located close to the flight line and was the Air Force's entire repository for all pressure suit operations, and consequently, had a high level of experienced personnel working there. PSD had the technical expertise and capability to do anything and everything with our pressure suits. To Habus, they were highly qualified "technicians" in every sense of the word.

As *the* experts, they routinely briefed us on the effects and hazards of high altitude physiology. An altitude chamber, located inside PSD, trained Habus to better understand the effects of high altitude physiology. PSD was also responsible for our survival training and instructed aircrews during their annual water survival refresher course and parachute training. The parachutes and ejection seat survival kits were inspected and maintained by PSD personnel.

Although not considered a military uniform, the David Clark Co. model 1030 pressure suit was *the* most prized uniform for aspiring Habus—it meant they were one step closer to flying the aircraft! My day finally arrived for fitting the $120,000 pressure suit. Before donning the pressure suit you were given a locker in the PSD changing room to store personal effects and your military uniform while flying. Each crew was issued four pairs of long underwear and thick white socks to be worn under the pressure suit. The long underwear provided a layer of warmth inside the pressure suit and reduced skin irritation from the inner liner of the suit.

The UCD

The question most frequently asked about the pressure suit was, "how did crew members go to the bathroom?" This was accomplished by the Urinary Collection Device (UCD), my next item to be fitted. The UCD had a large, thick rubber condom exterior. Inside was another thin, rubber condom attached at the open end, and tapered down as it went inside the large outer condom. The trick was to cut the tapered condom to the correct diameter of your penis so that it fit snugly (but not tightly!) around it. Velcro held the UCD in place to your underwear. At the far end of the UCD was an exit tube that connected to the pressure suit tubing. As you can well imagine, there were plenty of pranks played on each other with the UCDs!

All the UCD tubing and connections were located inside the pressure suit and not accessible during flight. The UCD exit tube was connected to a small rubber hose inside the pressure suit and continued down the left leg and entered an open/close valve. To make sure the UCD connection didn't come undone in flight, black electrical tape was wrapped around the snap-on connection for extra insurance. The open/close valve was located in a zipper pocket near the left knee and was the only thing accessible from outside the pressure suit. Another tube exited the valve and continued down the left leg to a lower zipper pocket. Inside the pocket was a plastic container with a highly absorbent sponge to collect and hold the urine.

As you can tell so far there was ample room for error! To use the UCD properly you had to inflate the suit slightly. This provided a positive pressure flow from inside to outside the suit when you opened and locked the open/close valve. If you felt a chilled, slight draft running across your penis with the valve open, you were somewhat confident it would work correctly. Feeling the draft told you at least everything was ready to flow in the right direction. In my 765 hours in the Blackbird, I never had to use the UCD, however, I've known other Habus who used it before they even got into the aircraft.

Just in case you're wondering—there weren't any provisions in the pressure suit for passing solid waste. I know it's happened to other Habus, as Don and I were personally involved in one such incident during a short TDY deployment to RAF Mildenhall in January of 1977. We were the mobile crew and had just launched the SR-71 on a very long mission to North Yemen when we received word back that the pilot had intestinal diarrhea during his first air refueling. We knew he would return if his problem was serious, but he elected to press on with the sortie.

During his descent into Mildenhall we talked to the pilot on UHF radio and learned he was in extreme pain—not with intestinal problems, but from having sat in his mess for well over eight hours. The diarrhea was so acidic that his bottom was nothing but raw flesh. We rushed the pilot out of the aircraft and into the PSD changing room. The pilot quickly got out of his pressure suit, and we immediately drove him to the BOQ for a shower. Later that day, the pilot attributed his intestinal problems to the "seafood special" he had eaten the night before at the Mildenhall Officers' Club. For several days afterwards all he wanted to do was stand up.

I use this somewhat humorous story to illustrate a serious point among our crews. Call it self-esteem or personal pride, but Habus never aborted an operational mission unless it was a life-and-death situation or involved the safety of the aircraft. The very fact that every operational mission had a back-up crew, ready and eager to take your place in case you were sick, added emphasis to complete the sortie regardless of how bad you felt at the time. Don actually threw-up once while we were flying and made the decision to press on. I've personally known of crews flying F-4 combat missions over North Vietnam aborting for lesser reasons.

The Suit

The Model-1030 pressure suit we wore came in 12 basic sizes. From there everyone was individually fitted for adjustments in arm length, glove size, and foot size. Although the pressure suit was a six layer outfit, three layers are significant. The outer most layer (exterior) was made of a fire retardant material called Nomex. It contained zippered pockets on the upper and lower legs, Velcro patches on the upper legs to secure your checklist, and most importantly, the parachute harness connections to mate you to the parachute. A pencil pocket and the American flag patch with your name below, were sewn on the left shoulder.

The exterior layer also gave us access to two important valves, each located around the bottom of your rib cage. The adjustable valve on the left side was connected to a cooling air supply which controlled the amount of cool air coming into the pressure suit. Aircrews could sweat profusely inside the suit if there was no cooling air. The source for cooling air came from either the aircraft's air conditioning system or from the portable liquid oxygen converters we carried with us while being transported to and from the aircraft.

The valve on the right side was the critical pressure controller. In the event of a loss of cabin pressure, the suit controller sensed the loss and immediately inflated the suit. The controller was considered a critical life-saving component, and as such, had both a primary and back-up system. One system was a dial-type pressure controller and the other was a push-to-pressurize valve. By manually "pushing" or "dialing" the respective valves you could inflate the suit as needed.

Because it was called a "pressure suit" most people thought we flew with the suit inflated all the time. Nothing could be further from the truth. It only inflated when necessary to save your life—you merely wore the 50 pound suit. Fully inflated, the metal helmet neck ring could actually rise up over your chin, so a tie-down strap with pulley leverage dangled in front of your chest to hold the neck ring firmly in place.

The inner layer, called the bladder, was made of a rubber compound and became inflated, much like a balloon, when air pressure was added. The rubber layer was irritating to bare skin, thus the need for a comfort liner made from lightweight Dacron material. Also located inside the bladder layer was a network of tubes to direct cooling air to the extremities.

Between the outer layer and the bladder of the suit was a tightly woven mesh netting designed to provide rigidity and keep the bladder from inflating too much. The netting was woven in such a manner that it utilized the same principle as a familiar child's toy. Remember the Chinese finger pull—when you put your two fingers in and then tried to pull them apart. What happened? You discovered the harder you pulled, the harder it was to get your fingers out. The same principle applied to the suit—the more pressure exerted by the inner layer against the webbing, the more rigid it became.

SR-71 missions were considered too critical to be delayed or canceled because of a leaky or faulty pressure suit and thus, a second, back-up suit was made for every Habu. I would guess I had to use my back-up suit, helmet, or gloves over a dozen times due to a fault in my primary suit. Sometimes, you wore the back-up suit just to exercise it, or while your primary suit was out of commission for routine maintenance.

After donning the suit it had to be checked out thoroughly before leaving PSD. Sitting in a large overstuffed reclining chair, the suit was connected to a pressure testing unit and fully inflated to make sure it held pressure satisfactorily on both systems, and that the communications and face heat worked properly. Testing results were recorded for trend analysis of each suit.

People often asked what it was like being inside a pressure suit. Many believe it would be claustrophobic while others thought it would be too cumbersome to enjoy flying the aircraft. Neither was true for me. After several years of flying the SR-71 I came up with my own description. I've always thought that being in the pressure suit must feel similar to what a baby feels like inside its mother's womb. The surrounding pressure suit environment is so controllable and comfortable, and you feel very snug and enclosed. With the suit on and lying back in the reclining chairs, it was very easy to fall asleep. Often there would be takeoff delays for one reason or another, and we weren't notified until after suit-up. Crews were now faced with two choices—de-suit and do the entire process all over again or remain suited up. If you chose to remain suited, you reclined in the chair until it was time to go. If you simply closed your eyes, nap time had arrived; it was that relaxing inside the suit.

The Helmet

The helmet was adjustable only in terms of the face seal—a latex rubber liner (later changed to foam rubber) surrounding the front of your face. The face seal was designed to trap and contain the 100 percent oxygen in front of the crew member's face for breathing. An external adjustment knob on the side of the helmet allowed the crewmember to tighten or loosen the face seal to suit his comfort.

A microphone was located inside the helmet, positioned directly in front of your lips. An adjustable dial on the outside of the helmet allowed you to move the mike closer or further away from your lips. It also served another purpose it wasn't designed for. If you dialed the mike closer to your lips and pushed it up with your tongue, it could be used to scratch your nose if it got itchy! By wriggling your head inside the helmet it was possible to rub your nose up against the mike. Also, by using the food tube probe, crews could position the "straw" inside their helmet to scratch. What relief—just pray you didn't have to sneeze!

The clear helmet face plate was the final locking mechanism that made your pressure suit a sealed unit. The glass face plate was connected to a metal ring on the bottom called the "Bailer bar." By lifting up on the Bailer Bar, the entire face plate rotated up on top of the helmet for storage. Rotating the Bailer Bar down, and locking it to the bottom of the helmet, sealed the face plate. When the Bailer Bar was locked, a flow of 100 percent oxygen was initiated inside the helmet. A dark-tinted sun visor also rotated up and down to block out the brilliant sunlight. Former SR-71 pilot, Lt. Col. Terry Pappas (Ret), tells about a unique experience with his Bailer Bar.

> As a new pilot, I was flying my second sortie in the airplane in June of 1986. It was to be my first flight at Mach 3 in the SR-71B, and we planned to have the traditional "Mach 3" party afterwards at the squadron. Several people had come in from out of town for the big event.
>
> On my first subsonic flight, my IP, Lt. Col. Jerry Glasser, had taught me that it was an acceptable technique to unlock and raise the helmet's Bailer bar while flying in the traffic pattern, as long as you weren't going back to high speed and altitude conditions. This allowed me to open the face plate and wipe the sweat out of my eyes occasionally, and still leave the dark visor down as a sun screen. The PSD instructors had encouraged us during training to keep the suit and helmet sealed until engine shutdown, so I was reluctant to comply with Jerry's suggestion at first. Finally, I relented and did so for the last half hour of pattern work on that first flight.
>
> Two days later, Jerry and I were strapping into the cockpit for my first Mach 3 flight. As I was doing the preflight checks, I noticed it was hard to see in the front cockpit because the sun was coming up over the horizon and it was shining right into my eyes. I put my helmet in the now familiar configuration of dark visor down and Bailer bar up.

A few minutes later into the checklist, we challenged each other on the configuration of our helmets, Jerry said, "Bailer bar, latched and locked." I repeated the same back to him, but must have been distracted by something in the cockpit, because I didn't complete the step. My face plate was down, but I failed to lower and lock the Bailer bar.

During the engine runs I remember noticing some unfamiliar odors as I ran each engine to 100 percent power. It didn't occur to me at the time that I shouldn't be able to smell ANYTHING with a properly sealed pressure suit and breathing 100 percent oxygen. Finally we got clearance from the tower, and it was time to make my second ever takeoff in the Blackbird.

I pushed up the power, released the brakes, and lifted the throttles up and forward into afterburner range. Now it's full blower and things are happening real fast. It's about two minutes from brake release to level off at 24,000 feet, so I had my hands full of 100,000 pounds of airplane screaming upward. We usually flew with the cabin pressurized at 26,000 feet, so as I leveled off at 24,000 feet enroute to the air refueling, 24,000 feet represented the partial pressure of oxygen in my lungs. As most Air Force pilots know, the Time of Useful Consciousness (TUC) at that altitude varies with each person and the level of work at hand. Fighting that 50 pound pressure suit and the workload of flying the Blackbird for the second time allowed me about three minutes of consciousness from the moment I climbed through about 12,000 feet.

I began to feel tingling sensations all over and got warm and uncomfortable, some of my typical hypoxia symptoms, but they were different now because of the suit. I was concentrating so hard on flying this machine that I didn't notice my symptoms, particularly since I had only experienced them once before in the pressure suit, four months earlier. Within a minute of leveling off, my control over the aircraft began to deteriorate. Jerry noticed that I was flying sloppy, and he said so. With a comment like that from my instructor I fought even harder to maintain precise control of the Blackbird. Jerry told me later that he had asked me a few questions to see if I was all there. He asked, "What's your airspeed?" And I replied, "400," which was true. Jerry then asked, "What's your heading?" And I said, "400," which was impossible. He immediately took control of the aircraft, declared an emergency, and began a recovery to Beale.

My recollection of the next several minutes of the flight is somewhat incomplete—I think I was out cold. I remember regaining my faculties as we were descending through 9,000 feet toward the field. At the time, I couldn't understand why Jerry wouldn't let me fly the airplane. I still didn't know what had happened. When we taxied clear of the runway I really had a sinking feeling. There must have been a dozen vehicles with red flashing lights waiting for us, and they weren't there to congratulate me for flying Mach 3 either!

We shut it down, and the first guy to reach the cockpit was the senior civilian PSD supervisor, Mr. Tom Bowen. As Tom knelt down beside me on the platform, he reached forward, put his hand on my helmet and pulled my face plate up. I thought to myself, "He's not supposed to be able to do that, because I had not unlocked my Bailer bar yet." That's when I suddenly realized, I never locked it! Naturally, I was sent to the hospital for numerous tests to determine if I was okay and to see if there was any explanation for my physiological incident.

Everything checked out fine and three days later, Jerry and I successfully flew again, to include the Mach 3 party afterwards. Thanks Jerry, I still owe you one!

Early face plates were made of very expensive Pittsburgh Plate Glass, which later changed to a high quality plastic material. Imbedded in the face plate was a grid work of extremely thin electrical wire, providing us with face heat. The wires were heated to prevent condensation from forming on the inside of the face plate as we breathed. Once connected to the aircraft systems, a rheostat in the cockpit allowed crews to individually select whatever face heat temperature they required. With the rubber face seal trapping the face heat and 100 percent oxygen around your face, it was easy to dry your eyes out after a four hour mission. Often you were desperate for tears to form just to moisten your dry eyes. New crews soon learned if you kept your eyes closed long enough, tears would begin to form. There was certainly no way of using eye drops!

The helmet mated to the pressure suit's metal neck ring with a metal ring of its own. It fit inside the pressure suit neck ring and was locked into place by a lift-and-pull locking device. Located at the bottom of the helmet was a small hole that allowed us to drink fluids and eat "tube food" in the pressure suit. Everyone was encouraged to drink plenty of fluids while flying to prevent dehydration. The small feeding port remained sealed until the plastic feeding tube was pushed through. Fluids were kept in plastic squeeze bottles with long tubes on top, similar to what athletes and bikers use for races. Our food was contained in a large sealed tube, resembling a giant size toothpaste tube. When the feeding tube was threaded onto the "tube food" top, it broke a thin metal seal, to keep the food fresh. The food came in various selections, such as macaroni and cheese, beef and gravy and several puddings for dessert.

Boots and Gloves

To accommodate our feet, the pressure suit utilized a single layer of heavy material, making it look as if we had "booties" on our feet. Over the pressure suit "booties" we wore thick, leather boots. Stirrups were attached to the heals of each boot by strong Velcro straps—similar to the stirrups F-104 crews used. The stirrups attached in a "ball and socket" manner to retractable cables located on the bottom of the ejection seat. The cables automatically retracted and locked your feet into the correct seating position, precluding them from flailing around and possibly breaking your legs during a Mach 3 ejection. While taxiing in from a mission, it was customary for crews to raise the heel of each boot, releasing the stirrup and saving time getting out of the cockpit. This required the pilot to take his feet off the rudder pedals momentarily, usually releasing one at a time.

After one night mission, a pilot was doing this maneuver when his stirrup became snagged on the cockpit floor and locked his foot in place. With one foot locked to the floor of the aircraft he had no means of steering. The SR veered off the taxiway and onto the grass. His RSO sensed something was amiss and asked, "Joe, where are we going?" The pilot was helpless to steer the aircraft; all he could do was watch and plan his next move. His only hope of stopping the aircraft was to immediately shut down both engines, which prompted the famous response from his RSO, "Joe, why's it so dark in here?" No damage was done, other than to the pilot's pride.

The gloves were one item that had to be perfectly tailored to fit each individual. Nothing was more irritating than flying the SR-71 with a pressure suit glove where the fingers were either too long or too short. Each glove had a locking metal ring, mating it to the sleeve of the pressure suit. Cooling air supply tubes ran down the inside of your arms and had to be placed inside the gloves during the suit-up, to preclude sweaty hands while flying. To display our agility, Habus routinely demonstrated to PSD visitors how they could pick up a thin dime with a fully inflated pressure suit.

Altitude Chamber

Located inside the PSD facility was an altitude chamber. Attached to the normal altitude chamber was an additional airlock chamber that allowed Habus to test their pressure suits at 85,000 feet and at high temperatures. It was a small altitude chamber, incorporating heating elements and the SR-71's ejection seat. The purpose of the chamber was to expose new crew members to the mating of the pressure suit to the ejection seat, build his confidence in the suit, learn how to operate and control the suit's temperature and pressure, and finally, to experience a loss of all cabin pressure at 85,000 feet (called a Rapid Decompression, or "RD" for short).

Every time Habus flew, they put their lives in the hands of PSD technicians. Wearing the pressure suit made it next to impossible to strap yourself into the ejection seat and make all the necessary connections satisfactorily. Consequently, crews were taught to extend their arms out each side of the cockpit and sit there patiently while PSD technicians on each side of the cockpit did all the mating to the aircraft and ejection seat. Trying to help them out merely hindered the process. They were extremely professional and safety conscious at their job, alert at all times to the dangers of becoming lax.

In the small altitude chamber, surrounding mirrors gave the crew member an unrestricted view of how the technicians accomplished strapping you into the seat. You had time to stop and ask questions and discuss each item on their checklist. Once strapped in, they sealed the chamber and started the climb in altitude. The chamber ride consisted of first climbing up to a low altitude to check for any sinus problems you might have developed, and then it was on up to 85,000 feet.

On the way up, the first thing to grab your attention was a flask of water sitting on the inside window sill. It slowly began to bubble as you passed through 63,000 feet, then to a rapid boil, and finally evaporated as you climbed higher. It's placed there to give you an appreciation of what would happen shortly to your blood without a pressure suit on. Upon reaching 85,000 feet, heaters are turned on to around 233°C. It's a strange feeling when your body is extremely comfortable, and yet, you see threads on the exterior of your pressure suit giving off wisps of smoke from heating. It's hard to believe your suit can give you this much protection from such a harsh environment.

To prepare for the Rapid Decompression, the greatly reduced air pressure now surrounding you (85,000 feet) is captured and saved in the larger altitude chamber, connected to your chamber by huge air valves. Once the thin air is captured, they descend our small chamber back down to 26,000 feet—simulating the cabin altitude of the SR-71 flying along at 85,000 feet. Since the RD happens so quickly, the supervisor briefs you on what to expect before throwing the decompression switch. I was told there would be a loud, explosive "BANG" accompanied by immediate fogging, and then rapid clearing inside the chamber. Simultaneously, the pressure suit would fully inflate. He recommended that the pressure suit tie-down strap be pulled tighter in preparation for suit inflation. After the briefing the supervisor asked if I was ready.

"Ready as ever," I replied. Peering through the thick glass window, that separates you from them on the outside, I watched the PSD technician slowly raise the red safety cover guard and put his thumb on the switch. When he moves the switch, instantly your 26,000 foot cabin altitude will be at 85,000 feet. It went exactly as he described—a loud "BANG," fogging, suit inflation—all simultaneous, followed by rapid clearing of the fog. They kept crews inflated at 85,000 feet for as long as they liked, to practice various cockpit chores in the rigid pressure suit. I was surprised that trying to pull on your tie-down strap or even turning your head in the helmet was more difficult than I imagined in a fully pressurized suit. *The* most important task was to be able to reach for the ejection seat handle, located between your legs. Hopefully, Habus would never experience an RD for real, but for now, they had a chance to practice one in a controlled environment.

The chamber was rapidly descended back down to 25,000 feet where we opened our helmet to observe our personal hypoxia symptoms without oxygen and checked our sinuses before descending to ground level. Once the chamber was back down at ground level, we practiced removing all the suit connections in order to get ourselves out of the cockpit safely. Then back to the dressing room to de-suit, and the chamber ride was complete.

CHAPTER FOUR

KC-135 "Q" MODEL TANKERS

Without air refueling the range of the SR-71 was limited to around 2,000 nautical miles (nm). Multiple air refuelings extended the range of the aircraft to the limits of crew endurance. Many of our missions have exceeded 12,000 nm. Forward basing of the aircraft permits faster response, shorter range, shorter duration missions, fewer air refuelings, and greater overall efficiency.

The KC-135Q model tankers were "unique" within the Air Force and thus, earned the "Q" model designation. At Beale there were 35 "Q" model tankers flown by the 349th and 350th Air Refueling Squadrons to support the SR-71's worldwide operation. At one time both squadrons belonged to the 100th Air Refueling Wing on Beale, but in 1976 someone made a *very* wise decision to place the two air refueling squadrons under command of the 9th SRW, since they were our exclusive means of refueling and went TDY everywhere the SR-71 went. It wasn't until the early '80s that we also began using KC-10s as a tanker aircraft.

A special bond developed between our tanker and SR-71 crews that didn't exist throughout the Air Force. They took considerable pride in their work because of the exclusive SR-71 refueling. They knew, and so did we, that the SR-71's mission success was directly related to our ability to get refueled in the air. They were always there, somewhere in the murk and dark of night, with a full load of JP-7 waiting for us. It was a comforting feeling to have Beale tanker crews, who you knew well, doing your refuelings. I have never known of a missed air refueling with the SR-71 because of tankers not being there.

The KC-135Q crews and their aircraft were "unique" from the rest of the Air Force in several ways. The aircrews were the only ones certified in our "unique," radio silent rendezvous procedures and their boom operators were the only ones qualified to refuel the SR-71. The Q-model tankers had special plumbing between their fuel tanks, allowing them to move JP-4 and JP-7 fuel between various tanks. Their engines could burn either JP-4 or JP-7 fuel. If the SR-71 landed somewhere JP-7 fuel was not available, we used the "Qs" to ferry our fuel. We could refuel the SR-71 on the ground, utilizing transfer hoses between the two aircraft.

Other than the fuel, the ARC-50 radio (pronounced "arc") was the second most important item aboard the tanker. Both the SR-71 and KC-135Q had the ARC-50 radio installed. The radio used standard UHF frequencies to communicate but had "unique" features associated with it that allowed coded (secure) communications and variable power levels for the transmitter (up to 100 watts). With the tanker and the SR-71 on the same UHF frequency, and the correct secret codes set in, we had range and bearing to each other's aircraft. Over the open ocean it was not uncommon to pick up the tanker at ranges of 300 miles or greater with 100 watts of transmitter power.

When more than one tanker flew together they were referred to as a "cell." Depending on the amount of JP-7 to offload, there would be either two, or sometimes three, KC-135Qs in a cell. Often, we took our gas from two tankers (called a "split offload") and had a third tanker there as an airborne spare. On important missions the airborne spare provided redundancy in case either of the other two was unable to transfer fuel or had to abort for an inflight emergency. In the early 80s, money for tanker flying time started to become tight, so SAC began to reduce the number of tankers to refuel the SR-71 to the minimum necessary—often only one!

It was important for the tankers to be in the air refueling track 30 minutes prior to the SR-71's arrival to check on weather conditions. The SR had no weather radar capability whatsoever, and therefore crews relied heavily on the tanker's weather recommendations. Frequently, the tankers had to move the Air Refueling Control Point (or ARCP—the rendezvous point for us and the tankers) because of bad weather, necessitating a different arrival route from the SR-71.

A rendezvous with the tankers was always one of two types. A "hot" rendezvous originated from a high Mach cruise leg and supersonic descent, while a "cold" rendezvous was a subsonic arrival, generally right after takeoff. It was extremely critical for the SR-71 to start a "hot" rendezvous descent at a precise point in order to accomplish a satisfactory rendezvous with the tanker. Once the throttles were brought out of afterburner to start down, there was little the pilot could change in the descent profile to modify the bottom out point.

Every time we flew there was a minimum amount of fuel we were required to have at each ARCP, called our "Bingo" fuel. Bingo fuel was computed so that you could arrive at the ARCP, not refuel for one reason or another, and still be able to divert to your alternate with a minimum of 10,000 pounds of fuel remaining. It may seem like a lot of fuel remaining at destination for other airplanes, but when you consider a missed approach and standard instrument pattern (ILS) for a thirsty SR-71 burns around 3,000 pounds of fuel, that's not much fuel in reserve. Just pulling up for quick visual pattern to a landing burned over 1,000 pounds of fuel.

In "theory," whenever crews computed they would be below Bingo fuel, they were supposed to abort the mission and proceed to their alternate landing base. In reality, most Habus took an educated gamble, rather than abort a mission. As long as the refueling and alternate weather were good, it was a gamble worth taking. If crews knew they were going to be below air refueling Bingo during cruise, one option available was to call the tankers prior to descent and have them move the ARCP closer to the SR-71's descent track, saving precious fuel. However, depending on where the ARCP was located, this option was not always possible.

At one time or another practically every Habu has been below Bingo fuel, searching for their tankers in the weather, knowing only too well their alternate bases were right at weather minimums. Not a pleasant feeling! Once the tankers were sighted, you were anxious to join up and commence refueling. The sweetest words Habus in this predicament ever heard were the boom operators saying, "You're taking your gas!" The tankers were our lifelines—they knew this and accepted the responsibility with pride.

The SR-71's air refueling system could receive fuel at approximately 6,000 pounds per minute from either a KC-10 or KC-135Q. All of our six tanks could be filled in about 15 minutes at a refueling pressure of 65-70psi. Once hooked up and transferring fuel, the boom would automatically disconnect whenever fuel pressure exceeded 70psi, which was the normal disconnect procedure when our tanks became full.

The critical need to refuel the SR-71 created a position on the air refueling switch, called "MANUAL OVERRIDE," providing an emergency means of manually locking the boom into our receptacle. Occasionally, the tanker's boom nozzle wouldn't stay locked into the SR-71's receptacle for one reason or another and necessitated the use of "MANUAL OVERRIDE." In this switch position, the SR pilot squeezed the trigger switch on his stick grip, opening the locking mechanism that holds the boom secure. After the nozzle was seated in the receptacle, the pilot released the trigger switch, locking the boom securely. The automatic disconnect feature of the boom was deactivated when using this mode; consequently, the pilot had to pay close attention to stay within the refueling envelope.

We also utilized the "Q" tankers as our normal means of transportation back and forth to Kadena and Mildenhall. The tanker leaving Beale was called the "deployer," and the tanker returning to Beale was called the "re-deployer." It was squadron policy to try and say good-bye to the departing crew on the morning they were leaving Beale. Every Habu available met in the Base Operations snack bar to have a cup of coffee and say, "so long" to the departing crew. This small gesture added yet another touch of class to our squadron.

Upon return to Beale six weeks later, most Habus showed up at Base Operations to meet the arriving crew. Their families and friends were also there to welcome them back. One crew at Beale was always assigned the task of keeping the family informed of the arrival time, meeting the tanker, helping out in hauling baggage, and to take the arriving classified mail bag to the squadron.

CHAPTER FIVE

THE SR-71'S ROOTS

It's hard to image the fastest jet aircraft in the world today was developed before 1962. The prime architect of the SR-71 was C. L. "Kelly" Johnson, head of Lockheed's Advanced Development Projects (ADP), better known as the "Skunk Works." In 1943 Kelly organized the "Skunk Works," a small unit of technical and production specialists, to build America's first production jet fighter. The XP-80, the prototype of the F-80 Shooting Star, was completed in less than five months. This effort exemplified Kelly's credo—be quick, be quiet, be on time. For 30 years he headed Lockheed's "Skunk Works" and played a leading role in the design of more than 40 of the world's most advanced aircraft—among them the SR-71, U-2, F-104, and P-38.

I recall, early in my SR-71 career, Kelly Johnson flying up from Burbank to Beale (as Lockheed ADP personnel routinely did) in their Lockheed Jetstar to attend one of our squadron monthly aircrew meetings. I was highly impressed with his ability to answer our detailed questions about the SR-71, and also by the fact that a Lockheed senior vice president would take the time to attend one of our aircrew meetings. Sadly, on 21 December 1990, Kelly Johnson died at the age of 80. He was a giant of his time—revered, admired, honored, and dedicated to excellence in building aircraft. An aviation genius, he achieved what was thought to be impossible.

Designed with slide rules and built in total secrecy, the SR-71 was well ahead of its time. New technologies and frontiers had to be explored to build an aircraft capable of continuous Mach 3 flight, where heat from skin friction alone would build up inside the aircraft to 300°F. The nose of the aircraft would heat up to 800°F, the windshield over 600°F, and the exhaust section reached 1,200°F at Mach 3. All these extreme temperatures were developed flying through an air mass with a temperature of -70°F.

Titanium was the only lightweight metal of the time that could sustain the heat and still provide the strength necessary to maintain aircraft integrity. Although difficult to work with as a metal, titanium was chosen to be the primary metal comprising over 90 percent of the SR-71's airframe. Because of the extreme heating and cooling cycles over its lifetime, each aircraft actually became stronger (annealed) every time it flew.

Everything on the airplane had to be specially designed. The hydraulic fluid, lubricating oil, fuel, engines, and variety of other complex systems, all had to be developed to overcome the extreme heat encountered at Mach 3 speeds and the hostile outside pressure and temperature environment above 80,000 feet. Even a special black paint for the aircraft's exterior had to be developed to withstand the extreme heating.

In August of 1959, the CIA awarded a contract to the Lockheed "Skunk Works" for the development of a Mach 3 aircraft called the A-12. In January of 1960, the contract to build a dozen A-12 aircraft was awarded. The first flight occurred on 26 April 1962 in aircraft 924 and was flown by Lockheed test pilot Lou Schalk from the secret test site at Groom Lake, Nevada. The early test flights barely exceeded Mach 1 because the J-58 engines from Pratt & Whitney were not fully developed and J-75s were used instead. It wasn't until January of 1963 that the first J-58 powered A-12 flew. Soon they were exceeding Mach 3.

Two of the A-12s were modified to carry the D-21 ramjet reconnaissance drone on top of the aft fuselage. The 42-foot titanium D-21 drone was powered by a Marquardt RJ43-MA-11 ramjet and was to be launched from the A-12 at Mach 3. Aircraft 940 and 941 were modified to carry the D-21 drone and included a rear cockpit for a second crew member. Once modified to carry the drone, the A-12 aircraft were called the M-12. The back seat crew member (called the Launch Control Officer) was in charge of safely launching the drone from the M-12. Once launched, the Mach 3.35 drone followed a preplanned flight profile with camera ON/OFF points also controlled by the navigation system. The 11,000 pound D-21 drone had a range of around 3,000 nm and could fly as high as 95,000 feet. Following its mission, the drone flew to a point over friendly territory, and its palletized camera unit was ejected and recovered by a modified C-130 aircraft, equipped with a Mid-Air Recovery System (MARS), where it would be taken for processing. As the D-21 continued its descent, it would soon self-destruct by a barometrically activated explosive device.

After three successful launches, on 31 July 1966, Lockheed pilot Bill Park and launch crew member Ray Torick climbed aboard 941 to launch the D-21 drone. At launch separation the drone hit the tail section of the M-12 causing it to pitch up abruptly. The fuselage forebody separated from the rest of the aircraft with both crew members inside. Both men ejected successfully, however Torick drowned in the ocean before being rescued by the Navy. After the loss, Kelly Johnson canceled the M-12/D-21 program.

B-52s at Beale were then modified to carry the D-21 drones, one under each wing on inboard pylons. The B-52s flew to Guam in darkness and launched the drones into China during daylight. Only a few missions were flown before the project was canceled. As of this writing, seventeen D-21 drones were stored at Davis-Monthan AFB, Arizona, four of which were delivered to NASA's Dryden Flight Research Center on 2 June 1994, for possible flight research projects. The Museum of Flight in Seattle, Washington, displays the world's only M-12 mated with its D-21 drone.

The Air Force became interested in using the A-12 as a high altitude interceptor to defeat a new generation of Soviet bombers. The next version of the aircraft, an Air Defense long-range interceptor, was proposed by Kelly Johnson in March of 1960 to General Hal Estes II, in Washington, D.C. It was to be called the YF-12A and had a two-man crew. By coincidence, I had the pleasure of working for Brig. Gen. Hal Estes III, 14th Air Division Commander, as my immediate boss at Beale AFB, and meeting his father during a visit. He talked fondly about the start of the YF-12 program as he toured the base.

On 7 August 1963, Jim Eastham flew the first YF-12 (tail number 934). Three YF-12As were built and tested (934, 935, 936), but finally lost out to funding for the F-111, a favorite of then Secretary of Defense, Robert "Strange" McNamara. Two of the YF-12s and an Air Force SR-71 were given to NASA for high speed research while the third YF-12 (934) was extensively modified to produce the dual controlled SR-71C trainer (981). The NASA program terminated in October of 1979.

The YF-12 carried the advanced Hughes ASG-18/GAR-9 fire control and missile system (forerunner of today's F-14 Phoenix system), later designated the AIM-47 missile. The radar modification to the nose of the YF-12 degraded directional stability to such an extent that three ventral fins had to be added. Two shorter fixed fins were mounted under each engine nacelle, and a larger, retractable fin was located under the aft fuselage. It retracted to give the necessary ground clearance on takeoff and landing.

Back in January of 1961, Kelly Johnson made a proposal for a dual-role strategic reconnaissance bomber (designated the R-12) to the Secretary of the Air Force and Col. Leo Geary (now Brig. Gen. Ret), Pentagon project officer for the YF-12. The proposal for the R-12 never got very far. As the "Skunk Works" continued development on the YF-12 it encountered very strong opposition in the Air Force from those trying to save the B-70 bomber program. While this flurry of activity was going on, the "Skunk Works" proposed an advanced strategic reconnaissance aircraft to the Air Force, and on 28 December 1962 a contract to build six SR-71 aircraft was issued to Lockheed.

The first SR-71 prototype (950) was driven on two flatbed trucks from Burbank to Palmdale's plant 42 for final assembly on 29 October 1964. Two months later, on 22 December 1964, Lockheed test pilot Bob Gilliland flew the first SR-71 aircraft. The pace of testing the flying envelope and operational characteristics of the SR-71 picked up momentum with the Air Force also testing and evaluating three SR-71s (953, 954, and 955).

Everything about the aircraft turned out to be "unique." At Mach 3 cruise, heating of the entire aircraft length (107 feet) forced it to "grow" several inches in flight. To give you an idea of Mach 3 speed, imagine a

30-06 rifle bullet fired over San Francisco and being able to sustain its muzzle velocity (3,000 feet/sec) all the way to New York City—the SR-71 would arrive first (3,100 feet/sec)! It's hard to imagine an aircraft built in the early 60s, utilizing Radar Absorbing Material (RAM) to produce less than a ten square meter target for enemy radars to find. The mere thought of a stealth aircraft back then was only for dreamers, but Kelly managed the impossible! It was a sad day, on 5 February 1970, when the Skunk Works received word from the Pentagon to destroy all the tooling for the Blackbird so that it would never be built again. A total of thirty SR-71As, two SR-71Bs, one SR-71C, fifteen A-12s, and three YF-12s were built by Lockheed.

The 4200th Strategic Reconnaissance Wing (SRW) was activated at Beale on 1 January 1965, the only unit to fly the SR-71. A year later, on 7 January 1966, Wing Commander, Col. Doug Nelson, along with instructor pilot, Lt. Col. Raymond Haupt, delivered the first SR-71 to Beale. It was the "B" model trainer, aircraft 956. The second SR-71B followed shortly, and "A" models continued to arrive steadily through late 1967. The unit designation was changed to the 9th Strategic Reconnaissance Wing (SRW) on 25 June 1966. Shortly after the Strategic Air Command was inactivated on 1 June 1992, the 9th Wing became part of the newly created command called the Air Combat Command (ACC), and its designation was shortened to the 9th Reconnaissance Wing.

CHAPTER SIX

TECHNICAL FEATURES OF THE SR-71

E ven as complex and highly sophisticated as the aircraft was, it went 17 years straight without an accident. That's an accomplishment equaled by *very few* aircraft in the Air Force inventory. In the following paragraphs I have attempted to describe in sufficient detail those systems "unique" only to the SR-71. A large part of the technical data in this chapter comes from notes I took while going through my SR-71 training. By the very nature of the SR-71 program, Habus were subjected to a tremendous amount of facts and numbers they had to use on every mission, and consequently, the technical data became firmly implanted in our memories. The once classified SECRET Dash-1 was also used when my notes and memory failed me.

I've tried to simplify all the technical data and still give the reader an SR-71 pilot's and RSO's perspective on how the various systems operate. SR-71 crews used a large library of acronyms for ease of conversation with one another which are presented in this chapter exactly as we used them in normal conversation. The acronyms are pronounced precisely as you read the letters, or I have provided their correct pronunciation.

Two terms Habus used often when they talked about flying the SR-71 were the "Accel" (pronounced "Ax-cell") and "Decel" (pronounced "Dee-cell"). Whenever the aircraft began its acceleration and climb we called it the "Accel," and the descent and deceleration the "Decel." In both of the maneuvers, you couldn't do one event without the other, i.e., if you wanted to accelerate from subsonic to Mach 3 you *had* to climb, and if you began your descent at 80,000 feet to meet a tanker, you *had* to decelerate.

Fuel System

The SR-71 burned JP-7 fuel. A one-of-a-kind fuel that used an additive to raise its flash point so the fuel would not break down at extreme temperatures. In an emergency situation, crews were authorized to refuel with JP-4 or JP-5, however, this limited the aircraft to Mach 1.5. These emergency fuels were to be used *only* if the crew was low on fuel and had to use any tanker he could find to avoid the loss of the aircraft.

All 80,285 pounds of JP-7 were carried in six main fuselage tanks, numbered 1 through 6, moving forward to aft. Located in each cockpit was a large fuel quantity gauge, with a selector switch beneath it, to read each tank quantity individually or total fuel onboard. Tank-1 (13,770 pound capacity) was the forward most tank and had a smaller separate tank called Tank-1A (1,655 pound capacity) that gravity fed into Tank-1.

Tank-2, next moving aft, held 12,970 pounds. Tank-3 was the largest, holding 16,160 pounds, and by its central location in the aircraft fuselage and forward wings had little change on the aircraft's Center of Gravity (CG) as fuel burned off normally. Tank-4 was next and contained 9,550 pounds of fuel. Tank-5 was the last of the fuselage tanks with a capacity of 11,550 pounds. Two wing tanks in each wing, numbered Tanks-6A (7,601 pounds) and Tanks-6B (7,020 pounds), gravity fed their fuel into a Tank-6 sump (called the "dog house") located at the extreme aft portion of the fuselage.

Besides cooling the aircraft down, fuel was used as a cooling medium for other components throughout the aircraft. A temperature controlled valve diverted cooling fuel above 148°C back into Tank-4, and fuel below 143°C into the engines and afterburner, if within engine consumption requirements.

If the automatic fuel transfer system was working normally there was little for the pilot to do except monitor CG readings as float switches and transfer valves did their magic. The automatic fuel management sequence basically burned fuel from the fore and aft tanks (1 and 6) and worked inward. A continuous reading CG gauge was located in each cockpit.

If the CG was not where the crew wanted it to be, the pilot could manually move fuel around between tanks to change the CG with two switches. If he needed to move the CG forward, the Forward Transfer Switch was turned on, moving fuel in the right hand manifold forward into Tank-1 (at 950 pounds per minute). If he wanted the CG to move aft he had to hold the Aft Transfer Switch down to move fuel in the left hand manifold into Tank-5 (at 233 pounds per minute).

A crossfeed valve connected the left and right fuel manifold to insure fuel supply during single engine operation. A fuel dump switch could be opened by the pilot in an emergency, to reduce gross weight quickly for an immediate landing. When opened, fuel dumped overboard at a nominal rate of 2,500 pounds per minute (depending on the number of boost pumps operating and fuel remaining) out the dump mast located at the extreme aft tailcone.

We took off with either 45,000, 55,000, or 65,000 pounds of fuel, and air refueled to full tanks. Takeoff with a full load of JP-7 was possible, but not practical. Fuel leakage, tire and brake heating, abort criteria, and single-engine performance were all stacked against you the closer you were to an 80,000 pound fuel load. Palmdale crews were the only ones making takeoffs with a full fuel load, primarily because they didn't have easy access to tankers like we did, and many of their flight tests missions were of short duration and didn't require air refueling.

Two dewars located in the nose wheel well, holding 106 liters of liquid nitrogen each, were used to purge the fuel tanks of all volatile vapors, preventing autogenous ignition of the fuel system. Mach 2.6 was the maximum speed we could fly without an inert atmosphere of nitrogen gas in the fuel tanks. Another purpose of the nitrogen gas was to prevent ambient air pressure from crushing emptying fuel tanks when the aircraft descended down into greater air pressure. We found the aircraft could deplete all of its liquid nitrogen on longer missions, and so a third dewar, containing 50 liters, was added.

The fuel tanks formed the exterior skin of the aircraft and, consequently, always leaked when the SR-71 was cool. Shallow drip pans were placed under the aircraft after refueling to capture the dripping JP-7. In each aircraft's maintenance record was a picture of the underside of the aircraft to identify the precise location and number of Drips Per Minute (DPMs) at each leak. Over the years, many sealants had been tried to permanently stop the leaks between the six main fuel tanks but were never successful. The extreme heating and cooling cycles, as well as the large pressure changes of the fuel tanks, created a situation where all maintenance could do was minimize the amount of leakage. As the aircraft and fuel warmed up with increasing speed, the sealant did its job, and the tanks were tight.

When JP-7 dripped onto the hangar floor it made the surface very slippery. I'll never forget the day I almost witnessed an SR-71 accident because of JP-7. Don and I were the mobile crew at Det 1 recovering the SR-71 from a mission. We led it into the hangar area, parked the car, and got out to watch him taxi into hangar-3. As the pilot slowly nosed the aircraft into the hangar everything appeared normal until the main landing gear transitioned from the outside concrete onto the hangar floor. Suddenly, everyone in the hangar saw the wheels were not turning and the brakes locked up, as the SR-71 slowly slid past its normal stopping point. Everything appeared to be happening in slow motion as the aircraft continued sliding through the hangar, out of the pilot's control.

Instinctively, every person in the hangar knew the pilot was in trouble and immediately grabbed onto any part of the aircraft they could reach, in an attempt to slow it down. Crew chiefs were throwing chocks in front of all the tires, and we were hanging onto the right wing tip. Everyone holding on was merely sliding on the hangar floor along with the aircraft. The chocks were not working, but simply being slid along with the SR. It was a helpless feeling. Idle thrust of a light SR-71 is so great, the aircraft requires constant braking just to keep a normal taxi speed. Now the pilot was faced with a crucial decision—keep the engines running and hope the brakes would begin to grab hold or shut down the engines, eliminating the idle thrust and rely *only* on accumulator pressure for braking. All these decisions had to be made in a split second!

The pilot elected to shut down one engine as he continued sliding through the hangar. On the other side of hangar-3 was a blast fence, used to deflect jet engine thrust upward during taxi out. Soon, the nose of the aircraft was sliding out of the hangar and heading directly for the blast fence. Fortunately, as the main gear slid outside the hangar floor and onto the concrete, the brakes finally took hold and the aircraft came to a stop with the pitot tube resting about ten inches from the blast fence.

The circumstances creating the mishap were unusual. JP-7 had dripped onto the hangar floor as normal, followed by an afternoon thunderstorm, blowing rain onto the hangar floor and mixing with the JP-7. You couldn't ask for anything more slippery than a mixture of JP-7 and water standing on a smooth surface. As a result of that incident all the hangar floors were covered with a sand and epoxy mixture to provide good braking action under all conditions.

The SR-71 was the first aircraft to use its own *fuel* for hydraulic fluid—called the Fuel-Hydraulic system. An engine driven pump provided 1800psi of recirculated fuel to actuate various engine components and then returned it back to the aircraft's fuel system to be burned. Fuel was used in actuators to control the afterburner (AB) nozzles, which maintained the proper Exhaust Gas Temperature (EGT) and controlled thrust output. Fuel was also used in engine actuators to shift the two-position Inlet Guide Vanes (IGV's) from their axial position to the cambered position, and back again.

As fuel was burned off during cruise everything became warmer because there was less cooling fuel available, and what fuel did remain became warmer and warmer. The hot fuel sometimes caused problems in the Fuel-Hydraulic system. Former SR-71 pilot and 1st SRS Commander, Col. "Pat" Bledsoe (Ret), describes aircraft heating problems encountered when he set the 1,000 kilometer closed-course speed record in 1976.

> When John Fuller and I were doing our mission study for the record-attempt flight, we found that the plan called for a speed of Mach 3.2, and a bank angle of 42 degrees around the curved portion of the course, with a projected average speed of 2,040 mph. We figured we could better 2,100 mph if we flew at Mach 3.3, and thought we could do that without exceeding the maximum Compressor Inlet Temperature of 427°C or the autopilot bank-angle limit of 45 degrees.
>
> Early in the morning of 27 July 1976, we launched in aircraft 958 and headed northeast. We went supersonic north of Reno, then turned south towards Edwards as we continued to accelerate and climb. We crossed the Edwards starting gate at 6:55:13.7 A.M., at 76,181 feet at Mach 3.3, in minimum afterburner. We were well below the optimum altitude for the existing gross weight, but that was intentional because FAI rules for closed-course speed records required the aircraft to exit the course at least as high as the entry altitude, so we planned to climb all the way around the course.
>
> As soon as we crossed the starting gate, I pushed the throttles up about halfway toward maximum afterburner and let the aircraft start

climbing. At this point the CIT was about 415 to 420°C, and everything looked good. Just about the time we started our left turn around the pylons, I noticed a slight fluctuation in the right engine exhaust nozzle. It was causing the right EGT to fluctuate and we could feel the airplane yawing with the variations in thrust. I watched it for a few seconds, and it seemed to be getting worse, so we decided to ease off on the speed, hoping that a lower airframe temperature would allow the exhaust nozzle controller to stabilize. I eased back on the throttles and allowed the Mach to settle at 3.28. The CIT went down a few degrees, and the fluctuations stopped for a couple of minutes but then they began again, so we backed off a little bit more to Mach 3.25. The fluctuations decreased in frequency, but never completely stopped. We held 3.25 until exiting the course at 7:13:09.4, at 81,776 feet. As I eased the throttles back toward minimum afterburner, the right afterburner blew out. Rather than attempt a relight, we decided to just decelerate and descend earlier than planned to let the airplane cool down.

We were a little disappointed when the official average speed turned out to be 2092.3mph. Still, that's pretty fast for an airplane with a malfunctioning nozzle. Because of the necessity to fly a constant curve outside the course pylons, the actual ground track of the airplane was 1,042 kilometers, so I suppose we did average more than 2,100 mph. Anyway, John and I were satisfied that we got all that 958 could give us on that particular day.

To ignite the JP-7 for engine start, and to light the afterburner section, a liquid chemical ignition system was used. Talk about "unique!" The liquid chemical, triethylborane (TEB), had the physical property of exploding when exposed to air. Mounted on each engine was a sealed tank, inerted with nitrogen gas and filled by maintenance with 600cc of TEB prior to each flight. During engine start, rising fuel pressure in the fuel control signaled the ignition system that a metered amount of TEB could be injected into the engine combustion section, after the pilot moved the throttle from cut-off to the idle position. Preceded slightly by fuel, the TEB exploded and ignited the JP-7. Anyone watching an engine start from behind the aircraft could see the tell-tale green flash of the TEB exploding, igniting the engine.

Each time a throttle was lifted up and moved forward into the afterburner range, another metered shot of TEB would light the AB fuel. Each engine's tank contained enough TEB for at least 16 metered shots to light either the engine or afterburners. Located on the throttle quadrant were TEB remaining counters for each throttle, reset to 16 by maintenance or crews, and mechanically clicked down a number every time the throttle was moved to start the engine or the AB was lit. The AB's lit hard and rarely together. In the event you ran out of TEB, or had a leaking tank, the afterburner could be lit by a catalytic ignitor. The catalytic ignitors are made up of a ceramic disk and two sets of pure platinum screening disks. When the turbine gets hot, the platinum glows and allows afterburner fuel to light off. Since the SR-71 cruised in AB, its AB throttle range was relatively large, allowing for vernier control at all speeds.

The aircraft performance charts provided data for "minimum," "mid-range," and "maximum" afterburner throttle positions.

Former RSO, Lt. Col. Doug Soifer, tells about the accidental making of one of the most unique pictures ever captured of the SR-71 inflight.

> *On our very first TDY to Mildenhall, Mike Smith [the pilot] and I were lucky enough to be there for Air Fete—the big annual air show at Mildenhall. We got to fly the first day and thought we did a good job. During the 20 minute sortie we had a real hard kick during one pass when we went to afterburner and pulled up tight. We didn't think much about it until we landed and were overwhelmed by people as we stepped off the jet and asked us what we did. We had no idea what they were talking about until someone brought over his camcorder and showed us the tape.*
>
> *During that pass we had "13 fireballs" come out of the plane's exhaust. It looked beautiful, and people wanted to know if it could be done again. They used the picture of us with the flames coming out for the next year's Air Fete poster. Mike and I became known as the "Fireball Twins." The maintenance people figured it was the TEB shooting out of its container and igniting the JP-7. With that start, we had an exciting six weeks in England.*

Engines

The basic Pratt and Whitney J-58 engine had its early beginnings in late 1956. When Lockheed and Pratt and Whitney got together to identify the engine and airframe parameters for the SR-71, the enormous advances in technology that had to be developed became apparent. The engine inlet had to be capable of sustaining temperatures in excess of 800°F under certain conditions; the fuel inlet temperatures would reach 350°F at times; fuel temperature at the main and afterburner fuel nozzles would reach 600 to 700°F; lubricating temperatures would vary from 700°F to 1,000°F in some localized parts of the engine.

The J-58 engine was every bit as innovative as the aircraft. It was the first dual cycle engine put into service. At subsonic and transonic speeds it was a standard, single-spool turbojet engine, and it essentially transitioned to a ramjet engine around Mach 2. In fact, at cruise, the rotor of the engine actually has a small negative thrust load on the engine. Other significant features of the J-58 engine include: first and only engine rated for continuous afterburning; engine oil can withstand 550°F with no degradation; first use of fuel as hydraulic fluid; extensive use of high temperature nickel and cobalt alloys; and use of metal seals on plumbing joints. Mr. A. J. "Arnie" Gunderson, our J-58 expert at Pratt and Whitney, provided the following statistics.

> *The engine is 20 feet long, four and a half feet in diameter, weighs 6,500 pounds, and puts out in excess of 32,000 pounds of thrust while consuming 65,000 pounds per hour of JP-7 and flowing 326 pounds per second of air. These are all sea-level parameters. At cruise, the engine has*

grown six inches in length, two and a half inches in diameter, is consuming 11,000 pounds per hour of fuel, and is sucking 800°F air to cool itself off!

Three years and four months after the go-ahead, the first "Blackbird" took to the air. It was powered by two afterburning J-75 turbojet engines to wring out the aircraft at subsonic speeds. As soon as Lockheed felt comfortable with the aircraft, a J-58 was installed in one side. After several months of subsonic flight tests, J-58 engines were finally installed on both sides.

In full AB, each Pratt and Whitney J-58 engine produced more horsepower than the ocean liner, the *Queen Mary* produced. Each engine inlet compressor case utilized a two-position, variable inlet guide vane to maximize engine thrust at specific times. The inlet guide vanes were set in the axial position for takeoff and acceleration to intermediate supersonic speed, and the cambered position for normal cruise. Having the IGV's in the axial position (parallel to the airflow) resulted in more thrust for takeoff and acceleration. They shifted automatically to the cambered position at about Mach 2.0—similar to shifting a car into fifth gear for cruise. Whenever we reached the maximum CIT of 427°C, that was as fast as we were allowed to fly. The engines were not certified beyond that temperature.

The massive engine had two features not found on other conventional jets. The Exhaust Gas Temperature (EGT) was automatically adjusted to keep its temperature within limits by electric "trimming" motors located on each engine. The trimming circuits were activated when the throttles were at full military power or above, and kept the EGT within a nominal band of 790-800°C. The pilot could also manually trim the EGT. The other feature was called the "derich" system, designed to protect the turbine from severe temperatures. If the EGT reached 860°C the fuel-to-air ratio of the engine was automatically reduced ("deriched") to keep the EGT below 860°C. Once the engine "deriched" the pilot could rearm the system and return the engine to its normal state.

The J-58 engine had a single rotor, nine-stage 8.8:1 pressure ratio compressor, utilizing a compressor bleed bypass at high Mach. When opened, bypass valves bleed air from the fourth stage of the compressor, and six large ducts routed the air around the compressor and turbine. The bleed air re-entered the turbine exhaust around the front of the afterburner where it was used for increased thrust and cooling. The transition to bypass operation occurred between 1.8 to 2.0 Mach. At those speeds the J-58 engine was starting to use the supersonic air flow to produce additional thrust.

Periodically, maintenance would test run an engine at night at their test stand facility. To fully appreciate the tremendous amount of power each J-58 produced, a night visit to the J-58 engine test cell on Beale was needed. The facility was located adjacent to the flight line and tested all the J-58 engines overhauled by maintenance before installation in the aircraft. The area surrounding the engine was roped off to keep visitors from getting too close to the engine during the test run. Everyone was briefed on the sequence of events they were about to witness, and issued both ear plugs and ear muffs to protect them from the tremendous noise.

After the idle run, to warm up the engine and check for fuel, oil, and hydraulic leaks, it was powered up to full military power for further checks. Again the engine was checked over by maintenance personnel and the OK given to advance power to the "min" AB setting. A few maintenance checks at "min" AB the power was advanced to "max" AB and The AB exhaust flame was truly a beautiful sight to behold. It produced a perfect blow-torch flame with nine highly visible concentric, circular shock waves forming inside. As power was increased from "min" AB to "max" AB, the blowtorch grew from about 20 feet long to about 30 feet. Certain parts of the engine became translucent from the extreme heating and appeared as if you could actually see inside the engine during the run. "Arnie" Gunderson explains.

> *It is true that after about 10 minutes of running at max, with little or no external lights, all of the internal parts in the turbine and forward afterburner areas are visible as heat shadows. It does look like you are actually looking through the engine at the vanes and various spraybar attachment points.*

The AB engine noise was so loud that its sound waves caused your entire body to shake. Standing 20 feet to the side of the engine you could try holding your teeth tightly together, but they still rattled! In max AB at sea level, the AB section reached temperatures of 3,200°F and at the distance of a football field behind the engine, exhaust temperatures were still 311°F at a velocity of 150 knots. Every visitor who saw a J-58 night engine run went away overwhelmed by the sheer power and beauty of the spectacle.

I'll always remember night flying in the SR-71 and looking back at the ABs through the aircraft's periscope. At high altitude they formed a brilliant blue flame that came to a small point, much like a gas Bunsen burner or a propane welding torch. In absolute silence inside the pressure suit, I could advance the throttles from min AB to max AB and watch the blue flame grow larger and brighter. I'd think to myself, "Such unbelievable power at your fingertips, if only all the aviators in the world could live this experience!"

Starting the huge engine was accomplished by a direct mechanical drive to initiate engine rotation. The large starting cart used to turn the engine over was called a "Buick" because it originally had two large block Buick V-8 engines, mounted beside each other, providing over 600 horsepower to rotate the J-58 engine. When Buick engine parts became scarce, maintenance converted over to using large block Chevrolet V-8 engines. The "Buick" engines didn't have mufflers, just 16 straight pipes coming off of the exhaust manifold. Through a series of gears, the two Buick engines drove a vertical shaft, extending upward and connecting directly to bottom of the J-58 engine.

The "Buick" start cart was wheeled into position just inside the wing tips with the vertical shaft directly beneath the engine. An engine access panel was removed, allowing the vertical shaft to connect directly to the engine. When the pilot called for engine start, the crew chief gave the signal to his assistant, standing under the engine, to pull out the manual throttle on the "Buick" control panel. Applying full throttle to the "Buick," the noise reverberating inside the hangar sounded like a 3,000 horsepower dragster revving up, and at night, flames could be seen shooting out of each exhaust pipe. A sight and sound to behold! The "Buick" turned the engine over slowly at first and then faster and faster, until the J-58 was ignited and stabilized at idle, about 4,000 rpm.

The reason for a direct-drive starter was because their were no air starting carts capable of supplying a sufficient volume of air to rotate the huge J-58 engine. The special lubricating oil used throughout the engine was so thick that it had to be preheated to a minimum of 70°C before the engines could be rotated. Whenever the SR-71 landed somewhere other than a home base, it was a major task to transport the large and cumbersome "Buick" (about 4 feet x 10 feet) just to start the engines, thus a portable air start system was developed in the late 1970s. Eventually, the SR-71 shelters (hangars) at Beale were equipped with large air tanks to store compressed air to rotate the starter adapter. Soon "Buicks" were becoming extinct, and eventually the air start method became preferred by maintenance.

Inlets

At Mach 3.2 cruise, over 80 percent of the thrust created comes from the inlet, 20 percent from the engine. Because the variable geometry inlets are *the* key to the SR-71's outstanding performance, I have devoted considerable discussion to their understanding. The inlet totally surrounds each engine and refers to its associated movable spike and modulating forward and aft bypass doors, all working in harmony to provide optimum aircraft performance.

The purpose of the inlet spike was to control and position the supersonic air flow at the throat of the inlet for optimum performance and to prevent supersonic air from entering the engine. The sharp-pointed movable spike was locked in its full forward position at subsonic speeds. As speed increased, the spikes unlocked above 30,000 feet at 1.6 Mach and moved aft into the throat of the inlet on a programmed schedule, depending on Mach number. The faster you flew, the further aft they traveled, approximately one and five-eighths inches per 0.1 Mach.

Each spike was moved by a large hydraulic actuator, to a maximum travel of 26 inches aft into the inlet. The hydraulic spike actuator had to be able to withstand air pressures exceeding 15 tons under certain air flow conditions. To show the pilot the precise position of each spike as it moved aft into the inlet, a spike indicator in the cockpit had needles for each inlet (labeled L & R) and were graduated from 0 to 26 inches aft. As each spike slowly moved aft, their conical shape increased the captured air stream area by 112 percent and reduced the throat area by 54 percent.

Each J-58 has six, large diameter (about 9 inches) bypass tubes running along the sides of the engine. At high Mach, a portion of the entering air is bypassed around the compressor and turbine sections through these six tubes, giving the engine stall free operation. This bypass feature led to the description of the J-58 as being a turbo-ramjet engine.

Located on the top and bottom of each engine inlet were the forward bypass doors, used to relieve excess air pressure inside the inlet. The bypass door openings were a rotating band of exhaust ports, located a short distance aft of the inlet throat. At supersonic speeds, the louvered doors were controlled by a computer called the Air Inlet Computer (AIC) and modulated from open to close to exhaust excess inlet air pressure overboard. The doors began to open up at 1.4 Mach and reacted to the Duct Pressure Ratio (DPR) inside each inlet.

The DPR was a comparison of pitot pressure on the outer surface of the engine cowl and the static pressure inside the inlet throat. As the DPR increased, the doors modulated open as necessary to relieve excess pressure building up in front of the compressor. In the front cockpit, beside the spike indicator, was the forward bypass door indicator. It had separate needles for each inlet (labeled L & R) and was graduated in increments of ten percent, ranging from full closed to 100 percent open.

There was an inherent problem in having the forward bypass doors open more than necessary. As air bypassed overboard, it created a tremendous amount of drag on the aircraft as the slower exiting air hit the supersonic air stream. In some cases the induced drag was significant enough that the mission had to be aborted because of the excessive fuel consumption requirement to overcome the drag. To optimize performance, the AIC, controlling the forward bypass doors, was programmed to run on a tight schedule, i.e., keep the doors closed as much as possible without causing any problems. Crews referred to this as the inlet "schedule." On some aircraft, the doors were scheduled tighter than on other aircraft, as well as individual inlet schedules between the left and right doors on the same aircraft.

The easiest way to understand the complex relationship between an inlet's spike and door, is to consider the spikes as being "dumb" (since they moved strictly on a Mach schedule) and the doors as "smart" (since they reacted to the DPR and modulated accordingly). As speed increased and the spikes traveled aft on schedule, the forward bypass doors modulated to control increasing inlet air pressure. In case the automatic spike and door computers went haywire, Habus had manual controls, allowing them to position each individual spike and door.

When something went wrong with the inlets, the hardest problem was trying to figure out whether it was the spike, the door, or both creating havoc. If either spike was not on its proper schedule by even the slightest amount (a few inches), it could cause a forward bypass door to be significantly too far open or closed. Each inlet on the same aircraft often had slightly different spike and door positioning.

The spike and doors were biased by the aircraft's Angle of Attack (abbreviated AOA and called "Alpha") and yawing (called "Beta") motion.

As the aircraft began a turn, the forward bypass doors biased open about 3-10 percent more, and the spikes moved forward slightly, providing an extra margin of safety for poor inlet airflow during each turn. The steeper the bank angle, the more the AIC biased the doors open and the spikes forward. Although this caused drag to increase, having the doors biased open and the spike biased forward during turns was the conservative way to fly the airplane. The next section on inlet "unstarts" talks about the consequences of having the inlet doors too tight.

Pilots could always take manual control over the door operation, or the spike and door, but could never operate a manual spike by itself because of the way the system was designed. Flying supersonic with a manual inlet created all kinds of restrictions for the crew: Max speed above 70,000 was limited to Mach 3; max altitude was 80,000; max bank angle above 75,000 was 20 degrees. Further, every time the aircraft banked for a turn the pilot had to manually position the spike slightly more forward to provide a margin of comfort from "unstarts" (described later). The further the spike was positioned forward, and the more the forward bypass door was opened, resulted in less than optimum aircraft cruise performance. The fuel penalty associated with manual spike and door operation was sometimes sufficient to force a crew to abort the mission, depending on where the inlet malfunction occurred.

In normal Mach 3 cruise pilots liked to see the forward bypass doors automatically modulating anywhere between 3 to 5 percent open. If they opened much more than that, you could try flying slightly faster (somewhere around 3.03 Mach) to close them down or take over manually if they were too far open. Another component of each inlet system to help close down the forward bypass doors were a second set of doors, called the *aft* bypass doors.

Positioning the aft bypass doors was a manual operation by the pilot—no computers controlled them. Located outboard of the throttles, were individual left and right aft bypass control switches, with fixed positions of either "CLOSE," "A" (15 percent open), "B" (50 percent open), and "OPEN" (100 percent open). The aft and forward bypass doors worked in opposite directions to each other, i.e., if you opened the aft bypass doors, the forward doors tightened down; if you closed down the aft bypass doors, the forward doors opened up. That way the pilot could manually shift the aft bypass controls during the acceleration and cruise to keep the forward bypass doors from being too far open. The good news was that the aft bypass doors created little drag on the aircraft when opened.

During the climb and acceleration to Mach 3, as the aircraft reached 1.7 Mach and the forward bypass doors began to open, pilots shifted the aft bypass doors from the "CLOSE" position to the "A" position, forcing the forward doors to tighten down. After the IGV's shifted to their cambered position (around 1.7 to 2.3 Mach, depending on ambient temperature), the forward bypass doors opened excessively (around 20-25 percent open) and called for placing the aft bypass to the "B" position, closing the forward doors down again. Since the IGV's shifted independently (anywhere between 85-115 °C CIT), a very noticeable yawing motion of the aircraft took place from the increased drag as the forward doors opened up excessively. If the pilot was distracted by something in the cockpit at the time the IGV's shifted, the yawing motion got his immediate attention!

After IGV shift, the inlets were utilizing the supersonic airflow to produce considerable thrust. Hence, the inlet was now bypassing little air overboard, and the forward doors began to close down tighter and tighter as you accelerated. Approaching Mach 2.6, or as the forward doors closed down tight (to the point where you couldn't stand it anymore), crews returned the aft bypass switch to the "A" position, opening the forward doors slightly. At Mach 3 cruise, pilots had the option of flying with the aft bypass doors in either the "A" or "CLOSE" position, depending on how loose the forward doors were scheduled, what speed they wanted to maintain, and what the outside temperatures were. Flying above 3.05 Mach, the aft bypass was normally positioned to "CLOSE," depending on outside temperatures.

Unstarts and Aerodynamic Disturbances (ADs)

Anytime the inlet pressure became unacceptable to the AIC, a phenomenon known as an Aerodynamic Disturbance, or "unstart" took place. Habus shortened Aerodynamic Disturbance to a "AD" and used the terms "unstart" and AD interchangeably during discussions. An inlet unstart can only occur when the aircraft is supersonic and after an inlet has been "started"; that is, supersonic flow is established inside the inlet. The inlets usually "start" between Mach 1.6 and 1.8. As supersonic speed increases, the supersonic air flow inside the inlet slowly moves aft, to a position near an opening called the "shock trap bleed." The shock trap bleed is an exhaust port, located in front of the forward bypass doors, and is designed to prevent the supersonic air from going any further into the inlet and also provides cooling air around the engine.

The term "unstart" refers to a phenomenon of a supersonic inlet when the Compressor Inlet Pressure (CIP) becomes too great and has no place to go inside the inlet and therefore unstarts (shock wave expulsion) in order to relieve the excess pressure building up. An unstart is recognized in the cockpit by a loud "BANG" noise, accompanied by the aircraft rolling, yawing, and pitching, and a decrease of the CIP toward 4psi. The jet engine itself continues to run although the afterburner may blow itself out during an unstart.

An unstart was usually a very unpredictable and violent maneuver of the aircraft. The aircraft yaws violently towards the unstarted inlet because of the tremendous amount of drag immediately induced, creating both a rolling and pitch-up motion of the aircraft. At altitudes above 75,000 feet, aileron control may be ineffective in controlling the roll during an unstart unless the Angle of Attack is immediately reduced. The instant an unstart occurs, the pilot's first action is to arrest any pitch-up motion of the aircraft. They generally occurred when you least expected them—all relaxed and taking in the magnificent view from 75,000 feet.

As you became more experienced in the aircraft you could sometimes feel when an unstart was about to occur if the forward bypass door was closing down too tightly. A very subtle inlet "duct rumble" manifested itself throughout the airframe and gave you a clue that an unstart was imminent, unless the doors were about to open up, or you took corrective action by shifting the aft bypass doors closed.

The most severe unstarts occurred right at IGV shift and were often accompanied by an afterburner blow out, creating additional pitch, yaw, and roll of the aircraft. When the SR taxied in from a mission, experienced maintenance personnel and Habus could tell visually if the fliers experienced a "good," solid unstart by looking at the engine exhaust "turkey feathers." They were the overlapping slats of metal surrounding the exhaust, which opened and closed according to the afterburner's pressure output. A "good" unstart caused the "turkey feathers" to open beyond their limits and, consequently, jumped out of their overlapping tracks and became visibly tangled.

Inlet Restarts

The inlets had an automatic "restart" feature to aid the pilot in recovery from an unstart. The "restart" maneuver produced a tremendous amount of drag on the affected inlet and rolled the aircraft rapidly in the direction of the unstarted inlet. If you happened to be in a 35 degree banked turn when the inside inlet unstarted, its increased drag, plus the thrust from the outside engine, increased bank rapidly. To keep inlet drag symmetrical during a restart cycle, the inlets had a "crosstie" feature active above 2.3 Mach, forcing the opposite (good) inlet to sympathetically go through the same restart cycle. This helped to minimize the extreme rolling/yawing maneuver and prevented the good inlet from possibly unstarting, but now doubled the increased drag on the aircraft.

The restart cycle was automatically initiated when a Shock Expulsion Sensor (SES) sensed an inlet unstart. To recapture the supersonic air flow, the automatic restart cycle went through the following sequence: the forward bypass doors drive full open, the spikes rapidly move forward as much as 15 inches, spikes then retract to their scheduled position (about 4 seconds after shock expulsion is sensed), then the forward bypass doors close back down to their automatic operation after the spikes retract.

If the unstart didn't "clear" (correct) itself after one cycle, the automatic restart cycle would continue to repeat itself until the pilot took over manually. One restart cycle could decrease airspeed from Mach 3 to Mach 2.9 in about 15 seconds or less. If the restart cycle continued, the Mach would decrease even further. With an unstart, the pilot's primary concern is aircraft control, and then he tries to figure out which inlet unstarted and why.

Above 2.3 Mach (with crosstie) it was important to identify which inlet unstarted, and the pilot could do so by watching the spike and door indicators closely. Whichever spike and door needle (L or R) was moving to its restart position first was the unstarted inlet—the lagging indicator being the good (sympathetic) inlet. It really became confusing if you were already flying with a manual spike and/or door and had an unstart. Since a manual spike and/or door did not respond to the automatic restart sequence, it was extremely difficult to tell which inlet was the culprit. Later on, a digital upgrade to the aircraft (discussed later) included left and right unstart lights on the instrument panel to indicate which inlet unstarted.

Depending on where your head was at the time, it was not uncommon to bang your pressure suit helmet off the side of the canopy when an unstart occurred. Most unstarts cleared (corrected) themselves after one automatic restart cycle and were considered transient. You simply pressed on with the mission and paid more attention to inlet parameters. If the forward bypass door was causing the unstarts, it was simply a matter of taking over manually and positioning the door where it was supposed to be. However, occasionally unstarts didn't clear that easily and repeatedly went through the unstart/restart cycle. Continuous unstarts that wouldn't clear were generally caused by hydraulic actuator problems with the spike or a major malfunction of the AIC, requiring the crew to take over manual control of the inlet(s) and most probably descend to subsonic speeds.

Just below the spike indicator were left and right restart switches. They were used to override the automatic restart cycle if the inlet(s) wouldn't clear. Turning ON either (or both) restart switch drove the respective spike full forward and its door full open, creating a tremendous amount of drag on the aircraft, but provided the most conservative means of clearing the inlet(s). The spike and door remained there until the pilot was ready to turn the restart switch OFF. Once the spike was full forward and the door full open, the pilot placed the manual forward bypass door control knob to the 100 percent open position. Next, he turned the restart switch OFF, and the spike immediately retracted back into the inlet while the door remained 100 percent open. If the unstart did not repeat, the pilot assumed the spike was OK, but the door was the culprit and had to be controlled manually. If the unstart had repeated itself when the pilot turned the restart switch OFF, he would assume the spike was at fault and would have to run both a manual spike and door inlet. Every time you turned the restart switch OFF, we'd grit our teeth in preparation for another unstart as the spike started moving aft. A big sigh of relief if it didn't go "BANG!" again.

On the right throttle was a two-detent slide switch, also used to control the inlets. It was called the throttle restart switch and was located on the throttles for quick access when everything else had failed and you needed stable inlets immediately. Sliding the switch back with your left thumb to its first detent drove both forward bypass doors full open. Sliding it further back to the second detent kept the doors fully opened and now drove both spikes full forward. Sliding the throttle restart switch ON gave you no choice but to slow down and descend. The descent rate in this configuration is extremely rapid and was used for emergency descents necessitated by other serious aircraft malfunctions.

I would estimate, on average, that about one in every ten unstarts resulted in the afterburner blowing out (quitting). When it did, it required the pilot to be extra forceful in flying the aircraft on track. Normally, a single, automatic self-clearing unstart would not cause the aircraft to drift off its programmed flight path to any great degree. However, if you were already turning when the unstart occurred and the afterburner blew out, it took plenty of work to stay close to your flight track. First, the inlet had to be cleared before the afterburner could be relit. During this time, you were fighting to maintain aircraft control, stay on track, analyze what went wrong with the inlet(s), and deciding what to do about it—all at 33 miles per minute! You had your hands full. It was extremely easy to get suckered into the wrong analysis of the inlets and apply the wrong corrective procedures. It's happened to every Habu more than once! Former RSO, Col. Roger Jacks (Ret), describes his first inflight unstart.

> *My first experience with an unstart sent my heart right up into my throat. We had practiced unstarts numerous times in the simulator, and we had heard all the horror stories of how intense the experience could be. I have to admit the first unstart experience did not disappoint me. In fact, I was amazed that an aircraft could survive such a violent event. We were at approximately Mach 2.3, 60,000 feet, in a turn and climbing when Captain Kinego advised me one of the inlets showed signs of instability. Shortly thereafter—KER BLAM!—the aircraft slammed my head against the side of the cockpit and then I felt it momentarily become unstable as it yawed, pitched, and vibrated. I performed my job, reading the checklist for unstarts and monitoring the aircraft attitude while my heart was racing with anxiety. I was very grateful I was flying with a seasoned and talented pilot like Joe Kinego who easily diagnosed the problem and maintained aircraft control. I don't know if that first unstart was a white knuckle event in Joe's life as it was mine; I guess I didn't want to know. I can't say that unstarts ever became routine, but they did become more tolerable.*

Former SR-71 pilot, Lt. Col. Joe Matthews (Ret), recalls having unstarts early on during training.

> *Sometime during the late summer/early fall of 1983, Curt and I were starting our second accel to altitude after filling up from the tankers. During the first hot leg, the airplane had run "as advertised," no unstarts, smooth as silk, not a hiccup . . . that should have been our first warning! Instead we chose to ignore this information and went ahead with the second accel anyway. We were over southeastern Washington state around Mach 2.6, still accelerating in a climbing left turn headed westbound. The jet was just humming . . . then . . . BAM/SHUDDER! Left side unstart for sure, but it was accompanied with a Christmas tree display of additional caution and warning lights. Two of which made it through my bug-eyed vision to register on my brain, generator, and hydraulic pressure . . . I*

croaked out an "ADS failure, left side" to Curt who already had the check-list out.

> *The plane wanted to roll deeper into the left turn, and the nose just kept coming up. I took my left hand off the throttles to help push the stick forward and to the right. Finally, with both hands on the stick, it took absolutely full forward, full right stick deflection and a generous amount of right rudder before the airplane began to roll out. The nose stopped climbing and ever-so-slowly reversed itself and began to fall! I couldn't talk, the air wasn't getting past my heart which was still firmly lodged at the top of my throat. But eventually we got things under control, and the descent and recovery to Fairchild AFB was, thankfully, uneventful.*

> *Two things dominate my memory of this particular event. Deep down I know how very, very close we were to losing that airplane. The second thing . . . the simulator training simply saved our butts!*

Former SR-71 pilot Lt. Col. William Burk (Ret) recalls unstarts on his very first operational mission at Det 1.

> *My RSO and fellow crew member, Capt. Tom Henichek, and I had just finished training and were on our first operational tour. The mission was designed as two passes through the DMZ of South Korea. Everything went as planned through our initial level off at 72,000 feet and Mach 3. Proceeding up the west coast of South Korea over the East China Sea, we approached North Korea. We made a right turn to the east for our first pass across the DMZ with a CPA (Closest Point of Approach) to North Korea of 1.5 miles . . . not much room for error when you are traveling one mile every two seconds!*

> *On the east coast of Korea we made a 60 degree left turn, followed immediately by a 320 degree right turn over the Sea of Japan. This was to position the SR for our second westbound pass through the DMZ. As we started the roll out of our 320 degree turn at 78,000 feet and maximum Mach, we experienced a violent unstart. This was about as bad a position as one could be in for an upwing unstart to occur. The aircraft pitched up and left with an immediate stick shaker warning.*

> *With the stick full forward I allowed the left inlet to attempt an automatic restart which was followed by another violent unstart. At that point I put both inlets manually in the restart configuration and waited for the SR to slow and stabilize. With the stick still full forward, the nose of the aircraft continued to drift left and right in a 5 to 10 degree arc above the horizon. The nose wouldn't come down for 20 to 30 agonizing seconds. At this point I asked Tom our position relative to our track across the DMZ. He said we were right of track which would have us closing on North Korean airspace. I initiated a 30 to 40 degree bank left turn and attempted a manual restart of the left inlet. Neither manual or auto restarts were successful, so we started a deceleration and descent to subsonic speeds and 30,000 feet. Some quick calculations showed we could make it to Okinawa subsonic. As we got closer it became apparent that we were a bit short on fuel, so the standby tanker was launched, and we took*

on an additional 10,000 pounds. It was quite an exciting first mission, to say the least!

Hydraulic Systems and Flight Controls

An Accessory Drive System (ADS) was mounted forward on each engine which converted power from the engine to drive the hydraulic pumps, the AC electrical generators, and fuel circulating pumps. One of the more serious emergency procedures Habus could face was a failure of either the left or right ADS. If the ADS failed, it meant the complete loss of one electrical generator, two of the hydraulic pumps (spike and door on that side), and a fuel circulation pump. As soon as the pilot recognized an ADS failure, he immediately turned the throttle restart switch ON and began a decel. With no hydraulic pressure on the spike and doors, they were free to "float," causing repeated unstarts and possible engine flameouts.

The aircraft had four hydraulic systems. The "A" & "L" and the "B" & "R" hydraulic systems were located on their respective left and right engine. The L & R hydraulic systems powered their respective spike and door, the landing gear, brakes, air refueling system, and nosewheel system. The A & B pumps powered the flight controls with hydraulic actuators. The left and right elevons had 20 hydraulic actuators on *each* side, and the rudders had four actuators each. Either the A or the B system could independently power the flight controls in case of an engine failure.

Hydraulic fluid to run the actuators was designed to withstand the high temperature at Mach 3 without breaking down its chemical properties or loosing its viscosity. Since many of the SR-71's problems only manifested themselves at high temperature, maintenance had to duplicate this on the ground by what was called "hot gigging" the aircraft. It involved connecting the aircraft's hydraulic systems to a large maintenance cart that heated the hydraulic fluid to inflight temperatures. In a closed plumbing system, the hot hydraulic fluid actuated the flight controls, so maintenance could begin their trouble shooting analysis.

The large delta wing of the SR-71 did not lend itself to have separate elevator and aileron control surfaces but instead utilized elevons, a single control surface that combines elevator and aileron inputs. Mechanical pitch and roll inputs from the control stick were blended in a mixer assembly, located in the tail of the aircraft, to actuate the elevons and move the aircraft accordingly. The mixer was a very complex assembly of bellcranks, feel springs, bias springs, push rods, and other components that converted inputs from the stick and changed them into servo inputs. The servos, in turn, metered hydraulic fluid to the elevon actuators to provide a blended pitch and roll control.

The two large rudders were fully moveable surfaces, unlike conventional aircraft having a vertical stabilizer with a trailing rudder control. Each rudder assembly was canted inward 15 degrees for increased directional control and to reduce radar returns off the aircraft. Single engine operation called for considerable rudder input to compensate for the engine placement off centerline and the tremendous thrust it created in afterburner.

At cruise Mach, having the rudders streamlined was important for good imagery results as well as for aircraft performance. The rudder trim was located on the control stick and moved both rudders left and right. On the lower left console of the cockpit was a spring-loaded Right Hand Rudder Synchronizer switch. Holding the switch in either the LEFT or RIGHT position moved *only* the right rudder. To center the rudders, the pilot pushed the periscope up and visually aligned the left rudder with the fixed, bottom portion of the rudder by using the stick trim switch. Then he turned the periscope to see the right rudder. If it was not aligned, he moved the Right Hand Rudder Synchronizer switch to get perfect alignment. Even after you aligned each rudder they had to be checked periodically. The heat of Mach 3 cruise occasionally caused the hydraulic actuators to move the rudders. Colonel Joe Kinego (Ret) recalls an early experience of his with rudder alignment problems.

> During the first cruise leg, I noticed that the aircraft was a little out of trim, so I began to put in some rudder trim to correct the situation. Well, I kept on putting in the rudder trim, and the trim needle on the gauge kept moving to the right, but the rudder itself did not move. This was only my third or so flight without an instructor, and Roger and I began discussing the situation. I tried to move the rudders using the rudder peddles, but they would still not move. We flew around the route trying to figure this one out, and soon it was time to descend anyway. During the descent at approximately 1.8 Mach we felt a "thud" shake the aircraft, and the rudders began to move again. Following the refueling we elected to complete the mission, so once again we climbed to altitude for supersonic cruise. Once again I noticed that the rudders locked up and would not move during the cruise leg. We flew the leg and during the descent felt the same "thud" followed by normal rudder movement.
>
> When we got on the ground and debriefed the mission I told the debriefers what had happened. No one had heard of this problem before, and we were very new to the program, so there were a fair number of skeptics. I was called several times over the weekend to restate the incident to the maintenance personnel and tech reps. By early the following week, everyone had given up trying to find the problem and decided to fly the aircraft with a more experienced crew.
>
> Bob Helt was picked to fly, and he departed on another sortie. About two hours later we got a call in the squadron that he had declared an emergency and was coming back from the midwest because his rudders had locked up during supersonic cruise. As it turned out the rudder actuators were freezing up due to the heat buildup while cruising at supersonic speeds. I believe Lockheed resorted to Teflon type hydraulic actuators after that incident.

After we lost an SR-71 in a landing accident at Kadena in May of 1973, it was 16 years before we had our next SR-71 loss, in April of 1989. Unfortunately, it was also a Det 1 aircraft (974) which crashed into the Philippine Sea, just one fourth of a mile north of the island of Luzon. The crew had just leveled off at Mach 3 cruise, heading southwest out of Okinawa, when all hell broke loose. The left engine suffered a catastrophic failure and seized. Unknown to the crew, the shattered turbine blades ripped through an area of the aircraft severing the flight control hydraulic lines. During descent the crew realized the worst—they were losing *both* A and B hydraulic pressure. While many of the SR-71 emergency procedures, had numerous checklist steps to remedy the situation, the A and B hydraulic system failure checklist has only one step: EJECT!

While struggling to keep the aircraft flying and heading towards Clark AFB for an emergency landing, the flight control movements became increasingly exaggerated to keep the aircraft upright. Soon, full deflection of the stick would no longer move the elevons, and a bailout was imminent. Knowing the aircraft would eventually not respond to any stick movements, it was better to bail out while the aircraft was controllable, rather than uncontrollable, so the pilot ordered a bailout.

The crew parachuted safely into the water several hundred yards off shore. Shortly, local fishermen came by and pulled them out of the water and took them to a local village where they tried to phone Clark AFB to tell everyone they were safe and arrange for a pickup. As it turned out, the crew eventually ended up at the local mayor's home for food and drinks. They finally made radio contact with a Navy P-3 Orion looking for them, and a HH-53 helicopter picked them up shortly in a rice field and took them to Clark AFB for a physical examination.

A decision was made to locate and bring up the SR-71, which was resting on the shallow ocean floor. The Navy sent a floating salvage crane and Navy SEAL divers from Subic Bay in the Philippines. Colonel Al Cirino (Ret), former SR-71 pilot, was sent to head up the salvage operation and preside over the Accident Investigation Board. It took two weeks to recover all of the aircraft frame, engines, sensors, and camera equipment out of 120 feet of water. The wreckage was taken back to Okinawa for a complete analysis, and the engines were sent to the Pratt & Whitney Company in Florida for a closer evaluation. Their investigation determined that the left engine's main bearings failed and caused the subsequent engine seizure. The A and B hydraulic lines were severed by the compressor and turbine blades being thrown from the engine, causing the complete loss of hydraulic fluid. Until the investigation was completed, the entire fleet of SR-71s was grounded for 36 days by the Air Force. The good news was that the pilot, Dan House, and RSO, Blair Bozak, were safe and well.

Electrical System

The electrical system was simplistic. An AC generator was located on each engine's ADS, capable of supplying the entire aircraft electrical load in the event of a single engine failure. A Constant Speed Drive (CSD) unit kept each generator's electrical output regulated. Left and right generator switches in the front cockpit had three positions: the "NORM" position connected the generators to the normal AC electrical distribution buses; the "OFF" position disconnected them; and an "EMER" position provided unregulated AC electrical power and was to be used only when either generator could no longer supply electrical power. The unregulated emergency power was provided to run the fuel boost pumps, fuel transfer valves, pitch trim, and basic cockpit lighting.

Two Transformer-Rectifiers (TRs) converted AC into DC electrical power. Dual 28 volt DC batteries were capable of supplying reduced DC electrical power for 40 minutes if both generators were inoperative. An inverter, converting DC into AC electrical power, supplied emergency AC power directly from the battery to run emergency AC requirements in the event of a complete electrical failure.

Circuit breakers were located throughout both cockpits. Numerous emergency procedures required the pilot to locate and pull, or push in, particular circuit breakers located on the lower left and right console. In the pressure suit it was impossible to turn your head around far enough to see the far aft circuit breakers on the lower console. For that reason, all the circuit breakers in the cockpits that couldn't be seen were identified in our checklist by a row and column. They were labeled in terms of "back" and "down," so the RSO could call out from his checklist, "left side, back six, down four," and the pilot would know precisely where to reach and feel. It was an exercise in Braille for the pilot, as he reached behind his left side and felt back six rows of circuit breakers and then felt down (inward) to the fourth. Whenever you pulled a circuit breaker up that you couldn't see, pilots watched intently for the appropriate response to insure they pulled the correct one. Some circuit breakers were difficult to pull up with the pressure suit gloves, so each pilot was issued a small metal circuit breaker tool that easily popped them up.

Flight Characteristics

The SR-71 had no high-lift devices of any sort, other than the lift created by the aerodynamic body of the fuselage, called the "chine." The chines were the flared portions of the fuselage extending outward, starting at the pitot tube on the tip of the nose and extended aft to a point where they blended into both wings. The chines improved directional stability with increasing angle of attack at all airspeeds. However, their primary purpose was to provide a substantial portion of the total lift at high supersonic speeds and eliminate the need for canard surfaces or special nose-up trimming devices. Besides being aerodynamically functional, the chine contained various compartments, called "bays," to house electronics and sensors.

The mid-span location of the engines minimized drag and interference effects of the fuselage. The inboard cant and droop of the nacelles gives maximum pressure recovery at normal angles of attack for high-altitude supersonic cruise. The outboard portion of the wing's leading edge has negative conical camber to move the center of lift inboard and relieve loading on the nacelle. It also improves the maximum lift characteristics of the outboard wing at high angles of attack and enhances crosswind landing capability. There were no flaps, slats, spoilers, or artificial stall warning devices installed.

Unlike many other aircraft, Habus *never* practiced stalls in the SR-71. As Angle of Attack (AOA) increased, the aircraft reached a point where it departed from controlled flight rather than stalling out. A nose-up pitching moment developed as the AOA increased, which eventually becomes uncontrollable as the critical AOA was reached. Subsonic, the critical AOA for pitch-up is approximately 18 degrees. At high Mach cruise, extreme caution was necessary if Habus were flying at altitudes above those for optimum supersonic cruise because the AOA could exceed 7 to 8 degrees. At 7 to 8 degrees AOA, any pitch transients caused by unstarts, increased bank angles, etc., could easily lead to an uncontrolled pitch-up maneuver.

Since there was no stall warning, the SR-71 had an Automatic Pitch Warning (APW) system incorporated into the flight controls. Placing the "PUSHER & SHAKER" switch to the "SHAKER ONLY" position caused the control stick to vibrate vigorously when the *rate* of pitch change was sensed to be too great, or a predetermined AOA was reached. When you pulled too quickly on the stick and got the shaker, merely relaxing back pressure eliminated the shaking stick. In the "PUSHER & SHAKER" switch position, if you ignored the shaker warning and continued to pull harder on the stick, the pusher system activated. The pusher system physically moved the elevons down and literally jerked the stick forward out of your hand to reduce the AOA. When it activated at supersonic speeds, you knew you were in trouble and had better relax back pressure because if you didn't, a bailout was not far away!

Navigational Systems

The SR-71's high speed and sensitive missions demanded a navigational system that was highly accurate, reliable, and didn't depend on inputs from other sources subject to electronic jamming. Patterned after navigational systems used on ICBMs, the SR-71's Astro-inertial Navigation System (ANS) filled those requirements. Simplistically, the ANS was a star tracking navigation system. At least two different stars had to be tracked for optimum navigation performance. With a highly accurate chronometer (to the 100th of a second) supplying Greenwich Mean Time (GMT) and the Julian date, along with a 61-star catalog stored inside the ANS computer, it was possible to know precisely where the SR-71 was over the ground.

Selection of which star to track was made by the ANS computer as a function of latitude, longitude, day of year, time of day, aircraft pitch and roll, and location of the sun. The computer selected a star by going through its star catalog, which was arranged in decreasing star brightness, until it found a star. A telescope-like star tracker looked for the stars in an expanding rectangular spiral search pattern. The ANS window was located on top of the fuselage, just forward of the air refueling door and consisted of a round piece of distortion-free quartz glass (about 9 inch diameter) that allowed the star tracker to see through.

On the cockpit ANS panel a star "ON" light indicated that a minimum of two different stars had been tracked within the last five minutes.

Star tracking was automatic. However, the RSO could assist the system in overcoming conditions such as overcasts, changes of sky background brightness, long periods of ground time, and air refueling when the boom obscures the tracking window. Former RSO, Col. Phil Loignon (Ret), recalls a sortie he flew over North Vietnam that changed future ANS procedures.

> *Jim Watkins and I launched on a operational sortie. We had solid cloud cover to 60,000 feet and no star lock on at coast in. A viewsight fix revealed a position error, so I updated the ANS. After exiting North Vietnam, the "STAR" light came on, and our track showed a 10 nautical mile error. The inquisition by the 15th Air Force following that was something to behold. We had flown over Hanoi instead of 10 miles away. Our error had allowed intelligence to determine that a new device on the North Vietnam radar sites was actually an optical device for tracking low level fighters. Although I was thought to have "screwed up," Lockheed came through with the determinations that the ANS tracked a light bulb in the hangar and had induced a heading error. We changed our ANS turn-on procedures as of that date.*

By comparing the position of the stars to their known location, and with the exact time of day, the ANS could then compute the aircraft's precise position. A normal gyro compass alignment of the ANS required 36 minutes of warm-up time and provided the SR-71 with great-circle navigational accuracy of 1,885 feet (0.3 nautical mile) for up to ten hours of flying time. It still amazes me even today that astronomers have charted our solar system so accurately that it allows the ANS to calculate the SR-71's position so precisely. Things may change here on Earth from century to century, but the same stars guided both Christopher Columbus and Habus.

The heart of the ANS was a large, self-contained unit—about half the size of a large refrigerator—called the Guidance Group. A computer inside the Guidance Group computed auto-navigation, guidance and avionics control, and maintained a continuously updated account of navigational status and coordinate values. The computer also stored instrument and mathematical coefficients, predetermined data references that defined the stars, and the mission flight plan. For continuous accuracy, the computer initiated and evaluated self-tests periodically throughout the flight. Software corrections to the star data were provided for the supersonic shock wave over the star tracker window that refracts the star light and for pressure and temperature gradients acting on the window, causing optical lens effects.

The aircraft's flight plan and sensor operation for the entire mission were contained on a wide tape punched with holes and loaded inside the Guidance Group computer memory. The tape was made by the 9th SRW's Mission Planning Branch, a group of highly experienced Air Force officers who knew how to plan SR-71 missions down to the finest detail. Many former SR-71 RSOs worked as mission planners to provide expertise. As the tape ran inside the Guidance Group, the pattern of holes "told" the aircraft where to navigate, what bank angle for turns, when various sensors were to turn ON/OFF, and where to have the sensors "look" for intelligence gathering.

Prior to every flight, ANS maintenance personnel loaded the tape and ran the Guidance Group in their shop to insure the programming was correct. The Guidance Group was delivered to the aircraft several hours before flight. It was hoisted up by a crane assembly and slowly lowered into its air conditioned bay located directly in front of the air refueling door. Once inside its bay, numerous electrical, air conditioning, and computer connections were completed, mating the Guidance Group to the aircraft. An exterior aircraft panel containing the star tracker window bolted over the Guidance Group.

The RSO had all the ANS controls in his cockpit. On the ANS panel, the RSO had a constant digital readout of longitude and latitude, wind direction and velocity, time to turn, and distance to the next turn point. By use of his keyboard a variety of other information was available from the ANS display panel, such as ground speed and true air speed. As long as everything was working satisfactorily, the RSO monitored the readouts to insure their accuracy. At any time, the RSO could manually override the ANS's preprogrammed flight path and sensor action points, if required. It was an automatic abort if the ANS wasn't working correctly, and since Don had first-hand knowledge of that, he had total responsibility in making abort decisions concerning our navigational accuracy. If we were in clouds or couldn't achieve a satisfactory star lock-on, the SR-71 navigated by an inertial-only guidance system. The inertial system had to be aligned and was updated automatically by the ANS when it was navigating normally. By using fix points every hour, the inertial-only system maintained a navigational accuracy of two nautical miles per hour.

On one occasion Don flew with another pilot, then Lt. Col. Bob Crowder (Ret), to take the SR-71 to a remote island in the Indian Ocean, called Diego Garcia. It was a test of Det 1's capability to support and fly reconnaissance missions out of a bare-base, remote island. Diego Garcia's strategic naval location was also gaining popularity with the Air Force as a staging base to fly B-52s and tankers from. We wanted to prove our capability to fly the SR-71 from there as well. One of Beale's SR-71 shelters was secretly torn down overnight and erected on the island days later, JP-7 was shipped in and stored, and large ground-handling equipment was flown in from Det 1 on C-141s. An advance party of Det 1 maintenance people were sent to receive the aircraft. Don really didn't want to go on the trip because he had just planned his big Lieutenant Colonel promotion party about the same time he was due to return from Diego Garcia. His room was all ready for the party, so he left me with last minute instructions to have his promotion party regardless of whether he was back in time or not.

After several air refuelings, the aircraft arrived in good shape. Although no sorties were flown out of Diego Garcia, maintenance practiced all the necessary routines in order to prepare the aircraft for flight. After everyone was confident that the right equipment and supplies were in place to carry out numerous sorties, the return flight back to Okinawa was planned. Shortly after takeoff, Don's ANS went haywire, and they returned to Diego Garcia. Navigation to each air refueling track was over thousands of miles of open ocean and required a high degree of reliance solely on the ANS. On their second attempt they had to abort on the ground, again because of a bad ANS. On the third try, Bob and Don were prepared for an alternative means of navigation in case the ANS failed a third time. It was called dead reckoning! The ANS did fail inflight; however, they successfully proceeded on to all their air refuelings by basically pointing the nose of the aircraft straight ahead. All the crews met Don at the aircraft and told him his party was "gang-busters!" He was one day late.

DAFICS

In the front cockpit, along the right console, was the Automatic Flight Control System (AFCS). Originally, the AFCS was an analog system throughout the aircraft, later upgraded to a digital system. The new system, called the Digital Automatic Flight and Inlet Control System (DAFICS, pronounced "daf-eks"), was undoubtedly the most extensive upgrade and modernization effort accomplished on the SR-71 since it was built. In 1981, I recall having numerous meetings at Palmdale with Don and I, the Palmdale Flight Test crews and the Honeywell design engineers, trying to iron out where and how an integrated digital system could replace the analog system to make the aircraft more reliable and efficient. We sat around a large conference table, listening as Honeywell engineers told Habus there would be no such thing as unstarts if the inlets were digitally controlled.

They went on to explain that the only reason we currently had unstarts was because the analog system couldn't cope and react to inlet dynamics fast enough, and with a digital inlet system, unstarts would be a thing of the past. We were skeptical of their pronouncement. Unstarts were a way of life for Habus, and to be able to eliminate them completely sounded like a fairy tale. As it turned out, the number of unstarts were reduced considerably with the DAFICS upgrade; however, they were never eliminated. DAFICS was thoroughly tested at Palmdale, and after many flights to work out the "bugs," it was finally installed in the first operational SR-71 in mid-1983. It proved to be a highly reliable system and dramatically decreased the maintenance workload.

The heart of the system consisted of three triple-redundant computers that constantly compared inputs and voted among themselves. If a fault was detected in one computer, it dropped off and allowed the other two computers to continue to operate. The AFCS control panel was redesigned to incorporate extra warning lights and included a DAFICS preflight Built-In-Test (BIT) switch to check out the system after engine start. Activating the BIT switch tested the entire DAFICS system, including the flight controls and inlets, something we could not do previously. During the four-minute preflight test, the aircraft made a very noticeable "howling" noise as the spikes moved back into the inlets for their checks.

A DAFICS analyzer panel was located in one of the chine bays (E-bay) and gave maintenance personnel an immediate readout of what was wrong if the DAFICS test didn't check out satisfactorily. From the DAFICS analyzer panel, maintenance could easily adjust the Air Inlet Computer (AIC) schedule of the spikes and doors, if needed.

The Stability Augmentation System (SAS)

The Stability Augmentation System (SAS, pronounced "sass") was designed to do exactly what its name implies. During normal flight conditions, the SR-71 experiences many small changes in attitude due to air loads or control inputs. These attitude changes are sensed by three pitch-, six yaw-, and two roll-rate sensors in each axis. Small attitude changes detected by these sensors are sent to the DAFICS computers, which in turn, electrically command transfer valve positions of the SAS servos. Transfer valves are used to convert the electrical signals into a proportional hydraulic flow and move the SAS servo actuators accordingly. The SAS servos position the flight control surfaces to compensate for the original sensed rate of attitude change. All this happens in a fraction of a second.

Although difficult to hand fly, aircraft controllability without SAS has been demonstrated to Mach 3.2. At supersonic speeds, aircraft control with the SAS off is extremely sensitive and stick control movements needed to be kept to the minimum necessary. A pitch change of only one degree at Mach 3 became an instant 3,000 foot/minute rate of climb or descent! Crews that have experienced the complete loss of their SAS at high Mach numbers have stated they had their hands full just keeping the aircraft upright. That's precisely why the SAS had triple redundant computers. Flying subsonic without the SAS was not too difficult, although the aircraft tended to wallow around slightly.

Whether the SR-71 was digital or analog equipped, the pilot still used the AFCS in the same manner for flying the aircraft. The AFCS panel was located on the forward portion of the pilot's right console and was divided in two sections. The top half of the AFCS contained the pitch, roll, and yaw SAS switches. Engaging each SAS switch energized their respective transfer valve, permitting hydraulic flow to fine tune the flight control surfaces. Large taxiing movements of the aircraft on the ground with the SAS switches engaged caused the rudders to slam against their full deflection position because of the yaw rate gyro's input. I know because the first time I was told by Kadena tower after landing to make a 180 degree turn on the runway, it felt like all hell broke loose when the rudders started banging away. I immediately stopped the aircraft and asked mobile if we had just fallen into a ditch or something, it was that bad. I soon discovered I forgot a landing checklist item—SAS switches OFF!

The Autopilot

On the bottom half of the AFCS was the autopilot. The basic autopilot had two solenoid-held switches, one for the pitch axis and the other for roll. Once engaged, the control stick was disabled and small, serrated pitch and roll wheels on the autopilot control panel now controlled aircraft movement. Only a small portion of each wheel was exposed on top of the autopilot panel. The pitch and roll wheels permitted small adjustments by moving the aircraft approximately one degree in pitch per 15 degrees of wheel rotation and one degree in roll per 8 degrees of rotation. To aid in making small finger inputs to the wheels and to keep from tiring out the pressure-suit-enclosed right hand, a clear plastic hand rest folded down in perfect position to rest the heel of your hand. The pilot then flew the aircraft by rotating the pitch wheel up and down with his index finger and the roll wheel left and right with his middle finger or ring finger.

In this basic autopilot mode, the pilot flew the aircraft through each wheel just as if he had control of the stick. There was no altitude hold function or automatic throttle control features incorporated into the autopilot whatsoever. Consequently, during cruise Habus controlled the aircraft's pitch attitude with the pitch wheel and airspeed with the throttles.

The basic pitch and roll switches had to be engaged first before *any* of the sub-functions of the autopilot would operate. Solenoid-held switches on the autopilot controlled the three sub-functions of aircraft heading, navigation, and airspeed. When the "HEADING HOLD" switch was engaged the aircraft would hold the heading at the time of engagement.

To the left of the HEADING HOLD switch was the "AUTO-NAV" switch, which stood for automatic navigation. It was an either/or situation between these two switches—only one could be on at a time. In the AUTO-NAV mode the ANS was running the show and navigated the aircraft accordingly to stay on track by banking and turning. It took some adjustment learning to have the AUTO-NAV fly the programmed track while you controlled pitch with the wheel and airspeed with the throttles. You definitely needed to anticipate what the ANS was about to do, in order to coordinate pitch and power.

Although we practiced hand flying the SR at Mach 3, it was not an easy aircraft to maneuver at those speeds and altitudes. Straight and level you could hold track accurately, but turns presented a greater challenge to stay on course. After hand flying a 90 degree turn you were doing well to be within a mile of your track. One mile might not sound too far off track considering you're traveling at Mach 3 and 75,000 feet, but it could make a significant difference on the intelligence you were sent to gather. It was practically impossible to hand fly the aircraft smoothly and precisely enough to obtain *good* imagery when the sensors were operating, particularly for radar imagery. We had a minimum requirement that the basic pitch and roll autopilot had to be engaged during all sensor operations. Most flights in 956, with two instructor pilots onboard, were hand flown entirely—it was a "pride thing" between seasoned pilots to show you could fly it without the autopilot.

The manner in which the ANS turned the aircraft was truly "unique." All supersonic turns made by the ANS were constant radius turns. A typical 32 degree bank turn at Mach 3 (1,721 KTAS) had a turn radius of 70 nautical miles. The mission planners chose the bank angle to achieve the desired sensor results and still stay within the required geographical airspace. If the mission planners had scheduled a bank angle of 35 degrees or less, the ANS would not command a bank greater than 35 degrees, even if a higher bank was required to keep the aircraft on course. If the turn was planned for bank angles between 35 and 42 degrees, the ANS could command up to its maximum bank angle of 45 degrees to keep the SR-71 on course. At speeds above Mach 2.9, mission planners used a maximum bank angle of 42 degrees, allowing a margin of 3 degrees to accommodate aircraft trim requirements or a greater ground speed than expected. Once on course, the ANS could keep the aircraft within 300 feet of the "Black Line" drawn on our maps.

The pilot's objective throughout a turn was to fly as close to a constant ground speed as he could. If the ground speed remained constant, the bank angle should remain relatively constant. If you didn't pay close attention during turns and the ground speed increased, the bank angle would increase to the ANS limit (45 degrees) to keep the aircraft on track, and if that didn't do it, the aircraft slid outside the turn. Quite often the sensors were working during turns and required a specific bank angle to cover the area of interest on the ground. By varying bank angles from that programmed, or sliding outside the turn, it was possible to miss your target. Wind velocity between 70,000 and 80,000 feet (typical cruise altitude range) probably averaged around 5-10 knots although many Habus have seen them higher than 100 knots flying out of England into the Northern latitudes.

Crew coordination became important since the RSO had the only ground speed and true airspeed readout. In our particular case, Don would tell me how many knots fast or slow we were entering and during the turn, and I translated that into a Mach increase or decrease with the throttles. If the aircraft was heavy, sometimes a descent of 2,000 to 3,000 feet prior to the turn was necessary to maintain the Mach speed throughout the turn.

The last switch on the autopilot was called the "KEAS HOLD" (KEAS, pronounced "Keys"). KEAS stood for Knots Equivalent Air Speed and is calibrated airspeed corrected for compressibility effects of altitude and airspeed. Once the aircraft was supersonic, the only speed (other than Mach) we talked about was KEAS. The KEAS HOLD position of the autopilot was used exclusively during the "Accel" and "Decel" when holding a constant airspeed was critical.

Whatever airspeed you engaged the KEAS HOLD switch at, the autopilot held constant by varying pitch. During the "Accel" we engaged the KEAS HOLD switch at 450 KEAS, and the autopilot held that speed constant until reaching what was called the "KEAS bleed schedule." The KEAS bleed schedule began at 2.6 Mach and automatically decreased the KEAS 10 knots for each tenth of Mach speed increase, i.e., at 2.6 Mach/450 KEAS, 2.7 Mach/440 KEAS, 2.8 Mach/430 KEAS, etc. The bleed schedule kept the aircraft from exceeding its maximum KEAS, and a red KEAS warning light on the instrument panel illuminated if the KEAS was exceeded by 20 knots above the bleed schedule.

On one particular simulator mission with Don, my airspeed got lower than I wanted during an emergency, and I began cursing and mumbling to myself that I needed more KEAS. The next thing I saw was this huge set of keys on a ring, flying past my left shoulder and landing in the cockpit. I broke out laughing as the instructor pilot said over the interphone, "You wanted more KEAS, you got 'em!"

Planning the Navigation

The SR-71 Mission Planning Branch developed all our missions. For every new mission they had to do what was called a "feasibility study." This process entailed looking at the area of interest to insure it could be covered adequately by the SR, the intended route of flight, foreign country overflight considerations, placement of air refueling tracks, and where best to originate the mission. Once it proved feasible and the OK was given to develop the mission, planners went into high gear working out the details. Specifics such as: what suite of sensors to use, where and when each sensor should be ON/OFF, where to best utilize the air refueling tracks, fuel requirements, where the JP-7 was coming from, timing of the mission, etc., etc., all had to be planned out in excruciating detail.

Along with the mission tape for the ANS, the planning branch also developed the aircrew's computer generated flight plan. The RSO's flight plan was much more detailed than the pilot's, since it included data telling him when specific sensors were ON/OFF and where his navigational fix points were located. Mission planners drew the route out on maps and pasted computer generated labels along the track to show specifics such as elapsed time, fuel remaining, Mach, altitude, heading, bank angles, coordinates, and distance to the next turn point. Habus referred to the line drawn on our maps, depicting the route of flight, as the "Black Line." After the mission maps were made, 35mm pictures were taken of the entire route and developed into a roll of film, to be placed in each cockpit's moving map projectors.

The pilot's map projector was on the forward instrument panel and sat right between his knees. The 35mm mission film was loaded before flight and preflighted by the mobile crew. After the pilot turned his projector ON he had a 4 1/4" x 4 1/4" moving map display of the entire route with all its labels. Placing the map projector switch in "AUTO" allowed the film to move over the projector screen in concert with the aircraft's true airspeed. A spring-loaded, fingertip slewing switch in both cockpits allowed us to fast forward or reverse the film wherever we wanted, in a matter of seconds. Once Habus became familiar with all the mission materials, they found they could fly the entire mission with reference to the map projector alone.

The map projector's 35mm film always started with the title frame, displaying the specific mission number we were flying and date of revision. During preflight, the mobile crew checked the mission number and date against the flight plan and ANS to insure all three had the same mission number and date of revision. Would you believe the next frame was usually a photo taken from a Playboy or Penthouse magazine, to keep the crew company at 80,000 feet? The mission planners enjoyed surprising us with a different photo each time. The RSO's map projector consisted of a 9 x 9 inch glass projection screen giving him a larger presentation and greater detail than the pilots.

Approaching level off, the pilot disengaged KEAS HOLD and slowly retarded the throttles to maintain the Mach. Just below the airspeed indicator was the Triple Display Indicator (TDI), displaying KEAS, altitude, and Mach speed. The TDI received inputs from the Air Data Computer and became our primary reference since it compensated for pitot-static errors and provided accurate speed and altitude readouts at supersonic speeds. The selection of values for any two of the three—KEAS, altitude, or Mach—automatically defined the value of the third, regardless of ambient temperature. For instance, if cruise was scheduled at Mach 3.0 and the desired initial cruise altitude is 72,000 feet, then the KEAS should be 396 knots. A chart in our checklist provided the data for all three inputs.

The large Attitude Director Indicator (ADI) and the Horizontal Situation Indicator (HSI) in the center of the panel looked and worked exactly like the displays in a T-38, but with minor modifications. The only major difference was their tie into the ANS to provide navigational inputs. In the "NAV" position of the mode selector switch, the bank steering bar gave commands to keep the aircraft on track. It worked just like flying an ILS in a T-38—keep the bank steering bar centered and you were either on course or heading back to course.

However, the pitch steering bar became very "unique." It received inputs from the vertical gyro in the ANS and reflected the vertical velocity of the aircraft. Pilots ignored the pitot-static vertical velocity and used the pitch steering bar on the ADI to establish supersonic climbs and descents. It never gave us an actual vertical velocity speed, only a pitch steering bar displacement from level flight. The pitch steering bar indicated zero vertical velocity when it was aligned with the small airplane symbol, and provided a scale sensitivity of approximately 1,000 feet per minute for each quarter-inch of displacement. The minimum vertical speed which could be sensed by the ANS and displayed by the bar was about 55 feet per minute.

It took some practice to interpret the pitch steering bar on the ADI during climbs and descents. When you rotated the pitch wheel up on the autopilot, the miniature aircraft as well as the pitch steering bar climbed above the horizon line. Pilots soon mastered ADI techniques and learned the perfect Mach 3 cruise/climb attitude was to have the pitch steering bar just barely touching the horizon line on the ADI. That pitch attitude produced just about the right amount of climb to be in harmony with the rapid fuel consumption, for maximum range cruise performance.

Mission Recorder System (MRS)

For ease of maintenance, the aircraft was equipped with a Mission Recorder System (MRS), that recorded every three seconds on magnetic tape, various parameters of the aircraft and its associated systems (engine, hydraulic, DAFICS, electrical, ANS, etc.). The MRS also recorded signals from various aircraft data sources, including analog transducer sources, digital information sources, cockpit and external voice communications, DEF systems, and event information sources. After flight, maintenance removed the MRS tape and through a computer process converted the electrical inputs into meaningful information. The MRS maintenance shop distributed the recorded information to individual maintenance shops for experts to look over and see if anything was going wrong with their particular system. When crews had difficulty describing maintenance problems on specific aircraft systems, such as the inlets or engines, they occasionally went over the MRS data along with maintenance to describe what they saw or felt in the cockpit during the time(s) in question.

Communication and Navigation

The remaining communication and navigation equipment was scattered throughout both cockpits. There was an ILS receiver and a outer marker beacon light located in the front cockpit. The RSO had the IFF/SIF transponder and HF radio in the back cockpit. There was a TACAN set (pronounced "tack-ann") and ARC-50 UHF radio in each cockpit, and a VHF radio added to the front cockpit in the early 1980s. There was no low-frequency ADF or weather radar onboard the SR-71. Interestingly, the A-12 aircraft used an onboard HF radio telemetry system to relay vital aircraft data back to a ground station on Kadena. Aircraft parameters such as hydraulic pressure, fuel flows, throttle angle, ejection seat, Mach, CIT, etc., were constantly being transmitted back to Kadena whenever the aircraft was flying.

The Horizontal Situation Indicator (HSI) displayed navigational information from the ANS, INS, TACAN, and the ILS receiver. By placing the "DISPLAY MODE SEL" switch in either of these positions the HSI displayed the appropriate navigational information. The DME displayed a maximum range readout of 1,999 nautical miles.

The ARC-50 UHF radio had an "INT/EXT" (Internal or External) switch located on its control head. In the internal position, the radio was a standard UHF radio. However, in the external position it became a "unique" UHF radio. In the external mode, the transmitted signal is encoded to appear as noise to all receivers except those equipped with a compatible de-coding device. A selectable "mission address code" feature prevented intelligible reception by stations which might possess the necessary equipment, but didn't have the classified codes set in. Communication, ranging, and Automatic Direction Finding (ADF) occurred between two stations as long as they had the same address code.

Thumb-wheel rotary selector switches were used by the RSO to dial in the classified five-digit code. A sixth digit was the range address code. Depressing an "interrogate" push-button switch on the panel initiated range and bearing interrogations in the external mode. A continuous ranging switch on the panel illuminated to indicate continuous ranging and direction finding by both stations. Using the ARC-50 in the external mode had a high resistance to jamming, and allowed message privacy over the radio.

To check the accuracy of our position, the RSO used the optical viewsight in front of him, enabling him to see beneath the aircraft. The viewsight was also useful to observe any activity below the aircraft and report back on the cloud conditions in areas of interest. As long as there were no clouds, the RSO could optically see and zoom in on the terrain below. An electro-optical video viewsight was later added to the rear cockpit for vertical viewing and ANS position fixing and was displayed on a 5 inch cathode ray tube.

Defensive Systems and SR-71 Vulnerability

No SR-71 has ever been lost or damaged due to hostile action. The aircraft was extremely difficult for enemy radars to find. Featuring the original stealth technology, the SR-71's wings, tail, and fuselage were constructed with special composite materials, called iron ferrites, that absorbed radar energy rather than returning it to the sender. At cruise speed and altitude, the radar cross section (a measure of radar reflectivity) of the SR-71 represented a target of less than ten square meters. For comparison purposes, the radar cross section of an F-15 fighter is somewhere around 100 square meters. Even if the aircraft could be found on radar, its detection was so late that there was simply not enough time for a missile to lead our aircraft for a successful "kill."

The only published and acknowledged missile firing at an SR-71 occurred on 26 August 1981. SR-71 pilot, Maj. Maury Rosenberg and RSO, Maj. E. D. McKim, were making their final pass on the Korean DMZ, heading southwest, when North Korea fired two Soviet SA-2 surface-to-air missiles at their aircraft. E. D. was the first to notice anything out of the ordinary by his DEF set automatically jamming the missile's guidance system and lighting up his cockpit displays. After E. D. informed Maury of his DEF indications, he looked out to the right, just in time to see the missiles go by. The incident caused quite an uproar in the press, and we became much more cautious in future passes through the Korean DMZ. Crews often had no idea they were even being fired at. Ben Rich, in his book, *Skunk Works*, states that over 100 Surface-to-Air missiles have been fired at the SR-71.

Even though the aircraft was difficult to find on radar, we carried very sophisticated Electronic Counter Measure (ECM) equipment, called the Defensive systems, to electronically jam and deny the enemy our range and bearing. All the Defensive systems (DEF, pronounced "deaf") were on the RSO's left console. He could control the jammers manually or let them run in the automatic mode so they would electronically jam a specific threat frequency when first detected. The DEF systems were constantly being updated to counter the latest enemy early-warning radars, surface-to-air missiles (SAMs), and air-to-air radar guided missiles.

Each DEF upgrade was assigned an increasing letter of the alphabet. Throughout my time with the program we used DEF A, B, C, E/F, G, A2, C2, H, M, and the very latest, DEF A2C. Depending in what part of the world we flew, the DEF software could also be modified to counter changing electronic threats. Whenever the United States "acquired" the latest Soviet radar technology, we often tested our current and new DEF systems by flying SR-71 sorties against the Soviet radar for evaluation purposes. These sorties were flown over the highly classified area north of Las Vegas, Nevada, known popularly as Groom Lake.

Turning the DEF system on made some Habus apprehensive, for good reason. On two occasions turning on the DEF systems at Mach 3 created problems no one was prepared for. In the late 70s, the SR-71 crew of Col. Bob Helt and Col. Larry Elliot (Ret) were flying out of Det 1 on a night operational sortie. When Larry turned the DEF set ON, the aircraft immediately experienced a power surge that disengaged all of their SAS channels. Bob experienced severe unstarts and large excursions of the aircraft in pitch and roll. Fortunately, Larry instinctively realized the "cause and effect" relationship and immediately turned the DEF system OFF. After a wild night ride consisting of unusual attitude recoveries, Bob finally brought the aircraft under control, re-engaged the SAS, and aborted the mission.

A similar experience occurred with the crew of Majors "Stormy" Boudreaux and Ted Ross, flying an operational sortie out of Beale in 1985. When Ted turned the DEF set ON, all three DAFICS computers shut down at Mach 3, leaving "Stormy" with his hands full of airplane. In both cases, the sudden, large electrical demands created perturbations, causing the computers and their associated SAS and inlets controls to shut down. Former RSO, Lt. Col. "Geno" Quist (Ret), remembers a similar incident with his DEF.

> On 13 November 1982, Nevin [Maj. Nevin Cunningham, the pilot] and I were the lucky ones to take 980 back from Kadena to Beale. The mission included a pass by the Kamchatka Peninsula, and Petropovlosk in particular. As we were preparing for the mission, the DEF system "Tech Rep" came to me and said, "Not real sure about this DEF system, we've had some problems with it and need to send it back to Beale." A DEF problem on this particular mission was cause for abort back to Kadena, since we had to accomplish the operational part of the mission enroute. Usually the DEF system was tested shortly after departure, and definitely prior to the entering "sensitive area." This time however, I had a bad feeling, so I simply turned it on—it looked OK—and pressed on with the mission. As we were leaving the "sensitive area" and turning towards our next refueling off the coast of Alaska, I decided to run a test of the system—just for maintenance reasons. This was probably the only time in my SR career that I didn't tell Nevin I was testing the

DEF gear. When I hit the test button, every light in the aircraft blinked, the autopilot kicked off, and I heard this, "What the hell did you do?" I quietly and quickly turned off the DEF, and we safely landed after a 4.8 hour crossing of the Pacific.

As the 9th SRW Commander in 1988, I was once invited to SAC Headquarters (building 500) to hear what intelligence analysts had recently learned about the latest Soviet defenses and their threat to the SR-71. When I arrived at building 500 I was met and escorted by a Second Lieutenant who introduced me to about six other Lieutenants. They sat me at the head of a table and for the next hour briefed me on the current Soviet threat to the SR-71 by use of slides, graphs, and charts. The entire briefing was based on their latest computer modeling, and to top it off, none of them knew I had an SR-71 background. They were merely told by their boss that a Colonel from Beale, who was interested in their threat analysis would drop by for a briefing. I made it clear to the Lieutenants that their analysis was pure "hog wash" and full of so many holes that they needed to restructure their briefing before giving it again.

They were literally dumbfounded when I told then I had flown the SR-71 for seven years, and assured them I could fly the aircraft anywhere in the world and return safely—under my rules—not some computer's rules! Without embarrassing anyone, I recommended to their boss on the side, that his Lieutenants need to know who their audience is before giving future briefings. The Lieutenants did more research on the SR-71's vulnerability and came up with a different conclusion, as Lt. Col. "Geno" Quist recalls.

During my Pentagon years (1986-1990) there was a continual case brewing about the vulnerability of the SR-71 to enemy missiles. It came to a head during the final days of the Pentagon budget decision to cancel the SR-71 program. The Pentagon "experts" advocating the demise of the program had no clue as to the true vulnerability of the SR to surface-to-air threats—so they decided to broadcast the word (dis-information) that it was "vulnerable." I asked for, and received, a document from SAC which, as far as I know would be true to this day, indicating that the threat to the SR-71 from any source, surface or airborne, is at best "LOW." For some reason nobody paid attention to the SAC study.

On several occasions, as Don and I approached Soviet airspace, I could see several Soviet fighters streaming their contrails off in the distance. The contrails showed them in a clockwise circular orbit. As the SR approached you could easily follow their contrails and watch each of them come out of their orbit as they headed directly for us. Once we saw the contrails coming towards us disappear, we knew the fighters were initiating their climb in an attempt to intercept us. Knowing there were Soviet pilots out there who would try to shoot you down if they were so ordered heightened your senses as they approached. I often wondered how they felt, knowing we were up there and their inability to do anything about it. Nothing ever came of their attempts, and I usually smiled to myself, realizing their frustration and dilemma. It was because of these experiences, and others related to me by Habus, I could tell the SAC Lieutenants to go "back to the drawing board" in their computer model and factor in the human element.

On 6 September 1976, Soviet pilot, Lt. Viktor Belenko, defected to Japan in a MiG-25. A book called *MiG Pilot* was subsequently written, in which the author describes a Soviet pilot's frustration in trying to intercept and shoot down an SR-71.

> *American reconnaissance planes, SR-71s, were prowling off the coast, staying just outside Soviet airspace but photographing terrain hundreds of miles inland with side-angle cameras. They taunted and toyed with the MiG-25s sent up to intercept them, scooting up to altitudes the Soviet planes could not reach, and circling leisurely above them or dashing off at speeds the Russians could not match.*

Lieutenant Belenko himself further describes the intercept problem.

> *They had a master plan to intercept an SR-71 by positioning a MiG-25 in front of it and one below it, and when the SR-71 passed they would fire missiles. But it never occurred. Soviet computers were very primitive, and there is no way that mission can be accomplished.*
>
> *First of all, the SR-71 flies too high and too fast. The MiG-25 cannot reach it or catch it. Secondly, as I told you, the missiles are useless above 27,000 meters, and as you know, the SR-71 cruises much higher. But even if we could reach it, our missiles lack the velocity to overtake the SR-71 if they are fired in a tail chase. And if they are fired head-on, their guidance systems cannot adjust quickly enough to the high closing speed.*

Don and I, as well as many other Habus, had flown numerous "Tomcat Chase" and "Eagle Bait" sorties against our best fighters—the Navy's F-14s and the Air Force's F-15s. We flew the SR to provide the fighters radar practice at finding, tracking, locking on, intercepting, and simulated firing of their sophisticated F-14 "Phoenix" missile and the F-15's AIM-7M "Sparrow" at a high-altitude, high-speed target. The "Tomcat Chase" missions were flown over the Pacific Ocean and "Eagle Bait" missions in the Nellis AFB training area.

In order to maximize scarce, high-altitude/high-speed intercept practice for the fighters against the SR-71, we "stacked the deck" in their favor to avoid a multitude of missed intercepts, and consequently, wasted time. The practice intercepts were conducted in a very controlled environment, favoring a successful outcome by the fighters. Both the SR-71 and fighters were on a common Ground Controlled Intercept (GCI) frequency, so the fighters could be vectored for the head-on intercept, and we could talk to each other to help set it up. We flew a precise straight line track, that was made known to the GCI controller and fighters well in advance of our arrival. All aircraft had their transponders on for positive radar identification, and no DEF systems were to be used. We kept the SR-71 at a constant altitude, airspeed, and heading as they maneuvered for their head-on attack. GCI controllers provided constant range and bearing for the fighters to their target (the SR-71), so they could hunt for us on their aircraft radar. Even under these highly controlled flying conditions, the F-14s and F-15s had extreme difficulty achieving a satisfactory SR-71 "kill."

The majority of missed intercepts for the fighters were because of two parameters that influence the intercept geometry greatly: the altitude difference between the SR-71 and the fighters, and the extreme closing velocity between the two aircraft. At the start of the "Eagle Bait" missions, the F-15s discovered that their Fire Control System (FCS) speed gate (the computed closing velocity between two aircraft) was not large enough to accommodate their extreme closing velocity against the SR-71. Software changes to their FCS computers solved that problem. If the fighters didn't climb and remained at 25,000 feet, for example, their missiles found it extremely difficult to climb up 55,000 feet (against gravity) to achieve a "kill" against the SR-71.

Several factors further complicate matters for the fighters to achieve a "kill." Their air-to-air missiles are aerodynamically optimized for maneuvering in the "thicker" air below 50,000 feet. Their small aerodynamic fins do not provide sufficient maneuverability to make tight turns in the thin air of 80,000 feet. As the missile races towards the SR-71 at Mach 3 or greater, the closing velocity between the two now becomes Mach 6, or about one mile every second! The missile's predicted impact point in front of the SR-71 has to be perfectly planned early on by the fighter's FCS because as they race towards each other at Mach 6, it becomes increasingly more difficult for the missile to maneuver. The proximity fusing of missiles, like the Mach 3 AIM-7M "Sparrow," also requires the missile to explode in front of its target, sending its lethal warhead in for the kill.

Until the latest technology of Air-to-Air missiles came along (the AMRAAM, a fire-and-forget missile with a range of about 35 miles), all the long-range Soviet and US missiles required the aircraft's radar to continue tracking the SR-71 long after the missiles were launched. They had to remain locked-on to the SR-71 in order for their FCS to relay tracking information back to the missile, so it could make appropriate corrections, racing towards the target. By turning on our DEF systems we could easily deny the fighters any meaningful radar information to guide their missiles.

All I ever heard on the radios from the fighters as they sped underneath us was, "Ah damn it, we're too late!" We tried for years to get SAC Headquarters approval to practice the same intercepts with Det 1's SR-71s against Kadena's F-15s. Every Det 1 Commander, particularly Col. Lee Shelton, pushed to get the practice intercepts approved because they believed a lot could be learned by both aircraft. Eventually SAC gave in to Colonel Shelton's repeated requests and approved the practice intercepts. In order to get high enough to take a reasonable shot at us, F-15 crews were given special permission to do a zoom-climb to 50,000 to

55,000 feet before a simulated AIM-7 launch against the SR-71. They had permission to be above 50,000 feet for a maximum time of 90 seconds without wearing a pressure suit. Former SR-71 pilot, Capt. Steve "Griz" Grzebiniak, writes about the Kadena intercepts.

> *We flew the HABU as a high-altitude target for the F-15's only on our infrequently scheduled "DEBBIE" training sorties. We were the fighter's "training aid," but it provided us with some valuable training and insight as well. I think it's common knowledge that our aircraft and pilots are the finest in the world and if anyone could shoot down an SR-71, it would be one of our own.*
>
> *Our pre-briefed mission required us to fly a specific track, at Mach 2.8 and no higher than 70,000 feet. In addition, we were required to fly over a designated point in space (the IP) and call our time out from the IP in one minute intervals starting five minutes back. If that wasn't enough, we would dump some fuel at the IP to help the fighters get a visual "tally" on us. After each mission, we would debrief by phone, and the F-15 drivers would report "four AIM-7's launched, four kills on the HABU."*
>
> *The next target sortie Jim and I flew had a different outcome. We were scheduled to make two passes over the intercept track. The F-15 guys were excited to have another chance to "smoke" the HABU. On the next pass, Jim and I flew the plan as briefed. One minute calls from the IP, on course, on altitude, Mach 2.8, "here's some fuel dump guys, come and get us." The next pass was different. I said to Jim that our F-15 jockeys are the best in the world, let's give them a challenge. Jim and I knew that we were flying our favorite jet, tail number 962—she never let us down. We came down the track to the IP, making our one minute calls, but there was no fuel to dump because we were at 86,000 feet and Mach 3.2. The inlet doors were slammed shut and the jet was purring like a kitten. I made a shallow 10 degree bank turn, not so much to foil the F-15's intercept, but to allow Jim to see the contrails flailing below us.*
>
> *In the phone debrief after the mission, the F-15 flight lead reported "four shots and four kills" on the first pass and mumbled something about radar problems and no kills on the second pass. Even with the world's best planes, pilots, and missiles, it would take "a golden BB" [a lucky blind shot by the enemy] to bring down a HABU.*

Mission Bays

All the sensors and other mission equipment were located in "bays"—separate compartments extending from the nose of the aircraft back to the wing roots. Each bay had an alphabet-letter prefix for ease of discussion and location (i.e. F-Bay was the forward cockpit and L-Bay was the forward, right mission bay). The right side of the chine had five large bays (D, L, N, Q, and T) and the left side four bays (K, M, P, and S) for housing mission equipment. A-Bay was the removable nose section, J-Bay the nose wheel well, and G-Bay the rear cockpit. Directly behind the rear cockpit was C-Bay to house a camera, R-Bay holding all the radio equipment, E-Bay containing all the electronic equipment, and H-Bay with air conditioning equipment.

To keep high temperatures out of the bays they were air conditioned and insulated with layers of silicone-impregnated fiberglass cloth, precompressed fiberglass slab, and aluminum foil. All the intelligence sensors inside the bays were of the "remove and replace" type—none permanently stayed aboard the aircraft. They were truly one of kind, making them very expensive and required extensive maintenance preparation between each mission.

When we were lucky enough to fly an SR-71 to one of the Dets or other locations, Habus usually took along a hang-up bag for clothes to wear on arrival. There's very little room in either cockpit to stow anything extra, so we handed over our hang-up bags to the crew chief to load into one of the empty aircraft bays. If the crew chief knew which bays were well insulated and air conditioned, and how to place the hang-up bag inside the bay, your clothes arrived safely. If he didn't know, your clothes arrived like Don's once did when we landed in Okinawa—completely charred! The crew chief laid Don's hang-up bag too close to a glass window and over one-fourth of his nylon bag ended up melting on his clothes.

Intelligence Sensors

The primary imaging sensor for the SR-71 was located in the nose of the aircraft. It was either a photographic camera or a radar imaging camera. The radar sensor was originally used as our "fallback" sensor in case the target weather was not suitable for photographic coverage. As our radar sensors became more sophisticated and produced greater resolution, it was no longer a fallback sensor. Prior to each operational mission with the camera onboard, we had to obtain target weather approval from SAC Headquarters in order to launch. Each photo sortie was required to have a certain percentage of cloud free coverage (usually around 70 percent cloud free) in the target area before the OK was given to fly.

It often seemed as if the weather personnel at SAC could never get it right. There were times, after we were already airborne, clouds had moved into the area of interest, and the primary camera picked up little intelligence. On the other hand, many of us had flown with the radar sensor onboard, when the weather turned out to be perfect for photographic coverage. Habus and many others spent long hours waiting for the weather to clear up over the target before they were either launched or canceled. Most crews liked radar missions better, because they were not dependent on target weather and were always a "go."

There were many days the entire Det went through the complete drill of preparing the aircraft, loading sensors, briefing the mission, getting the tankers airborne, and then canceling at the last minute because of a poor target weather forecast by SAC Headquarter's Global Weather department. The total effort that went into preparing for each sortie was tremendous.

A classic example of this "drill" occurred in March of 1979 when Don and I, and pilot Buz Carpenter and RSO John Murphy, were deployed TDY to RAF Mildenhall with the SR-71 (972) to fly a specific reconnaissance mission into Yemen. Tensions were building between them and Saudi Arabia. All four of us did a weather drill for four consecutive days until the clouds finally cleared in the target area to launch. Every morning we went through the same routine—a 0200 wake up for a 0500 takeoff—only to end up with the crew in the cockpit ready to go and the mission canceled.

Every night we had to be in crew rest by 1800, which left little time for socializing. Consequently, after each cancellation we de-suited and drove directly back to our BOQ rooms to start our 0600 party. Our friendly British "senior citizen" BOQ maids, Elsie, Janet, and Phyllis, arrived for work around 0800 only to find the four of us drinking wine, listening to loud music, and enjoying life. Jokingly, each morning the three maids came into our room, along with a bible, and pretended to be reading scripture to us for our sinful behavior. They thought we had partied all night long for four days in a row and were still partying each morning as they came to work! Little did they know the truth.

Our two primary sensors were either the high-resolution Optical Bar Camera (OBC), used for taking panoramic photography or the side looking radar system known as the CAPRE (Capability Reconnaissance, pronounced "caper"). The entire nose section of the SR-71 contained either sensor and was removed and replaced after each operational mission.

The OBC camera utilizes a continuous moving roll of film. In operation, the camera takes photographs while scanning from left to right across the SR-71's flight path. Camera operations are automatic; however the RSO manually controls its operating modes: vertical exposures or stereo photography. The OBC's terrain coverage was 2 nm along the ground track and extended 36 nm to each side of the aircraft (further if banked). Sufficient film was onboard to cover approximately 2,952 nm, or 1,476 nm in the stereo mode.

We always flew with the very high-resolution Technical Objective Cameras (TEOCs, pronounced "techs") onboard for specific target areas. The TEOCs were installed in the left- and right-hand mission bays and could be pointed from zero to 45 degrees to the side of the aircraft. The ANS controlled the TEOC camera automatically. At zero pointing angle, the TEOCs covered a 2.4 nm square area and, at a 45 degrees pointing angle, covered a five by six nautical mile diamond shaped area, 14 nm from the side of the aircraft. Each TEOC had enough film for approximately 1,428 nm of coverage. I've seen excellent photos from the TEOC cameras showing MiGs falling out of the sky from attempted intercepts as they ran out of airspeed and ideas!

When we flew with the radar sensor, the RSO used the Recorder Correlator Display (RCD) to aid in navigation. The correlator developed the radar imagery inflight, by use of lasers, and displayed the imagery on his large RCD screen located directly below the RSO's viewsight. The only problem was, it took 60 seconds for the correlator to develop and display the imagery. Thus, the RSO was always looking at a moving radar picture of where the aircraft was 60 seconds ago, or about 33 miles behind us. The radar sensor provided the intelligence community with all-weather, day/night imagery and proved extremely valuable to the Navy in locating Soviet submarines in dock.

By 1986 we had a new state-of-the-art radar, high-resolution, imaging system, called the Advanced Synthetic Aperture Radar System (ASARS, pronounced "Ace-R's"). The ASARS views terrain by means of radar to the left and right of the ground track, at selected ranges. It was an improved version of the ASARS radar sensor that was flight tested during July of 1983 in the United States, and later operationally at RAF Mildenhall. The test data from those missions provided the means to enhance even further the radar capability of the equipment. ASARS and its associated support equipment and personnel were deployed to Det 4 at RAF Mildenhall in 1987 to begin flying operational missions. The system had plenty of bugs to be worked out at first, but after about 6 months it was declared fully operational and provided day/night, all-weather reconnaissance imagery of extreme clarity.

ASARS has the capability for search, acquisition (navigation update), and two high-resolution spotlight modes. The search mode is initiated and controlled automatically by the ANS or manually by the RSO. Acquisition and spotlight modes are initiated and controlled automatically only. In the search and spotlight modes, the imaged area is perpendicular to the ground track, or it can be "squinted" forward or aft up to 30 degrees. In the acquisition mode, the imaged area for a navigation fix point is 37 degrees forward of perpendicular. The ASARS can also be operated in turns.

In the search mode of operation the terrain coverage is a 10 nm swath, positioned 20 to 100 nm to the left and right of the ground track. In the large spotlight mode, the terrain coverage is approximately one nautical mile square; small spotlight mode, a rectangle approximately one nautical mile by one-third nautical mile. Both spotlight modes can be positioned 20 to 85 nm to the side of the ground track.

An Inflight Processor and Display (IPD) produced onboard radar images for the RSO as well. With all sensors operating, the SR-71 was originally advertised to gather intelligence over 100,000 square miles every hour; this increased to over 150,000 square miles per hour as our sensors became more sophisticated. The ASARS sensor required the nose section to be slightly modified in the shape of a "duck's bill," with obvious dimples on each side of the nose chine.

Another form of intelligence gathering is called ELINT (pronounced "E-Lint") and stands for Electronics Intelligence—the recording of electronic signals covering a broad range of frequencies of the electromagnetic frequency spectrum. ELINT includes collecting signals from the Electronic Order of Battle (EOB) at the low end of the frequency spectrum (like radar acquisition, tracking, and guidance signals) to the very high frequencies of the Soviet SA-10 missile.

The SR-71 was excellent for "stimulating" the enemy's electronic environment. Every time Habus flew in a sensitive area, all kinds of radars and other electronic wizardry were turned on to see if they could find out what was flying so quickly through their airspace. In fact, our missions were generally not ELINT productive unless "they" were looking for us with electronic signals. I recall several missions where we totally surprised "them" and consequently, didn't pick up any significant electronic emissions. It often made me wonder if there wasn't a more covert classified program in existence, that somehow gave advance notice of the SR-71's arrival, just so "they" would have their electronic defenses up and running for us to document.

To receive and record signals we used the Electro-Magnetic Reconnaissance (EMR) system, which was later upgraded by the EMR Improvement Program (EIP, pronounced "EEP"). Prior to the EIP upgrade, the EMR would literally sit there and record signals from hundreds of miles around the aircraft. It had no discretion on what signals it received, and made it very difficult to find specific frequencies out of the thousands recorded on one mission. The EIP was a highly sophisticated and programmable scanning system (called "smart scan"), capable of receiving only specific signals. It had the electronic logic to key off specific signals it found, then move on to look for other associated radar frequencies.

For instance, having once found the SA-10's long-range acquisition radar signal, the EIP would then look specifically for the SA-10's associated tracking and fire control frequencies. In another mode of operation, the EIP would let the electronic environment orchestrate the signal parameters it searched for. The EIP was very efficient at its job, at times often recording over 500 emitters on a single operational sortie from RAF Mildenhall, because of the large number of Soviet and Warsaw Pact electronic emitters. It was a Star Wars version of eavesdropping.

The EIP continuously recorded signals from horizon to horizon along our flight path, a distance of around 1,200 nm. If the system recorded a specific frequency for a short period of time, computers could plot the precise position of the transmitter on the ground within approximately one half mile, at a distance of 300 miles from the SR-71. Two electronic signals that were very illusive to intelligence gathering were that of the SA-5 and SA-10 Soviet SAM missiles. The Soviets didn't turn them on very often, knowing that its electronic signals would be recorded. Once recorded, future Air Force DEF systems could be developed or software programmed to counter the missile threats.

As of this writing, the two SR-71s being brought back into the Air Force inventory will be modified with a data link system to accept digital inputs from the ASARS and ELINT. The data will be recorded and, when the flight path permits, downlinked in near-real time to a ground station. The recording capacity of ASARS and ELINT intelligence is approximately one hour, or about 2,000 nm.

Cockpit Layout

The SR-71's front cockpit was somewhat snug with the pressure suit on, although comfortable. Headroom between the canopy sides was tight, as the canopy narrowed upward. Front cockpit visibility was restricted slightly because of the helmet and the small window panes surrounding the canopy. The RSO's cockpit was considerably roomier.

In the back seat he had two small window panes on each side and the ability to also see directly beneath the aircraft through his viewsight. The RSO's windows had shades that could be pulled down while the pilot used movable, metal shades on each side of the canopy sill, called "bat wings," to keep the bright sunlight out. All the cockpit switches and buttons were easily accessible and enlarged where necessary to accommodate the pressure suit gloves. There were no flight controls in the rear cockpit.

The flight control stick grip was similar to a fighter type but had various buttons located on it to suit the SR-71's needs. The top center button, for use by your thumb, was the four-position switch to run the pitch and yaw trim. To the left of it was the two-position transmitter and interphone switch—push forward, and you transmitted on the HF, UHF, or VHF radio. Pull back on the switch, and you talked to the RSO, crew chief, or tanker crew in the interphone position. On the front side of the stick grip was the trigger disconnect, used to disconnect systems immediately that had the potential to get you into trouble if they went haywire. Squeezing the trigger disconnected the air refueling boom and autopilot immediately, and interrupted the pitch and yaw trim, stick pusher, and the anti-skid system for as long as you squeezed the trigger. On the right side of the control stick was the rain removal button, used to squirt a gooey rain removal fluid onto the windshield. No one ever used it.

Most people find it amazing that all the SR-71 cockpit instrumentation was the round dial type. The YF-12s had vertical tape displays which seemed to be in vogue for modern cockpits of the time. The large Attitude Directional Indicator (ADI) was the pilot's primary attitude reference source. It received gyro inputs from either the ANS or the FRS (Flight Reference System), depending on which position the pilot had the switch. The FRS provided a back-up attitude and heading mode of operation in case the ANS failed. The FRS was later updated (around 1982) to a SKN-2417 INS, providing the aircraft with greater back-up navigational accuracy. Not all, but most of the switches and gauges were grouped throughout the cockpit according to their particular system function (i.e., electrical, fuel, air conditioning, inlets, etc.) for ease of locating and manipulating.

A periscope was located directly in front of the pilot's helmet. Pushing it up extended the periscope into the air stream about four inches, giving aft vision to the pilot. The periscope rotated 15 degrees in each direction allowing the pilot to see everything aft and just outboard of each rudder. Besides using the periscope for rudder alignment, it was very important to check the aircraft was not producing a contrail when we entered sensitive airspace. Contrails were very rare at our altitudes because it takes the right combination of temperature and moisture to produce them. Twice I've seen contrails coming from my aircraft above 70,000 feet. Contrails were most common on our Giant Reach missions flown off the Northern coast of Russia during the winter. The periscope was also used to insure fuel dumping had started or terminated and gave the pilot an excellent view of the engine nacelles in case of fire or other engine malfunctions. One peek through the periscope was worth a thousand cockpit warning lights!

Air Conditioning and Pressurization

SR-71s fly in an extremely adverse speed and altitude environment. Ram-air temperatures exceeded 752° F at design speed and outside air pressure was less than 0.33 psi near the limit altitude. To help radiate the extreme heat, the external skin surface was painted black. The air conditioning and pressurization system used hot, ninth-stage bleed air from each engine. As the hot bleed air traveled forward, it was cooled first by the air-to-air heat exchanger located in each nacelle and then by the primary air-to-fuel heat exchanger in each wing. The air then traveled forward to a cooling compressor and secondary air-to-fuel heat exchanger located in H-Bay, just behind the rear cockpit.

The only temperature control Habus had was over the cockpit and pressure suit. A temperature rheostat, located in the front cockpit varied the temperature as required. Since you couldn't feel the cockpit temperature with the pressure suit on, a cockpit temperature gauge was installed. On one operational mission, the rear cockpit didn't receive air conditioning for some unknown reason and became so hot that the RSO's plastic checklist pages began to curl and his grease pencil entries melted. Fortunately, his pressure suit kept him comfortable.

Crews could select to have the cockpits at a cabin altitude of either 10,000 feet or 26,000 feet by moving a two-position switch. We typically flew with the cabin pressurized at 26,000 feet because it provided better cooling air supply to our suits and, in the event of a high altitude ejection, the pressure differential between the cockpit and the outside atmosphere would be less. A cabin altimeter gauge indicated cockpit altitude between 1,000 and 50,000 feet. If the pilot needed to dump cockpit pressure quickly, he moved the cockpit dump switch ON, depressurizing both cockpits to the outside pressure. A windshield de-icer blew hot air over the outside of the left front window only, proving extremely useful in ice and heavy rain.

Oxygen Systems

Since your life depended on a constant oxygen supply in the thin atmosphere of 80,000 feet, the aircraft was equipped with three independent liquid oxygen sources, each one capable of supplying the crew's needs. Oxygen system one and two's control panels were located in each cockpit while the standby system was in the front cockpit only. The crew's 100 percent oxygen supply was routed from the control panels through their ejection seat survival kits, and into their pressure suit helmets.

Each crew had two 45 cubic-inch capacity emergency oxygen bottles located in their ejection-seat survival kits. Both of these emergency oxygen bottles were activated automatically upon ejection. The emergency oxygen supply was always available to Habus by pulling on the "green apple" of their emergency bailout system, attached to the right side of their pressure suit. The emergency oxygen bottles provided each crew member unregulated 100 percent oxygen for about 15-20 minutes—enough for an emergency descent to an altitude where sufficient oxygen was available. The oxygen supply was something crews always took for granted because it never failed and had four independent systems.

Ejection Seat

The SR-71 ejection seat was usable from zero speed and altitude (called a "Zero/Zero" ejection seat) to the maximum speed and altitude of the aircraft. The seat was a rocket-propelled, upward-ejecting unit. Most people believe an ejection at 2,200 mph would rip your body apart. However, the air is so thin at 80,000 feet that the actual "Q" forces (decelerating "G" forces) when your body first hits the air stream is a lot less than an ejection from a T-38 at 500 mph at sea level. To eject from the SR-71, you reached between your knees with both hands and gave a sharp, upward tug on the seat's large D-ring. To keep your arms tucked in tight to your body, crews were taught to hold on to the ejection D-ring as the seat fired from the aircraft.

The first, and most important event after pulling on the D-ring, was to have the canopy eject free from the cockpit. Unlike most high performance Air Force aircraft with ejection seats, you can *not* eject through the SR-71's canopy. After the sharp tug on the D-ring, the canopy unlocked and was thrusted free from the aircraft. To preclude a disaster from happening (like being ejected into the canopy) there was an interlock device installed that wouldn't allow the seat to eject until the canopy was first removed. So, if the seat didn't fire after pulling the ejection seat D-ring, our procedure was to reach to the left side of our seat and pull the "Canopy Jettison T-handle," an alternate means of removing the canopy. If the canopy was not gone then, your last option was to manually open the canopy locking lever and hope cockpit pressurization would push it off.

In case the ejection seat D-ring initiator between your knees didn't fire, a secondary ejection T-handle, located also on the left side of the seat, could be pulled to initiate an ejection. However, the D-ring between your knees must have been pulled first in order for the T-handle to be operative. When the secondary T-handle is used, the seat catapult fires *immediately*, without regard to the canopy. Both the front and rear cockpit's ejection sequences were independent of each other.

After pulling on the D-ring there was a 0.3 second delay to remove the canopy, and then a catapult gas charge was fired to initiate seat ejection from the cockpit. The gas charge had a duration of 0.15 seconds, sufficient to raise the seat above the canopy sills, at which point, a wire lanyard attached to the floor of the cockpit was pulled, igniting the seat's rocket motor. The rocket motor provided sufficient thrust and duration (0.5 seconds) to eject the seat approximately 300 feet above the aircraft.

Although the ejection seat was certified for "Zero/Zero" capability, your odds of a successful ejection increased as altitude and airspeed increased, giving the parachute sufficient time to fully deploy. To aid in low airspeed and/or low altitude ejections, the parachute incorporated an extraction gun that fired a metal slug, pulling the 35-foot diameter parachute into the air stream for immediate opening. If you were in a low altitude ejection (below 15,000 feet), pressure actuated (aneroids) initiators cut your foot retraction cables, opened your lap belt and shoulder harness, and activated the seat-man separator, pushing you free of the seat.

The only thing different about a high-altitude ejection sequence (above 15,000 feet) is that you remained strapped and locked into the seat during the free fall down to 15,000 feet. Once you've ejected into the thin air at 80,000 feet, the pressure suit inflated immediately, emergency oxygen was supplied, and a battery supplying face heat was activated. A stabilizing 6.5 foot diameter drogue chute attached to the top of the ejection seat kept the seat (and you) from tumbling during the long "free fall" ride (about 7 minutes) down to approximately 15,000 feet.

At 2,000 feet above the landing surface we pulled the "Survival Kit Release Handle" on our right side. After pulling the release handle the survival kit fell free below us, attached to a 25-foot lanyard. As it dropped, it activated a CO_2 cylinder, inflating the life raft. The survival kit contained standard Air Force survival items: a one-man life raft, day/night flares, desalinization kit, emergency UHF radio with spare batteries, first aid kit, thermal blanket, fishing gear, survival manual, and maps. Tethered between you and the survival kit was the inflated one-man life raft, ready for a water landing.

Everyone had to attend the Air Force's Water Survival Training at Homestead AFB, Florida. The four day school was designed to teach aircrews how to survive in open seas with only the equipment in their survival kits. The school culminated with Habus parasailing on the fourth day in the pressure suit to practice water entry, staying afloat, getting into the life raft, and a helicopter rescue.

There's an ejection story that happened to Lockheed test pilot Bill Weaver on 25 January 1966 in aircraft 952, the first loss of an SR-71. During their test flight an inlet problem, coupled with other problems, caused the aircraft to break up and the cockpit section became detached from the aft fuselage. With the incredibly high "G" forces created by the breakup of the aircraft, Bill Weaver blacked out. Coming out of his dazed state and regaining his senses he thought he was dead, believing no one could possibly survive what had just happened.

During the ejection, his visor iced over immediately, due to the extremely cold temperatures his warm face place was exposed to. Seeing nothing but brilliant white frost, he was convinced he had died and thought it wasn't all that bad. Soon Bill realized he wasn't dead and somehow had separated from the aircraft. Unable to see outside, he couldn't open his face plate visor until a safe altitude was reached. As soon as he felt the opening shock of the parachute he knew he had to be around 15,000 feet and could now safely open his visor. I was told that incident prompted the addition of the battery activated face heat into our ejection seat, if for no other reason than to be able to see outside.

The combination of the SR-71's ejection seat and pressure suit was extremely reliable. Ejections from the aircraft have ranged from sea level, to Mach 3 and over 75,000 feet. Throughout all the years of the Blackbird program no fatality was ever attributed to the ejection seat or pressure suit.

Drag Chute

The SR-71 utilized a drag chute system to aid in stopping the aircraft on a landing rollout. The drag chute compartment was located on top of the fuselage, between the rudders. When the pilot pulled on the drag chute T-handle on the instrument panel, the drag chute compartment doors sprung open, and a series of chutes went into action. The first chute to be ejected was called the "Pilot Chute" (42 inch diameter). When it hit the air stream its job was to pull out a slightly larger chute called the "Extraction Chute" (10 foot diameter) which produced aerodynamic lift. When the extraction chute hit the air stream it pulled out the safety pin holding the main chute. With the safety pin removed, the main chute (40 foot diameter) was free to deploy and decelerate the 60,000 pound (plus fuel) SR-71.

When the main drag chute deployed it gave a firm tug on the aircraft. To avoid possible damage to the rudders and main chute, the pilot pushed the drag chute handle in, jettisoning the main chute on the runway before reaching 55 knots on the landing rollout. All three chutes fell onto the runway and had to be retrieved before other aircraft could land. Obviously, if stopping distance was marginal, we always had the option of retaining the main chute until safely stopped.

One technique to minimize the landing distance was to pull the drag chute handle while the SR was just a few feet above the runway and ready to touchdown. The delay for all the chutes to open and finally blossom the main chute was around four seconds. Timed just right, the main drag chute blossomed right at touchdown. Obviously, if your timing was off it could ruin your day by slamming the aircraft onto the runway. Since any drag chute is most effective at higher speeds, it made a significant difference in your overall stopping distance to deploy it as soon as possible. I practiced the technique occasionally and used it only when runway and/or braking conditions were marginal (i.e., short runway, wet, snow, or ice).

On a rare occasion the drag chute doors opened inadvertently at high Mach creating problems. RSO, Lt. Col. Curt Osterheld (Ret), describes one such flight.

In January 1984, Joe and I were on our first operational tour at Det 1, Kadena AB, Japan. The mission profile took us west on an ELINT collection over the South China Sea and then east across the DMZ in Korea. We were in the accel after our initial refueling. At about Mach 1.5 we felt a sharp jolt that shook the aircraft violently. We both passed it off as clear air turbulence and pressed on. After a while Joe remarked that the trim didn't look right, so I "spun" [calculated] a manual CG (one of the fifty times I'd do it this mission) and confirmed that, for our fuel indications, it was correct although the CG seemed to be moving all over the place.

By now we noticed we were about 3,000 pounds low on the fuel curve and getting farther behind rapidly. The autopilot kept kicking off. The aircraft would not stay trimmed. At last, we were so far down on the fuel curve that there was no alternative but to abort back to Kadena. The descent gave us plenty of "unstarts" as I broadcast the appropriate HF messages, admitting our failure to the whole world. The "new guy" paranoia crept in as we wondered what we had screwed up. The approach to runway 05R was uneventful, and Joe made a perfect landing. Then, as we both spouted expletives, we realized there would be no reassuring tug from the drag chute. . .it had failed, or so we thought. Some judicious braking and a rapid-fire discussion over the radio about arming/disarming the barrier, and the SR was brought to a safe stop. As we taxied into the hangar, a lot of the maintenance folks were pointing, ashen-faced at our jet. And now, as Paul Harvey says, "for the rest of the story. . ."

The jolt we had felt early on in the accel was caused by the right drag chute door popping up into the slip stream and ripping loose from the aircraft. As the drag chute door departed, it acted like a can opener on Tank-6 and cut a 10 inch gash that allowed fuel to siphon out. The fuel leak caused our trim and CG transients that even the autopilot couldn't keep up with. With no drag chute doors, the drag chute had departed the aircraft and was lost at sea. We were grateful to the Lockheed engineers for designing the drag chute to lock to the aircraft only when the drag chute handle was pulled. . . . one can imagine the effect of the chute deploying inflight at Mach 1.5!

Landing Gear, Tires, and Barrier

The aircraft's main gear consisted of three wheels on each side, any one of which could support the SR-71 at normal landing weights and were rated for a maximum speed of 239 knots. Each main gear was equipped with anti-skid protection for slippery runway conditions. The front cockpit had an emergency gear release T-handle, permitting the gear to be released and free fall by gravity to the down and locked position when pulled out by the pilot. On all of the aircraft's Functional Check Flights, after extensive maintenance work was performed, it was routine to check out the use of the emergency gear release system to lower the landing gear. The T-handle was attached to a cable that had to be pulled out about nine inches and required up to 65 pounds of force to release the uplocks holding the gear doors locked. I recall one Habu pulling hard on the T-handle to test out the emergency system and broke the cable, leaving the T-handle and frayed cable in his hand. Fortunately, this was only a test of the emergency system, and normal gear extension was still available. We all thought it was funny, but maintenance didn't see the humor in it.

The 32-ply tires were silver coated to reflect heat and filled with high-pressure nitrogen for inerting. Depending on how well pilots landed, each tire was good for about 15-20 landings (full stop or touch-and-go). The main landing-gear wheel wells didn't dissipate heat well and consequently, the main gear remained quite hot after landing. Due to the remote island location of Okinawa, our Det 1 missions were planned to arrive back at Kadena at high Mach until the last possible minute before starting our decel. Consequently, the main landing gear assembly was generally too hot to touch after parking in the hangar. Every time Habus came to their final stop for engine shutdown, cooling fans were immediately placed in front or behind each main gear to cool down the brakes.

The nose gear consisted of two smaller tires used to steer the aircraft. By pressing the "Nose Wheel Steering" (NWS) button on the stick grip, the pilot engaged a holding relay that allowed hands-free steering of the aircraft through his rudder pedals. Nose wheel steering was limited to 45 degrees left and right.

The SR-71 had a "unique" departure end barrier (designation BAK-11/12 barrier) developed to stop the aircraft on the runway if all other means failed. It consisted of a set of pressure sensitive switch mats located about six feet apart, built into the runway to sense the nose gear rolling over each of them. After rolling over the switch mats, timing computers quickly calculated the speed of the SR-71 and fired off an air pressure charge that quickly pulled the barrier cable up into the air in time to snag the main gear and stop the aircraft. We were willing to accept minor damage to the main gear if it could save the aircraft. One BAK-11/12 barrier was located in the departure overrun of runway 14 at Beale, and the only other one was on runway 5R at Kadena, located about 2,000 feet short of the overrun.

The barriers were armed and disarmed in the tower on the barrier control panel by the tower controller on duty. The barrier air charging process had to be started about five minutes before the barrier could be armed. Once sufficient air pressure was available, a green barrier "CHARGED" light illuminated in the tower. On takeoff and landing the tower controller informed the pilot that the, "barrier is armed". My particular takeoff technique with the SR (staying low to the runway to build airspeed) sometimes created sufficient vibration and overpressure from the ABs to fire off the barrier on takeoff from Kadena. Tower personnel soon realized they needed to disarm the barrier as soon as "Snake & Nape" broke ground. (Don and I picked up the nicknames of "Snake and Nape," respectively, after my favorite, and highly compatible, ordinance load on F-4s in Vietnam).

There were very few totally successful BAK-11/12 barrier engagements by an SR-71; consequently, crews never planned on using it to stop them.

The SR-71's Lifeline—Det 6

Keeping all the aircraft supplied with parts around the world was a monumental job. Since everything was "unique" to the SR-71, an exclusive supply system had to be established. Our parts supply system was located at Norton AFB, California, and was called Det 6, which reported to the 2762 Logistic Squadron at Wright-Patterson AFB, under the former Air Force Logistics Command (AFLC). Their high level of engineering expertise and system updates constantly kept the SR-71 fleet modernized with new equipment. From a crew member's standpoint, working with Lockheed, Det 6, and the Palmdale Flight Test Center was a streamlined way of doing business if you wanted anything accomplished. If Habus needed something changed in the cockpit or the aircraft, Det 6 made it happen. They engineered the request and Palmdale tested it.

Det 6 was generally commanded by a former SR-71 crew member who knew about the needs and worldwide operation of the aircraft. The remainder of Det 6 personnel were civilians with a wealth of knowledge and experience in dealing with the SR-71. The Det 6 Commander also commanded Palmdale's SR-71 Flight Test facility (Det 51) and all of their personnel. They had a dedicated SR-71 test bed aircraft (call sign "DUTCH") and T-38 aircraft (call sign "TOXON") used for chasing the SR-71. There were two SR-71 qualified crews at Palmdale. Typically, one of the pilots was a graduate of the USAF Test Pilot School, and the other pilot was chosen from the SR-71 operational program at Beale. That way there was a solid blend of each crew's background, providing the right mix to flight testing requirements. Palmdale was also responsible for the complete tear down, overhaul, and update of aircraft systems that occurred about every three years for each SR-71.

CHAPTER SEVEN

OUR TRAINER—
THE SR-71 "B" MODEL

The first SR-71 to arrive at Beale was the "B" model (956) on 6 January 1966 and was flown by Col. Doug Nelson, the first 9th SRW Commander. At one time there were two SR-71 B-models. One trainer (957) crashed on final approach at Beale on 11 Jan 1968. Habus referred to the remaining trainer as either the "B" or "956."

Externally, its only distinguishing difference between an "A" model was the raised rear cockpit where the IP flew and the two ventral fins extending beneath the engine nacelles to provide additional stability. The IP flew in the rear cockpit with a student onboard or while giving a check ride to another Habu. He flew from the front seat if he was checking out a new IP, or from either seat if he was giving a Distinguished Visitor (DV) flight. The DV flights were set up to acquaint general officers and other key military personnel in our chain of command with the SR-71's unique capabilities. Occasionally we flew civilian DVs that had a direct influence on the future funding of our program, such as former Senators Barry Goldwater and Howard Cannon; others we couldn't understand why they got a ride, like the former president of Notre Dame University, the Reverend Theodore M. Hesburgh. Former 1st SRS Commander and SR-71 pilot, Lt. Col. Rod Dyckman (Ret), echoes the sentiments of most Habus concerning DVs flying the SR-71.

> *Most Congressmen and generals were too concerned about politics and public relations (PR) to concentrate on learning the most basic requirements necessary to be effective in the airplane. When I once flew with a Congressman, we did a television interview and other PR tactics that left us very scant on time to concentrate on the simulator and flying requirements. In most cases it was just another notch in the ego belt.*

The back seat of 956 basically squeezed everything in from the front cockpit of an "A" model, plus the necessary items from the RSO's cockpit, including the ANS, HF, and transponder. Although seldom used, the rear cockpit had a switch to raise and lower the gear, instead of a landing gear handle. The drag chute had a similar switch in the back seat to deploy and jettison the chute. A drag chute emergency-deploy T-handle was located between the IP's legs and worked off the same cable arrangement as the front seat drag chute T-handle.

Both cockpits used a control transfer panel, just forward of the throttles, to select which cockpit had control of the navigation equipment, fuel system, inlets, and autopilot. An associated yellow light on the transfer panel illuminated to tell each crew member who had control of which system. The aft cockpit throttle restart switch, when moved out of the OFF position, immediately switched control of the inlets to the aft cockpit, regardless of which cockpit had control. Also, the following controls in the aft cockpit could override the forward cockpit: aft bypass door controls, EGT trim switches, brake switch, restart switches, APW switch, air refuel switch, and the trim switch.

From the back seat the IP had no control over the air conditioning switches, cockpit temperature control switches, bay air switches, or the cockpit pressure dump switch. All the electrical systems and exterior lights were controlled from the front cockpit. The generator control switches, bus tie switch, battery switch, emergency inverter switch, and emergency AC bus switches were all in the front cockpit. The aircraft carried no reconnaissance or intelligence sensors.

Flying 956 from the rear cockpit was certainly no picnic. It was an extremely busy cockpit for the IP, having to perform RSO duties and safely monitor the student's flying performance. Fortunately, this is where our intensive simulator program paid big dividends. I never had a student in the SR-71 that wasn't thoroughly prepared and ready for his first five dual missions.

In the traffic pattern, where we spent a good deal of our flight time with 956, I raised the seat as far as I could tolerate because of the need to see the runway. The most difficult approach for an IP in the back seat was an ILS or PAR (Precision Approach Radar) because the high AOA on final approach, coupled with the long nose of the aircraft, blocked your entire view of the runway from about one mile out. From there through touchdown, IPs had to rely on their peripheral vision and experience to get good landings. Colonel Joe Kinego had a rule of thumb used by most IPs, "If you couldn't see the runway at one mile and all the way on in to the overrun, you were lined up well!"

Fortunately, Beale's runway was 12,000 feet long and 300 feet wide, giving us extra room for centerline alignment. Most IPs planned the 360 degree overhead pattern so their base turn was an angling final turn, rolling out on a very short final prior to touchdown. I planned my base turns to be in a constantly decreasing bank, planning to roll out just over the end of the runway. That way I kept sight of the runway until the last possible moment.

The "B" model flew and handled the same as an "A" model. It was good for a beginning pilot to experience an unstart with an IP onboard before he went solo. We were prohibited from inducing unstarts although easy to do if you wanted to show one to a student. For some strange reason, 956 always seemed to accommodate the IP's learning objective and unstarted quite frequently.

CHAPTER EIGHT

OPERATIONAL, SIOP, AND TRAINING MISSIONS

The highly classified National Reconnaissance Office (NRO) was created in the early 1960s to combine satellite reconnaissance projects underway at the CIA and Defense Department. The office was headed by the Assistant Secretary of the Air Force. The existence of the NRO was an official secret for many years, until its name and overall mission were made public in 1992. Allocation of NRO assets, including the SR-71, was controlled by the Director of Central Intelligence (DCI). Any user that needed intelligence acquired by NRO resources had to make a request through the DCI's office. A committee then reviewed intelligence requests daily, prioritized them, and directed the NRO to position satellites or aircraft as necessary. The SR-71 was part of this process and, consequently, was considered a national reconnaissance asset.

SR-71 operational sorties were flown under the rules of the Peacetime Aerial Reconnaissance Program, or PARPRO (pronounced "Par-Pro"). PARPRO was created for all military reconnaissance assets (air-breathing aircraft) and was managed at the Joint Reconnaissance Center (JRC) in the Pentagon. Every peacetime reconnaissance mission flown worldwide was continuously monitored from start to finish at the JRC, 24-hours a day (called "the watch").

The JRC was further responsible for determining the threat to our aircraft on each mission and obtained the appropriate approval authority to fly each of them. If the mission involved overflight of foreign countries, it was JRC's job to obtain the necessary permission from the State Department. Very few people in the Pentagon were knowledgeable on the SR-71's capabilities or had a SENIOR CROWN security clearance. For those reasons, a former Habu was usually assigned to the JRC and performed duty on "the watch," able to answer questions in case a mission didn't go smoothly.

Operational Missions

"Operational" missions were those that flew through what was called a "sensitive area." While gathering intelligence on foreign countries, we flew in airspace that was defined as a sensitive area. There we could expect any kind of reaction from a foreign country and had to be alert for any possibility. Flying in the sensitive area, all of our airborne equipment, systems, and navigation had to be 100 percent perfect, otherwise it was an automatic abort.

When Don and I flew through a sensitive area, cockpit communications were minimal. We said only what was necessary and paid strict attention to our job at hand. Your sense of awareness became keenly intensified as you wondered what you might see today. We logged our operational missions separate from all other types of flying activity, and after flying around 50 operational missions, Habus were awarded an Air Force Air Medal.

Being under command of the former SAC, they also wanted a final vote on each operational mission and, consequently, had to approve each one of them. Located at SAC Headquarters in Omaha, Nebraska, was another agency with functions similar to the JRC, called the Strategic Reconnaissance Center (SRC). The SRC had a staff of officers, who for the most part, were former crew members in their respective reconnaissance aircraft, SR-71, U-2, and RC-135.

SRC had to send an approval order, called the "Execution" message, for every scheduled operational mission. We could not fly without the "Execute" message from SRC. The "Execute" message was transmitted via secure communications directly to each Detachment Commander and included numerous other addressees who needed to know the mission was a "go." Once the Detachment received the "Execute" message it was up to them to make it work. Operational sorties flown out of Det 1 were called "GIANT SCALE" missions, and out of Det 4 were called "GIANT REACH" missions.

The majority of our operational sorties were flown repeatedly, with only minor changes to the track or sensor operations. Most of these "routine" missions were flown to gather what was called "Indications and Warnings" (I & W) intelligence on other countries. Flying over the same sensitive areas on a regular basis allowed intelligence analysts to determine such things as troop movements, changes to the EOB, and aircraft deployments—all good indications and warnings that something was about to happen. If the I & W intelligence indicated a high level of activity, we could then focus our intelligence gathering in greater detail on a particular geographic region.

However, some operational sorties flown at the Dets had a higher priority than others and, as such, included several means of insuring they would be flown successfully. The lowest level of priority had a spare SR-71 ready and waiting in case the primary aircraft broke. The next level had a spare crew in

The final touches to Det 4's logo are drawn on the rudder of aircraft 980. The dart sticking in the double two represents Det 4. Some of the artistry on other SR-71s was much larger and more detailed. The only approved method of writing on the aircraft's exterior was with chalk because it wasn't harmful to the skin of the aircraft at high temperatures. *Lockheed*

Airplane Arrangement

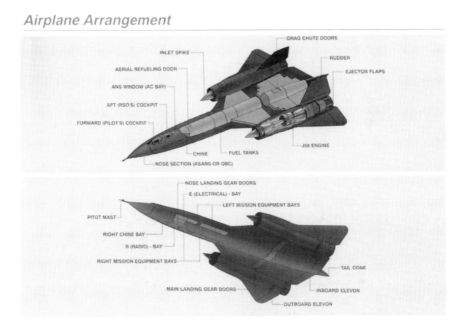

This diagram shows the location of all the major components of the SR-71. *Lockheed*

Sensor Data Collection *(Terrain Coverage at 80,000 Feet)*

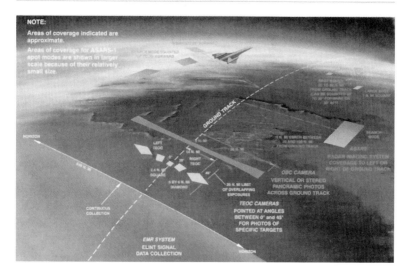

This unique picture shows the SR-71's continuous sensor coverage over the ground from 80,000 feet. It includes the ELINT signal collection, the Technical Objective Cameras (TEOCs), the Optical Bar Camera (OBC), and the Advanced Synthetic Aperture Radar System (ASARS). All of the distances are extended if the aircraft is banked. *Lockheed*

The entire nose of the SR-71 was removable. We flew with either an optical camera inside the nose called the Optical Bar Camera (OBC) or a radar imaging sensor called the Advanced Synthetic Aperture Radar System (ASARS). *R. Graham collection*

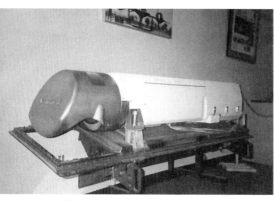

A TEOC camera mounted to its bay cover. The entire unit was raised up into the chine and secured to the fuselage. The camera lens section is covered in gold foil to insulate it from the heat. The lens aims down through the glass window pane. *R. Graham collection*

A J-58 engine on the test stand at night. The tremendous heating of the turbine and after-burner section of the engine makes it glow red hot, allowing you to see heat shadows on the inside of the engine through the metal. The circular concentric shock waves can be seen inside the exhaust plume. Standing beside the engine in full afterburner (AB) made your teeth rattle and body tremble uncontrollably from the exhaust noise vibrations. *Pratt and Whitney*

The crew of Tom Alison and JT Vida. Tom had just finished flying his last sortie in the SR-71B for a total of 966 hours. JT flew up from Palmdale to congratulate him on his last sortie. *Tom Alison*

The J-58 engine. The engine oil tank, mounted on the compressor case, is serviced to 5.15 gallons to cool the engine bearings and gears. The three large compressor bypass tubes (six per engine) duct air from the compressor section and help turn the engine into a ramjet at high Mach. *Pratt and Whitney*

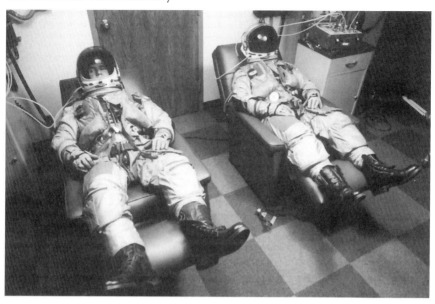

Terry Pappas and John Manzi are ready for testing and the final stages of suit-up at Beale. The suits are fully inflated and pressure-tested for leaks prior to every flight. After testing is complete, the boots are zipped, stirrups attached, and suits zipped closed. *Lockheed*

Fully decked out in the $120,000 pressure suit. If a loss of cabin pressure occurred at 80,000 feet, the suit inflated to save your life. This crewmember is carrying his liquid oxygen converter for breathing and cooling of the suit. *Chad Slattery*

The crew's transportation to and from the aircraft—the white PSD van. The mobile crew and their car are waiting for engine start. The car was equipped with two UHF radios for communication with the SR-71, the Command Post, tower, weather personnel, and other air traffic control agencies handling the aircraft. They also had a portable military VHF radio, nicknamed the "brick," for worldwide communications. *Lockheed*

Terry Pappas and John Manzi wait inside the PSD van for their aircraft to be readied. Cooling air to their suits is provided by the portable liquid oxygen converters behind their recliners. Velcro on the suit legs holds their checklists in place, and the stirrups on their boots lock to the ejection seat retraction cables. *Lockheed*

On mobile duty, Bill Orcutt wishes the crew a good mission before they climb up the stands. The two oxygen hoses leading from their pressure suit helmets connected to the aircraft's oxygen supply provide two independent sources of precious oxygen. *Lockheed*

A bare SR-71 ejection seat. Our shortest operational sortie was 57 minutes; and longest was just over 11 hours. The oversized D-ring, located between your legs, started the ejection sequence when firmly pulled. Just above the foot rests are the ball-and-socket foot retraction cables that connected to our stirrups. *R. Graham collection*

101

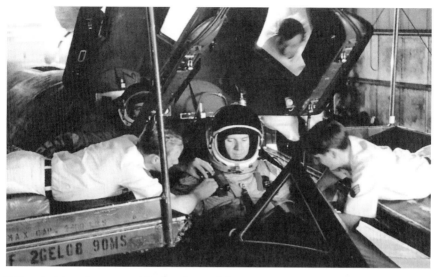

PSD technicians lie prone while they "strap-in" Terry Pappas. At some remote locations this had to be done with only one ladder and one technician, requiring them to lay across your body in order to reach the other side of the seat for attachments. *Lockheed*

A picture of myself strapped in and ready to go. The helmet's rubber face seal traps the 100 percent oxygen around eyes, nose, and mouth. The microphone is positioned just in front of my lips for transmitting. The pulley and cable around the metal neck ring attaches to the tie-down strap. The cord leading into my helmet is for the face heat. The two parachute straps are locked onto the pressure suit. *R. Graham collection*

RIGHT

SR-71 crews practice their formation skills. In the Beale area we flew low-level navigation routes, formation practice, aerobatics, instrument flying and "Pace Chase" with the SR-71. I had the diagonal stripe added to the aircraft when the crews said they wanted a distinctive look to our T-38s. *R. Graham collection*

This picture of the trainer (956) shows the pronounced raised rear cockpit. Due to its limited visibility, the Instructor Pilot (IP) in the rear seat had to use his peripheral vision to stay lined up with the runway on final approach, and his flying abilities and instincts to make a good landing. You felt as if you were flying on the end of a pin, with no outside visual references. *Lockheed*

Aircraft 960 lifts off from Mildenhall. The concentric rings of light coming from the SR-71's exhaust are individual shock waves formed by the supersonic air exiting the engine. The uninstalled maximum thrust of each J-58 engine was over 32,000 pounds. At Mach 3 speeds, the engines supplied approximately 20 percent of the total thrust, and the inlets supplied 80 percent. *Gary Jones*

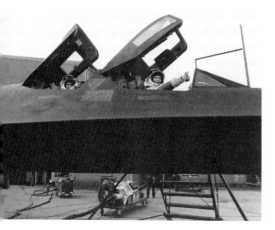

Pilot Bob Behler prepares to fly his last operational sortie with his RSO, Ted Ross, on 9 April 1985 from RAF Mildenhall. The individual ejection seats and pressure suits afforded a safe escape from the aircraft at all altitudes and airspeeds. *Gary Jones*

BELOW
One of Beale's KC-135Q tankers refuels a thirsty SR-71. Locked to the boom, the pilot had to rely on the tanker's director lights, located on the forward belly of the tanker, to maintain the contact position. Our average time locked-on to the boom was between 17 to 20 minutes to get a full load of JP-7. The tankers became our "eyes" when it came to avoiding bad weather. *Lockheed*

This photo was taken from an SR-71 stabilized in the pre-contact position. From here, the pilot will close in on the tanker to place the end of the boom nozzle about three feet in front of his windshield. The boom operator then flies the boom into the air refueling receptacle. The tanker's fore-and-aft, and up-and-down director lights are seen on the forward belly. *Lockheed*

Terry Pappas going through his cockpit checklist. Note his dark visor is half way down and the clear visor in the up and stowed position. When the metal Baylor bar ring (top of helmet) is brought down, it locks to the clasp at his chin level, starting the flow of 100 percent oxygen. *Lockheed*

In the early 80s, crews occasionally refueled from KC-10 tankers. They were able to fly at higher airspeeds than the KC-135Qs, making refueling easier for the SR-71 pilots. The high angle-of-attack (AOA) associated with a slow airspeed make the SR-71 more difficult to fly locked-on to the boom of a KC-135Q. *USAF*

The nose-high pitch attitude for landing is evident, as Palmdale's test aircraft (955) touches down. Forward visibility from the cockpit on final approach was blocked slightly by the long nose and chines. The 40-foot diameter drag chute reduced our landing distance considerably. *Lockheed*

RIGHT
Members of the 9th Reconnaissance Technical Squadron (9th RTS), Beale AFB, California, analyze the SR-71's intelligence. Through the use of portable vans, the 9th RTS developed, processed, and analyzed all our intelligence on a worldwide basis. *Lockheed*

John Morgan celebrates his 600-hour sortie with a cool refreshment at Kadena, while his pilot, Bob Crowder, joins in the festivities. John eventually achieved 1,000 hours in the SR-71 on 11 April 1985 at RAF Mildenhall. *Frank Stampf*

The moment every Habu trains for and eagerly anticipates. Roger Jacks is presented his "Mach 3" pin on his first flight by the 9th SRW Commander, Col. Pat Halloran. It was a festive atmosphere on the flight line with champagne, family, relatives, friends, and Habus participating. *Roger Jacks*

RIGHT
One of our Bachelor Officers' Quarters (BOQ) on Okinawa. Room 216 displays typical living quarters for our six week tours of duty. Habus spent considerable time and money upgrading each room with bars, carpets, pictures, stereo equipment, fresh paint, drapes, etc., to make living conditions more tolerable. *Frank Stampf*

LEFT
Joe Kinego (left) and Roger Jacks (right) after a mission. Notice Joe is wearing the newer dark brown pressure suit that was phased in around 1974. The old white suits produced unwanted reflections throughout the cockpits from the brilliant sunlight at 80,000 feet. The suit's tie down straps dangle from their neck rings, keeping the helmet ring in place during full inflation of the suit. *Roger Jacks*

In April 1977, Habus John Murphy, Don Emmons, Roger Jacks, and myself arrive at the entrance to Det 1 operations before a mission. The austere building was also used for the KC-135Q tanker operations. *Roger Jacks*

This is BOQ 318, our living accommodations for six weeks on Okinawa. It was built in the late 1960s with CIA funds for the A-12 pilots flying under the code name "OXCART." When the SR-71 began flying missions in 1968, all six Habus lived on the top floor, and our KC-135Q crews occupied the bottom floor. *Frank Stampf*

At his restaurant, Mr. Nakachi explains to a group of Habus the Okinawan's famous "Tiger Drink." Okinawans truly believed when a man drank the "Tiger Drink" he would have increased virility and manhood. I can personally vouch that the drink put most Habus to sleep more than anything else! *Curt Osterheld*

Refilling the endless supply of vodka and tonic for our "basic hooks" are Roger Jacks, myself, and Don Emmons. The tanks were located to the side of our BOQ and caused quite a commotion as people drove by. If you give a Habu a can of black spray paint and a stencil, anything can happen! *Roger Jacks*

An SR-71 crew practices a single-engine go-around at Mildenhall in full afterburner. It required around fifteen degrees of bank into the good engine, and ten degrees of rudder just to keep the SR-71 traveling straight ahead. The landing gear is on its way up. *Gary Jones*

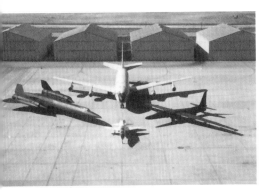

All of the 9th SRW aircraft at Beale AFB, California: T-38, KC-135Q, U-2, and the SR-71. I was fortunate to fly the first three aircraft routinely, and the SR-71 twice, as the Wing Commander. One of the SR-71 hangars in the background was secretly dismantled at night and reassembled on the remote island of Diego Garcia in the Indian Ocean for future SR-71 use. *R. Graham collection*

A side-by-side comparison of a YF-12 (936) on the left and the SR-71 (961) on the right. The rounded nose cone of the YF-12 contained the radar for its interceptor mission. Three ventral fins (not shown) were added underneath the YF-12 for increased directional stability. *Lockheed*

LEFT
A rare picture of the once highly classified project "TAGBOARD" program. The D-21 drone is mated to its mothership, a slightly modified A-12, and redesignated to M-12. The program was short-lived after an unsuccessful launch of the drone on 31 July 1966, causing the loss of the aircraft and the death of the Launch Control Officer in the rear seat, Ray Torrick. *Lockheed*

In July of 1985, an SR-71 was flown to RAF Fairford, England, on static display for visiting King Hussein of Jordan. The very next day, British nuclear protesters threw paint on the SR-71. There was no permanent damage to the aircraft. Several days later crews flew "low" passes over the protesters tents near RAF Fairford. Rumor had it that several tents were leveled and hearing problems lasted for hours afterwards. Dressed in their Habu party suits, left to right, are John Morgan, Steve Lee, Ed Yielding, Les Dyer, Bob Behler, and Det 4 Commander, Lt. Col. Barry MacKean. *Les Dyer*

Lockheed spent over a year making a film at Beale on the SR-71 called, "SR-71 Blackbird." They ended up with a movie that told a good story about the aircraft, the crews, and all the effort that went into producing one sortie. Discussing the photo session is Andy Stumpf, Robert Mehnert, and myself. *R. Graham collection*

In May 1973, aircraft 978 departed runway 5R at Kadena and collapsed the landing gear. The aircraft was damaged beyond repair. At the time I was flying F-4s at Kadena and a typhoon pushed the crosswinds out of our limits, and we canceled flying for the day. As I pulled into my driveway, I heard the roar of an SR-71 trying to land. I watched him disappear on final approach and thought to myself, "Good luck in these winds." Suddenly, I heard another roar of his engines as I observed him trying for a second approach at landing. The next day I went to my F-4 squadron and heard all the pilots talking about an SR-71 that crashed on landing. *R. Graham collection*

Mike Smith and Doug Soifer performing at RAF Mildenhall's annual Air Fete. This underside shot of the SR-71 captured a rare photograph of what maintenance believed was all the TEB shooting out of its tank to ignite the afterburners. The picture had been taken from several angles and became quite popular among aviation enthusiasts in England. Visible moisture is seen streaming from the chine and wing tips. *Gary Jones*

Lieutenant Colonels JT Vida and Ed Yielding pose before their 6 March 1990 record-breaking flight from Los Angeles to Washington, D.C. in 64 minutes, averaging 2,144.8 mph. On that historic event, aircraft 972 was turned over to the Smithsonian's National Air and Space Museum at Dulles International Airport. *Lockheed*

The salvage effort of the fuselage from aircraft 974. In April 1989, a double hydraulic system leak forced Dan House and Blair Bozek to eject into the Philippine Sea, a quarter-mile north of Luzon. They were picked up in good shape, and the decision was made to recover the aircraft. *Rod Dyckman*

After the final SR-71 flight on 26 January 1990 at Beale AFB, California, a planeside ceremony retires the colors for the last time. Mr. Ben Rich, co-designer of the Blackbird family of aircraft and President of Lockheed's famed Skunk Works, sadly watches the two Air Force sergeants fold the flag. *Lockheed*

The final SR-71 flight on 26 January 1990. A large crowd on Beale's flight line waits for pilot Rod Dyckman and RSO Tom Bergam to bring the SR-71 to a stop, right of the podium. Rod flew several awe inspiring passes over the field in final salute to the SR-71's 22 years of dedicated service. *Lockheed*

The SR-71's official "Certificate of Retirement" was presented at the ceremonies honoring its final flight on 26 January 1990. When SR-71s returned to the Air Force in 1995, former Habus had the retirement certificate stamped with the international "Prohibited" symbol. *R. Graham collection*

As the SR-71 program ended in 1990, some of our aircraft were fortunate enough to be flown to museums around the United States. This SR-71 was cut up and is being swallowed by a C-5 transport on its trip final to a museum. *Lockheed*

LEFT
The prime architects restoring the SR-71s back into service with the Air Force. Left to right, Bill Grimes, Capt. Mike Zimmerman, and former RSOs Don Emmons and Barry MacKean. Not pictured is Lockheed's SR-71 Project Manager, Jay Murphy. The "Buick" is positioned underneath and connected to the right engine, ready for start. *Lockheed*

the cockpit of a second SR-71 waiting for the word that the primary aircraft had broken and for them to launch. The highest level of insurance had the spare SR-71 flying the route directly behind the primary aircraft by about 30 minutes. Any one of these readiness levels was determined by the priority of the mission and the amount of time available to gather the particular intelligence (the "window"). The routine operational sorties were flown by every Habu. Some Habus were fortunate enough to be "at the right place at the right time" to fly special missions created by "hot spots" developing somewhere on the globe. Former SR-71 pilot and 1st SRS Operations Officer, Lt. Col. Mike Smith (Ret), talks about his one special mission.

Major Doug Soifer and I were still pretty new at the game when the first oil tanker convoys were to be escorted into the Persian Gulf past the Iranian threats of blockade. We were at Kadena, a young senior crew living the life of the Habu, when tasking came down for an SR-71 mission into the Persian Gulf to locate "Silkworm" anti-ship missiles. There had been considerable discussion at higher headquarters as to which Det to fly the mission from. Plans were made and re-made, maps were drawn and re-drawn, problems studied and re-studied until the powers-that-be finally decided that an SR-71 would fly from Kadena to the Persian Gulf and back, one of the longest missions ever flown in the SR-71. It would be a true test of both man and machine. Like every other Habu, we wanted this mission. It was special, it was first, it would cover territory that this jet had never been in, and would provide that test of skills and "stuff" that every aviator/adventurer seems to require from time to time.

At the time, there were always two jets at Kadena and, like everyone, we had our favorite. In the minds of Habus, one jet always ran a little better, made fewer noises, and had fewer problems than the other although these exotic jets seemed, at times, to favor a specific crew as much as the crew might favor the jet. At any rate, we had been getting along famously with 967 while the other crew and the maintenance guys thought that the other jet, 975, was the best of the two.

Colonel Tom Alison was the Det 1 commander, and he had us plan, and think, and study the mission for what seemed like weeks. Minor changes in routing or targets had the ripple effect of changing many, many details, and at times it seemed that the slow moving convoys would get in the Gulf before the SR-71. Of course, the best jet, 975, was the number one choice, and the other, 967 (our favorite), would be the airborne spare. Kadena was absolutely overrun with tankers and aircrews—the briefing room for the mission was full of crews and planners and supervisors, all there for us. The planned mission was more than 11 hours of flight time, 5 refuelings, thousands of miles between suitable emergency runways, and a target area so small that we would have to slow down slightly to stay on track due to the SR's large turn radius at high speed. The crew was more than ready.

The morning of our mission, 22 July 1987, was a beautiful, tropical island day and, at last count, 27 tankers would take off to get our one black jet to the Persian Gulf and back. We began the routine: normal crew brief, suit-up, and then got the word of a slight delay, the ANS isn't quite right. We elected to go out to the jet and wait for the fix, and in a few minutes we were told that they were finishing up. No sooner had we stood up than Colonel Alison rushed up to tell us that maintenance had dropped a part under the seat, and we would be taking the spare—967, our jet. We rushed through the preflight checks and taxied out.

Takeoff was a heavyweight[65,000 pounds of fuel] right to supersonic cruise—we were exhilarated. Our only shortage was our oxygen—which we used at a very high rate for the first hour—but after tightening up our helmet face seal a little, our oxygen use slowed to normal. We would laugh later that it had been our heavy breathing that was using up the oxygen. After the first refueling, the jet settled into its rhythm and flew perfectly for the entire flight. The crew in the airborne spare was right behind us, ready to take over if we developed problems.

We flew over places that were new to us . I saw inlet temperatures climb 70 degrees in less than a minute in level flight above 70,000 feet (this rare occurrence confirmed by the crew flying the spare 30 minutes behind us) and clouds so high and so white they seemed to glow over the Indian Ocean. Finally we arrived in the target area and flew through the Strait of Hormuz, right over the convoys. We had slowed to about Mach 2.5 to make the turns inside the Gulf and were listening to AWACS make the threat calls in addition to watching our own equipment. Fortunately, we were busy, and we finished so quickly that the threats didn't have time to become dangerous.

We had both been confident that we would get to the target; now came the tough part, we had to get home. Of course weather moved in to our last refueling. When we finally found the tankers, one had a bad refueling boom and the other had no director light. But refueling went OK. After one last supersonic leg, 11.2 hours after we left Kadena, we landed in the dark with no liquid nitrogen remaining. The maintenance and operations support guys were ecstatic, 967 had run flawlessly; no write-ups for the entire mission. It was the greatest feeling of my life!

In one regard, the SR-71's high speed worked against it. Because it traveled so fast, it had only a short amount of time to gather ELINT before it was out of range. To "listen" for longer periods of time we flew what were called "coordinated" sorties. On those sorties, other intelligence gathering assets, usually an RC-135 or EC-135 reconnaissance aircraft, were involved in our mission. At Det 4 the SR-71 also flew "coordinated" sorties with British RAF Nimrod aircraft and the German Atlantiques aircraft collecting ELINT intelligence. We used the SR-71 primarily to stimulate the electronic environment while other assets gathered the ELINT.

One question that routinely came up with an audience of civilians was, "What's it like spying on another country with the SR-71?" Habus had to be prepared with an answer rather than avoid the question. The point I always tried to make was the fact that we were *not* spying. Covert spying on foreign countries is highly illegal and people can be tried, convicted, and imprisoned for the act. By internationally agreed upon PARPRO rules, the SR-71 gathered intelligence overtly on foreign countries. For that reason, and by the Hague Convention of 1907, we wore the American flag on the left shoulder of our pressure suits, and our aircraft were painted with Air Force markings. If we ever went down in a hostile country there was to be no doubt we were Air Force crews, flying an Air Force aircraft. The list of countries we flew PARPRO missions in international airspace includes: Vietnam, Cuba, Libya, Nicaragua, Iran, Iraq, China, North Korea, Warsaw Pact countries, Persian Gulf region, and the Soviet Union. Keeping a watchful vigilance is not the same as spying.

We knew the Soviets were always closely monitoring our activities at Beale and the Dets, either by satellites or radio intercepts. A former SR-71 pilot, Col. Duane Deal, worked for me as the 9th Avionic Maintenance Squadron (AMS) Commander at Beale, housing all the highly classified and sophisticated electronic sensors used on the aircraft. He asked for permission to paint Russian words on the flat roof of his sprawling flightline maintenance building where all the sensors were kept. He told me his troops wanted to paint a slogan that was sure to be seen by Soviet satellites as they passed overhead on a daily basis. In large Russian lettering they wrote on the roof top, "You watch us, while we watch you!" I never received any feedback if the writing was ever seen by Soviet satellites, but the 9th AMS was proud of it being there, and so was I.

SIOP Missions

The Single Integrated Operational Plan (SIOP) was created for SAC and the Navy to use their nuclear weapons against a foreign country. The plan ranged from a very selective use of nuclear weapons to the complete use of nuclear bombers, ICBMs, and SLBMs. SAC's plans called for the SR-71s to be used in a Post-SIOP mission. Our role was to conduct nuclear Bomb Damage Assessment (BDA) after a nuclear exchange had occurred, so the senior civilian and military leadership could determine if follow on strikes were warranted.

Every Habu crew had to be "SIOP certified" annually. This entailed a full day of studying the highly classified SIOP war plans in the 9th Wing "vault." We spent considerable time in the vault familiarizing ourselves with all the SIOP rules, procedures, documents, and checklists. Crews focused on a specific SR-71 SIOP sortie that they could be asked to fly some day and studied every facet of the mission in excruciating detail until it was memorized.

The certification process consisted of the crew briefing the specific SR-71 post-SIOP sortie before the 9th SRW Commander or Vice Commander. The crew took about 30 minutes to brief the entire sortie, from start to finish, emphasizing what actions they would take along the route if certain scenarios developed. At the completion of the crew briefing, the Wing Commander asked if any of the experts sitting around the table would like to question the crew on any facet of the SIOP mission. If the Wing Commander was satisfied with their briefing and answers to the questions, he signed documents making them "SIOP certified" for another year.

Training Missions

We didn't need higher approval to fly training sorties. Generally speaking, all the training sorties were flown at Beale and the operational sorties at the Detachments. It was difficult to develop training routes in the United States because of the sonic boom created by the shock wave coming off the airplane at supersonic speeds. At 80,000 feet the sonic boom could be heard on the ground as a double thunder clap, the first clap being much louder than the second. Some of the major obstacles our routes had to avoid were: cities in excess of 30,000 people, all national park and recreation areas, national monuments, and winter skiing resorts.

There were also individual locations we had to avoid where our sonic boom supposedly created problems for farmers. They included such things as mink farmers who said their minks wouldn't mate, farmers who claimed their cows wouldn't give milk, and chickens that wouldn't lay eggs, all because of the sonic boom. At Beale we had a full time officer responsible for investigating all of our sonic boom complaints.

Don and I created a sonic boom that neither we nor the mission planners had anticipated. During our decel into the Andrews AFB Airshow in July of 1976, we inadvertently boomed a small country town in West Virginia and created a panic. The town's only industry was a dynamite manufacturing plant, and when everyone heard the long dreaded "BOOM!!" they were all convinced the factory had just blown up. Their volunteer fire department, along with the rest of the town's folk, raced out to the factory only to find it still intact. A local newspaper clipping, describing the false alarm, was later sent to Don and I at Beale.

At Det 1, when the opportunity presented itself, crews would make a Mach 3 pass over the island for all to observe. The mobile crew passed the word to maintenance control, and they announced over the Det's PA system the estimated time of the pass. It was impossible to see the SR-71 with the naked eye from the ground, so Habus dumped a small amount of fuel, creating an artificial contrail behind the aircraft, as they made their southerly Mach 3 pass over the island. Maintenance personnel and "Tech Reps" congregated outside the hangars to watch. From the time the aircraft was directly overhead, it took one minute and twenty seconds for the sonic boom to reach the ground. It was a small tribute to all the maintenance folks for their hard work; they loved to see (and hear) the labor of their work, and so did we! It was all part of the inherent camaraderie within the SR-71 community.

CHAPTER NINE

KADENA AB, OKINAWA, JAPAN (DET 1)

Following the deployment of three A-12s (930, 932, and 937) to Kadena in May of 1967 under the code name of "Black Shield," the first operational sortie was flown by pilot Mel Vojvodich. The last A-12 sortie flown by the CIA was on 5 June 1968 by Jack Weeks, who never returned from his fateful mission. His disappearance remains a total mystery as no aircraft wreckage was ever found. A decision was made to continue flying reconnaissance sorties from Det 1; however, it would be done in an overt manner with the two-seated SR-71s. The very first SR-71 operational sortie was flown at Det 1 on 21 March 1968 by Maj. Jerry O'Malley and RSO Capt. Ed Payne. Originally the detachment was called OL-8 (Operating Location-8), then changed in 1970 to OL-RK (Operating Location Ryukyu—the Japanese island chain including Okinawa). In 1971, the detachment changed to OL-KA (Operating Location Kadena), and finally in August of 1974 it was called Detachment 1.

At the time, Okinawa provided a well-suited location to fly sorties into Vietnam and also cover other areas of interest in the Pacific theater. Kadena had the support facilities, security, and room for construction that many other locations in the Pacific did not have. Facilities already built with CIA funds in 1965 included four large T-hangars, an adjoining maintenance complex, and living quarters for personnel; it made logistical and financial sense to continue flying SR-71 sorties from Kadena. Originally, only three SR-71s were at Det 1 but increased to four in the Spring of 1970 due to increased intelligence requirements. We always had a minimum of five KC-135Qs and five tanker crews TDY to Kadena to support the SR-71.

The entire Det was enclosed by a perimeter security system with a single entry point guard shack. At the main entrance you had to show the guard the correct security badges to enter the Det, had to know the cipher code to open the front door to Operations, needed the cipher code for the Operations Officer's office door, and lastly, the combination codes to open your safe. More numbers to remember!

Early on, Det 1 consisted of a PCS (permanently stationed) Commander and a few other key military personnel. Everyone else was TDY from Beale and flew to and from Okinawa on our KC-135Qs. During the late 1970s, the entire Det shifted to PCS personnel, including their families. Moving to a PCS operation greatly increased the responsibility for the Commander but also increased the efficiency and effectiveness of our Det operations. After that organizational change, the only personnel going TDY to Okinawa were the KC-135Q tanker crews, Habus, Lockheed "Tech Reps," and PSD technicians. At its peak the total Det manpower was over 300 men and women.

The position of Det commander was always filled by former SR-71 crew members who had made it up through the ranks to Lieutenant Colonel or Colonel. Although the position was a non-flying job, it was highly sought after because the locations were good, the operational flying great, and the commander didn't have to cope with the tons of paperwork and a multitude of meetings to attend, like back at Beale. Every Det commander was given the freedom to run his operation as he saw fit and reported to no one other than the 9th Wing Commander back at Beale. They were autonomous units, streamlined to accomplish the flying mission and unimpeded by the bureaucracy of a large wing structure.

Det 1 Routine

For Habus there was no such thing at Det 1 as a typical work schedule, since the flying activity changed from week to week. The Det was on contract with SRC to fly so many operational reconnaissance missions each month—typically 10 to 12 per month, or about one sortie every third day. If we aborted a mission, flying activity had to pick up to cover the reconnaissance targets missed. However, to keep from flying a predictable schedule, the sorties were randomly spaced throughout the month.

There were three combat-ready crews at Kadena at all times: One crew was the primary fliers for a given day, another crew was the back-up and also performed mobile duties while the third crew took care of any additional duties or had the day off. The flying "ladder," as we called it, rotated so that the next scheduled sortie had the previous mobile crew move up as the primary fliers, the "off" crew moved up as mobile, and the previous fliers became the "off" crew. Regardless of what mission came up next, we adhered to the flying "ladder" religiously, making other Habus envious of those fortunate enough to fly the special missions that seldom occurred. If you were the back-up crew when a special mission came down, jokes ran rampant about the possibility of the primary crew getting sick or falling off a bar stool, making them unable to fly.

On average we flew about three times a week. That was the best it would ever get! With weather cancellations, maintenance aborts, spared sorties requiring two aircraft, and everything else imaginable, you rarely saw a typical week of flying materialize. Thrown into the weekly schedule were all the tours and briefings Habus gave for public relations (or out of necessity), and soon the week became full of activities. The name of the game at our Dets was to "work hard and play hard." A classic tale by Col. Roger Jacks (Ret) emphasizes the point.

> The camaraderie and team spirit was unmatched when compared to any other flying experience. SR-71 aircrews, maintenance personnel, KC-135Q aircrews, mission planners, administration personnel, and Recce Tech squadron personnel worked hard and played hard at our Detachments. I recall a mission that, according to the Intelligence Shop, was going to be especially hazardous since it had been reported the "bad guys" were out to shoot down an SR-71. Everyone seemed to sense the potential for danger, and the resolve to successfully pull off this mission became intense. As we were cleared to taxi onto the runway and hold, my pilot, Maj. Joe Kinego said, "Look out the right side of the aircraft, you won't believe it." When I looked out the aircraft, I saw our maintenance crews all lined up down the right side of the runway saluting the aircraft. With a lump in our throats and pride in our hearts we launched out on the mission. Upon returning, the maintenance crews met us in the hangar with a large banner that said, "Welcome home Kinego and Jacks."

Many Habus emphasized sports and other healthy activities which consumed a large part of their free time. One day we were having a drink in Don's room when another RSO came in huffing and puffing from his daily jog. He started to berate Don and tell him how he needed to exercise to stay healthy, rather than smoke and drink all the time. Don sat patiently behind his bar puffing on his cigarette and sipping his vodka-tonic while the RSO ranted on and on. After he stopped his chastising, Don said, "Tell you what, I'll race you from the main gate back to 318 and see we'll who's in better shape." The RSO had no choice but to accept the challenge after all his talk about how unfit Don was in front of other Habus.

The big event was set, and several days later we drove them both to the main gate for the race. It was about two miles from the main gate to 318, mostly uphill. I followed alongside Don in the car with lights flashing. At about the halfway point I could see he was getting thirsty so I passed him a cold beer through the car window as he continued to jog on. Soon Don arrived at 318 and was back behind his bar, with a cigarette in one hand and vodka-tonic in the other. Dripping with sweat, the RSO finally entered the room huffing and puffing. From that day forward we never heard another word from him about any Habu being out of shape.

Your first operational sortie ended up with a tie-cutting ceremony at the bottom of the ladder. We were told beforehand, and also knew from seeing the previous ties, to pick the cheapest, most offensive tie you could find on the island. I completely forgot about wearing my necktie during the mission but was reminded of its presence when I pulled into the hangar and saw the Det Commander holding a pair of scissors. At the foot of the ladder Don and I were congratulated on our first mission, given champagne to drink, and had our ties cut in half. The bottom half of the ties were labeled with crew name and date, then placed on a picture board in Operations.

Another special Habu tradition crews eagerly anticipated after flying their first operational sortie was being given the HABU patch to wear on the left shoulder of their flight suit and jacket. This is the one patch that distinguished between those who had flown the SR-71 (VIPs, trainees, etc.) and those who had flown it on operational missions; there was no other way to earn the privilege and honor of wearing the HABU patch. Slipping into our flight suits back at PSD we realized Habus had already taken care of having the HABU patch sewn on the sleeve while we were airborne—it looked good, and we were proud to be part of it! Colonel Jacks recalls the special event.

> As a trainee I really admired the SR-71 crew members that got to wear the prestigious HABU patch on their flight suits. That was an honor that had to be earned by successfully flying an operational SR-71 mission. The patch was a long-time coming because the training program took approximately one year to complete. One of my proudest days was wearing the HABU patch on my flight suit. I have no idea who started the tradition, but it became one of honor and importance to the SR-71 crew member.

One of the most demanding, and shortest, SR-71 operational missions flown, we nicknamed the "Rocket Ride." It was an unrefueled, Mach 3 reconnaissance mission that made one pass through the Korean DMZ, lasting a total of 57 minutes. We stayed in AB from takeoff roll until ready to decel back into Kadena. The "Rocket Ride" was one mission every Habu tried to break a "time-to-climb" record we kept among ourselves. Timing started at brake release and finished when two parameters were achieved—reach 80,000 feet and be at Mach 3. Any crew who thought they had broken the record had to get the MRS tapes and prove their time. The fastest time I recall was just a shade over 14 minutes, set by Lt. Col. Jim Sullivan (Ret). Unless the "temp devs" were considerably colder than standard during the accel (minus 20 degrees or more), there was little chance for a record that day. Former Maj. "Geno" Quist, RSO, remembers his turn at flying a similar "Rocket Ride."

> On September 3, 1982, Nevin [Maj. Nevin Cunningham] and I were the primary crew to take an SR to the Toronto Air Show. The flight plan called for a 45,000 pound fuel load with a "hot" leg and a refueling in the midwest. We flew out over Lake Tahoe, and then were cleared for the accel. We had never had an accel with such a light load—by then the fuel was down to near 30,000 pounds—what a thrill, to say the least. When we felt IGV shift, the change in the acceleration was so great that the autopilot disengaged. Everything else went well, except as if to remind us who was in charge, we had three unstarts later in the flight!

Det 1 was not equipped to do depot-level maintenance overhauls on the aircraft, so about once every year all three aircraft were swapped out for SR-71s that had recently completed a major overhaul at Palmdale. Another major reason for exchanging aircraft annually was to prevent corrosion problems from developing on the aircraft. The salt water surrounding the island, coupled with its year-round hot and humid climate, made corrosion the aircraft's greatest enemy. When I was flying F-4s on Okinawa, corrosion to the aircraft's electrical system was starting to ground our aircraft. It took an aggressive corrosion control program of painting, ripping out old aircraft wiring, and encasing new wire bundles to preclude the F-4s from turning into rust buckets.

At first, SR-71s were ferried directly to and from Det 1 on a non-operational mission called "GLOWING HEAT." It was about a 5 hour flight from Beale to Okinawa, included a refueling after takeoff and another one south of the Aleutian Islands, extending off the west coast of Alaska. The last refueling could take you all the way to Okinawa, but with little gas in reserve. Everywhere around the world, whenever an SR-71 was airborne, a designated KC-135Q crew had their aircraft "cocked," ready for an immediate takeoff in case the SR-71 crew radioed ahead that they needed additional fuel in order to land safely. This was called the "strip alert" tanker and became a Habu's ace-in-the-hole for extra fuel.

When word got out about "GLOWING HEAT" missions coming up, crews lined up at the door of the Squadron Commander's office, volunteering to ferry an SR-71 over to Okinawa rather than take the 18 hour tanker flight. Colonel Joe Kinego (Ret) explains why:

> It was always a thrill deploying the SR to our Dets at Kadena and Mildenhall. When we traveled by KC-135Q (which was most of the time) a typical trip to Kadena would take anywhere from 18 hours to two days, depending on winds. Generally speaking, if we had to go through Guam we spent the night there due to the tanker crew's rest requirements. The Mildenhall trip was shorter, but still 12 to 15 hours depending on stops. Flying the SR over was about a four hour flight to either place if we went direct. Later in the program when we began flying operational sorties enroute, the time jumped to 6-8 hours. I can remember many times having breakfast at PSD before departing for the Dets and arriving there a few hours later in time for breakfast again!

During one of the aircraft swap-outs, the maintenance troops at Det 1 wrote sayings, poems, notes, messages, and drew art, on the entire exterior of the first SR-71 being sent back to Beale. Chalk was the only allowable writing instrument on the skin of the aircraft since it didn't damage the surface at high temperatures. When the aircraft arrived at Beale the writing received a lot of laughs by those of us greeting the aircraft and crew. There was so much chalk on the aircraft that it was hard to tell the aircraft was painted black. However, the maintenance hours required to get the chalk off was not such a laughing matter. The entire aircraft had to be washed down with JP-7 to remove the chalk. After that episode, the other aircraft arrived back at Beale with one picture drawn in chalk on each rudder. Some of the "nose art" was quite extensive, utilizing colored chalk and lots of detail, filling up the entire rudder.

As the three aircraft arrived at Beale, one every other day, the squadron made a festive atmosphere out of the event by having all the available Habus, along with their families, show up at Base Operations to welcome the arriving crew and aircraft. Maintenance parked the aircraft directly in front of Base Operations to make the event special for the families. A red carpet was rolled out from the foot of the ladder, and a welcoming party waited for the crew to step down. If "Tech Rep" Bill Brown was around, he brought his trumpet along for special occasions such as this to play the Habu "charge" as the crew exited the aircraft.

Every aircraft put on an arrival show of some sort, depending on their fuel state. I vividly remember everyone standing around on the grass in front of Base Operations, waiting patiently for the arrival of Majors Al Cirino and Bruce Liebman from Okinawa. They were overdue by several minutes, but mobile said they were in radio contact and should be arriving shortly. We waited and waited, everyone's eyes peering towards the north and west, from where they would be flying—at least that's what we thought. Suddenly, out of no where came this tremendous roar of afterburners as the SR-71 flew directly over our heads from behind, briskly pulling up to 10,000 feet heading due west. They had flown around behind us and completely surprised and startled everyone. I never saw so many adults flinching and ducking while children fell to the ground on their knees. Cirino and Liebman pulled off the surprise of a lifetime!

In the late '70s, we started to get more "bang for the buck" during swap-outs by adding on an extra refueling and flying an operational mission prior to landing at Okinawa or Beale. On one swap out it was decided to have both SR-71s fly an operational sortie and pass directly over one another near the city of Petropavlovsk, on the Soviet peninsula of Kamchatka, one heading for Okinawa and the other for Beale. There was slight concern at the time about the effect each shock wave would have on the inlets as they passed each other with a Mach-6 closure. As it turned out, nothing at all happened, and by dumping fuel they were the few Habus who got to observe a Mach-6 rate of closure from the cockpits. Former SR-71 pilot Det 1 Commander and 9th Wing Director of Operations, Col. Tom Alison (Ret), recalls the high speed pass.

> *We had two occasions to fly missions from Beale to Kadena which required very precise timing. On one, we were scheduled to pass a point off the coast of Petropavlovsk at the same time as another "Habu" was passing the same point in the opposite direction, headed from Kadena to Beale. After two air refuelings, and 3-1/2 hours of flying, we hit the spot within 10 seconds of our planned time and had the spectacular experience of seeing Lt. Cols. Bob Crowder and Don Emmons pass us, head on, about 5,000 feet below at a closure rate of over Mach 6.*
>
> *On the second occasion, we were again going toward Kadena from Beale. This time we had been through three air refuelings and flown over 4-1/2 hours. My RSO, Lt. Col. JT Vida planned it so we left the third air refuel-*

*ing right on time, and we passed Majors Lee Shelton and Barry MacKean
exactly "bang on" off the Soviet coast near Vladivostok. We continued on into
Kadena and were followed moments later by Lee and Barry. The Blackbird
watchers on Habu Hill had seen one SR leave but somehow two came back!*

Habu Lifestyle

Compared to other Air Force crews, we worked at making our
lifestyle comfortable at the Det. We were there so frequently that it became
incumbent for us to have nice quarters and cars to get around in. Bachelor
Officers' Quarters (BOQ) number 318 housed all the Habus and Q-model
tanker crews. It was built with CIA funds to specifically house A-12 crews
first deployed to Okinawa in May of 1967. It was a typical two story BOQ
with 20 rooms on each level. SR-71 crews had been living there since 1968
in six selected rooms (rooms 201, 202, 212, 214, 216, and 218). Since we
always kept three crews at Det 1, it was convenient for the base Billeting
Office, as well as for us, to set aside the six crew rooms and never book anyone else into them. Controlling the rooms this way, Habus were able to
arrange among themselves to be in the same room for practically every
tour. The lower level of 318 was occupied by Beale's KC-135Q crews and a
few staff officers.

Habus put in a lot of work making the rooms more bearable and
liveable for their six weeks on the island. Every room had its own bar, built
by Habus before us. Each crew had their own car while on the island. It
required an initial one-time car fund contribution of $75, and then $35 for
each 6-week tour, to cover insurance and maintenance. Just like the special
corner rooms were reserved for the senior Habu crew, so was the premier
car of the fleet. In this case, premier simply meant the best "clunker!"

In the late 1960s, corner room 220 was set aside for the crew's preflight meals and physical exams, given by the Habu Doctor. Early on in the
program a Beale Flight Surgeon was always TDY with the crews on
Kadena. In the early 1970s, the crew's preflight physical exam was no
longer given by a Flight Surgeon, and our PSD technicians took over the
job. The crews persuaded the Habu Doc to give up his office (the bedroom), so they could build a lounge they called the "Secret Bar." The normal entrance to Doc's office was boarded up and a large bar, stereo equipment, and refrigerator were added. The entrance to the new lounge was
through a small storage closet about two feet in width located in the
kitchen area. After entering the storage closet a secret entrance led directly into a large clothes closet of the former bedroom. After meandering
through the closet you finally arrived in the "Secret Bar". The bar soon
gained a reputation as "the" place for night life. The room had returned to
its original condition by the time I arrived although the stories and legends of the "Secret Bar" remained intact!

Many of the off-duty traditions at Det 1 began well before my
time but continued over the years as they passed down from one generation of Habus to the next. Big events included the "Sunday Daiquiri Party"
and the "Crew Party," both of which were deeply embedded in Habu tradition. The Daiquiri party took place every Sunday afternoon, after the

Det softball game. Sometime during each crew's six-week tour it was traditional for them to host a "Crew Party" for everyone.

After each mission we also had a traditional "Post-Mission Hooks" party. Habus used the cryptic term "Hook" to describe any alcoholic drink. At the end of each SR-71 mission debriefing session, a crew member would typically announce, "Hooks in 201!", letting everyone know he was opening his bar for drinks after everyone was done with their work at the Det. In the confines of 318 we could discuss our classified missions in a social atmosphere, exchange "how the mission went" stories, talk about how we could have done it better, and then all go out for dinner. It provided the social link between Habus and the Det-1 staff. Lieutenant Colonel "Geno" Quist (Ret) recalls a particular debriefing at one of his "Post-Mission Hooks" parties:

> On 12 October 1982 we flew 975 on an operational sortie out of Kadena. Everything went perfectly until the landing pattern. We had done one low approach and were turning base to final for another low approach prior to a full stop. Halfway through the base turn, the right (inside) engine chugged and I asked Nevin [Maj. Nevin Cunningham] what happened. He matter-of-factly said, "We just lost the right engine." I, in my infinite wisdom said, "Does that mean we are going to full stop this one?" I found out later during our "Post-Mission Hooks" discussions that my subsequent radio call declaring an emergency for loss of an engine caused quite a ruckus in the mobile car (Maj. Les Dyer and Capt. Dan Greenwood)—they nearly tore up their "Stars & Stripes" newspapers, and the Det Commander (Col. Randy Hertzog) nearly swallowed his pipe!! With only seconds to react from my radio call before we were on the ground, I can just visualize the mad scramble they must have been going through in the mobile car. Landing was successful and uneventful.

One of the traditional impromptu parties was to "no-notice" the Commander's home late at night, preferably after he was in bed. All the Det 1 Commanders knew they were eligible for "no-notice" parties from Habus. At night we generally announced our presence by "roof stomping" the Commander's house. This entailed climbing onto the roof of his house and stomping in unison to awaken he and his wife. We tried not to abuse our welcome and generally departed after a few hours of drinking. The "no-notice" was more of a hospitality check of the Commander and his wife, meant to keep them on their toes for the next time we might strike. "No-noticing" was the Habu way of socializing.

With long summer months on Okinawa, a lot of our free time was spent on "Secret Beach," a favorite Habu hangout north of Kadena, where crews could relax, catch some rays, and swim in the East China Sea. Two local eating establishments Habus loved to frequent were the Skoshi-KOOM on Kadena; and Mr. Nakachi's restaurant, the Paradise Garden. The Skoshi-KOOM was an annex of the Kadena Officers' Open Mess (KOOM), providing outstanding food, good drinks, and a place to socialize with Det personnel. All the employees of the "Skoshi" liked to have us around and prominently displayed a sign behind the bar which proudly read: "This is HABU Country"—and it was! On any day of the week you could probably find one or more Habus there after hours.

A rather small, out of the way club, the Skoshi had a bar, dining room, and an area that served as transient quarters for visiting personnel. The second floor dining room level had a balcony with a magnificent view of the East China Sea, particularly at sunset. The manager and his small staff, who were all Okinawan's, welcomed the Habus from Det 1, and this more subdued atmosphere was a welcome respite from the large main Officers' Club and its boisterous fighter-pilot stag bar. Colonel Alison relates the close bond between Habus and the Skoshi staff:

> Over the years the Skoshi became the place of choice for a large number of the Det 1 permanent party as well as the SR-71 crew members. The manager, Mr. Jack Oshiro, always made the Habus feel welcome while Ito in the bar, Kiyoko in the dining room, and Chef Higa in the Kitchen gave us the special attention that made us "regulars" at the Skoshi. I have many wonderful memories of my time on Okinawa, one of the most favorite is of sitting at the upstairs bar looking out over the East China Sea and watching the sunset. I remember how I used to remark to Lt. Col. Joe Vida as we arrived at the instrument approach fix for the landing at Beale and the radar controller would say, "Aspen, you're at Paradise" (the name of the fix)—I would simply smile inside my pressure suit helmet and say, "not really, it's actually 3,000 miles West!"

I first met Mr. Nakachi while having dinner at his restaurant called the "Paradise Garden." Over the years, my acquaintance with Mr. Nakachi grew closer and stronger. Soon I could not eat at his restaurant without his wife calling for him to join me. While we ate and drank he supplied a continuous stream of food and booze at our table, regardless of the number of people with me. Mr. Nakachi became friends with all the Habus I brought to his restaurant and the feeling soon became mutual.

One tradition Mr. Nakachi started among Habus was the ritual of drinking his "Tiger Drink." For Okinawans it was a very expensive drink, reserved only for special occasions. Sometime during the evening Mr. Nakachi would always politely offer a taste of the "Tiger Drink" to everyone. He kept the "Tiger Drink" in a large green urn made of Okinawan crushed glass, which sat as the centerpiece of his restaurant bar. He had one of his waitresses bring over a tray consisting of the "Tiger Drink," a ladle, tongs, and wine glasses for all.

He took particular pride in describing how the drink was made and the effect it had on males. Sitting on folded knees, he used the tongs to reach deep inside the urn and pull out from the liquid what appeared to be a seven inch long, very narrow, sub-miniature Christmas tree, with a long root structure attached to the base of the tree. After he pulled the dripping mass out of the urn and holding it in the air by his tongs, Mr. Nakachi began in broken English, "This is the penis of a Bengal tiger from Red China. Okinawan's believe the Tiger Drink will

125

bring virility and long life to all men who drink it." At this point he placed the tiger penis on a tray and passed it around for everyone to touch and marvel at.

While the Bengal tiger's penis was circulating around the table, Mr. and Mrs. Nakachi were busy ladling out the brandy mixture from inside the urn for everyone to sample. Habus that had drunk the "Tiger Drink" before were well aware of its potent alcohol qualities while the uninitiated were curious to taste the drink. As Mr. Nakachi made a toast to "all the Habus" I enjoyed watching everyone's expression as they slowly sipped the "Tiger Drink."

"Fragging" the New Crew

One tradition Habus enjoyed was successfully "fragging" the new crew. We adopted the Vietnam War-era term of "fragging," or "frags" for short, to indicate a practical joke Habus played on each new crew during their first tour to Det 1. Some of the frags were very elaborate while others were simple but highly effective. One of the more elaborate frags involved setting up a simulated operational sortie at Det 1 that was so real, even if the new crew suspected something was going on, they had no reason to doubt it. The "mission" was planned to be flown by the new crew when they were next on the flying ladder—about four weeks into their tour. To add credibility, an "actual" message was sent to the Det from SRC (by former Habus working there) to execute the sortie. It was to takeoff at 0600 on a Saturday morning.

The entire Det was at work on Friday to help the new crew plan their mission. It was decided that certain personnel had to attend the 0400 briefing for it to remain a believable mission. These included the Det 1 Commander, weather personnel, the DO, mobile crew, mission planners, the briefer, PSD personnel, intelligence personnel, and maintenance supervision. If any of these key positions were not at the briefing it would look suspicious. Everyone agreed to help out and the mission briefing went without a hitch.

After the crew was completely suited up and waiting to get out of their recliner chairs, the mobile crew came rushing in to tell them that their airplane was broken and should be repaired in about 25 minutes. Picking the right amount of time to repair the aircraft was important to making the frag work. If the delay was too long, some crews would de-suit and wait elsewhere in Operations. However, if just the right amount of delay was chosen, then the crew would elect to stay in the pressure suit, since it took about 15-20 minutes to completely suit up and accomplish the pressure checks again.

Just short of 25 minutes the mobile crew came back a second time to tell them that the aircraft wasn't repaired yet and now they were on a delay of unknown time—it could be fixed in 5 minutes or 35 minutes. To add realism in their presence, mobile received a call on the "brick" from maintenance reiterating the delay. This scenario was totally believable and happens occasionally with either the SR-71, tankers, or deteriorating weather being the culprit for delays. The recommendation to the new crew was to remain suited up until the mobile crew came back to tell them the airplane was actually fixed—they agreed! Of course, all this time the mobile crew and everyone else was just down the hall having coffee and donuts, deciding how to execute the next stage of the frag.

The one crucial element in making the frag successful was relying on the ease with which crews could drift off to sleep in the pressure suit while reclined in the overstuffed chairs. At this point, the PSD supervisor told the crew to relax and he'd turn out the blinding overhead lights and wake them up before the mobile crew came back. That sounded reasonable to them after being up half the night already and a long mission staring them in the face. After some time had passed, the mobile crew tiptoed into PSD, stole all their clothes and threw them into the car as everyone departed the Det for 318 to have Bloody Mary's and wait.

After sleeping for a while the crew finally woke up and couldn't figure out what had happened or how much time had elapsed. They called out for the PSD supervisor and with no response, unplugged their vent hoses and walked to the door only to find a long, dark, empty hallway leading down the Operations building. The light bulb clicked—they had been fragged! They helped each other out of their pressure suits, went to the lockers for their clothes, and realized they had been truly fragged—no clothes! In only their long underwear, socks, and white boots, they called for a base taxi cab to come to the Det security gate for a ride back to 318. They were greeted with laughter and drinks.

Another frag continued one step further than the preceding one, by actually having the new crew strapped into the cockpit. RSO Col. Roger Jacks tells the story.

It was our turn to fly the next operational sortie when the Operations Officers told us he may have to take us off the mission. He went on to tell us that intelligence had confirmed reports that the enemy had developed a capability to shoot down a SR-71, and they had every intention of doing so on the next sortie. He thought it would be better to have a seasoned crew fly the mission. Joe [pilot, Capt. Joe Kinego] and I were really mad and hurt at the same time that we were not viewed as being capable of flying any mission, no matter what the circumstances. We argued for over an hour with the Operations Officer when he finally said it was against his best judgment, but he would let us fly.

We spent the rest of the day mission-planning the sortie. I would be less than honest if I said I found it easy to go to sleep that night. The next day we started the ritual of readying ourselves for the flight. Then we continued on to the final mission briefing, PSD suit up, and strapped into the cockpit. Waiting to get airborne was the same feeling I had when I played football. Once the gear was on, you lived for the opening kickoff. My "kickoff" was lifting off the ground strapped to an aircraft cranking out over 68,000 pounds of thrust. But that moment never happened. Engine start never came.

Just as we were about to start the engines, the Operations Officer ran up the ladder to tell us the mission had been delayed at least 20 minutes. Maintenance also had an equipment problem they wanted to fix so they would be turning off power to the airplane for a few minutes. We did not know that one by one, they were quietly leaving the hangar. All of a sudden we were totally alone and became agonizingly apparent we had been had! With considerable effort we got ourselves out of the airplane, back to PSD, and helped each other out of the suits. When we arrived back to our rooms a big party was raging, and Habus roared with laughter while some maintenance troops yelled out, "Hey, where have you guys been?"

Some frags were not isolated to the new crew or to the Dets, as pilot Lt. Col. Rod Dyckman (Ret) explains:

It was time for Bergie (Capt. Tom Bergam, my RSO) and me to have our annual stan/eval simulator check ride. We bought the traditional bottle of booze for each evaluator as a bribe to pass the check ride. Our evaluators were Bernie Smith [pilot] and Denny Whalen [RSO]. After the pre-simulator briefing, Bergie excused himself for a nervous trip to the bathroom. While he was gone, Bernie removed two pages from Bergie's checklist—"ADS Failure" and the "Index" of malfunction.

During the mission, predictably, Bernie gave me an ADS failure. I told Bergie, "ADS left side, give me the ADS checklist." Bergie started looking through his checklist and couldn't find the ADS failure. "Come on Bergie, give me the ADS checklist." You could hear him cussing and hitting the side of the simulator as he rifled through the checklist. "Bergie, I need that checklist now!" He goes to the index, and there is no index!! The light bulb comes on. As he backs out of the simulator he sees all three of us enjoying his misery. Bergie hasn't forgiven me yet for being part of this frag.

Habus once fragged the 9th SRW/Det 2, our sister U-2 detachment located at Osan, Korea. Det 2 crews and personnel were known as the "Blackcats" and wore a U-2 patch depicting a black cat. They also had a Det 2 mascot, a black male cat called, Oscar. For Oscar to be the true Det mascot they flew him on a U-2 mission in one of the empty mission bays. After the flight he became crazed and was never the same again. They decided to have Oscar castrated to see if that would calm him down. At the Det's request, the vet saved Oscar's testicles, where they were proudly displayed in a glass jar in Operations for all to see. The inscription on the outside of the jar read, "Oscar's Balls—flown over 70,000 feet in a U-2." Colonel Tom Alison describes what happened next.

The frag of Det 2 concerning "Oscar's Balls" occurred in early December, 1978, and JT and I were the crew involved. It was the only time we ever had to divert/land away on a GIANT SCALE mission and occurred on a night sortie over the DMZ when we had a generator failure. We only had two land aways in over 120 operational sorties and six years (speaks highly of the jet). We diverted into Osan AB, Korea, at night, and the folks at Det 2 were extremely helpful in getting us settled.

The recovery team arrived the next morning, and the fairly routine generator replacement was accomplished, and everything looked good for an early morning departure the next day, which was a Saturday. JT and I had decided that, if at all possible, a frag was in order and had talked about what would be appropriate. The Det 2 Commander at the time was Lt. Col. Doyle Krumery. He had a large beautiful desk in his office that he was very proud of. With the help of a couple of crew chiefs, we entered the Det offices later that night and very carefully moved the prized desk into a shower stall in the PSD area. Not a scratch . . . we were very proud of ourselves!

On the way out of the Det we spied the jar with "Oscar's Balls" prominently displayed in the operations area. It was perfect. JT put the jar in a helmet bag and stowed it in the rear cockpit early the next morning. Since it was a Saturday and no Det 2 flying was scheduled, all the U-2 people slept in and no one had gotten to the Det to discover the jar with Oscar's balls was missing. All the way through engine start, taxi, and takeoff we expected to hear a radio call to come back immediately until the missing items were found. As it turned out, the desk in the shower caused so much of an uproar that Oscar was overlooked. I think our maintenance people even got loaded on the tanker and headed back to Kadena before the "the real frag" was discovered.

On our way back to Kadena, which was a "hot" flight, we decided how we were going to put the finishing touches on our frag. When we arrived back at Det 1, we got together with Chuck Weithoff, the SAS/autopilot technical representative, and a good friend. He fried two chicken hearts until they were just two little black, hard things, and then we took a needle and some dark thread and wove a short strand between the fried chicken hearts. It was rather easy to get another jar that was the same as the one that held the precious cargo. After filling the jar with water (I don't know what was in the jar with "Oscar's Balls"—we never had the courage to actually open the jar) we added the chicken hearts. It was amazing how they looked exactly like the original except they were burned black! Since the U-2 guys were so proud that they had taken "Oscar" flying in the "Dragon Lady," we put a label on the jar that read, "Oscar's Balls—flown Mach 3+ in an SR-71."

We then, appearing as contrite as we could, had the jar returned to Det 2 with our profound apologies because, we said, the jar had been stored in an aircraft bay that had gotten hot on the trip back to Kadena and "Oscar's Balls" had been fried! JT and I returned to Beale before the reaction traveled back to Det 1; however, knowing Doyle Krumery's explosive nature, it wasn't hard to imagine the conversation between him and the Det 1 commander, Lt. Col. Bob Cunningham.

Later, the real "Oscar's Balls" were returned to Det 2. However, the U-2 pilots vowed they would get even. Sometime later, when one of them was at Kadena they took from the Det 1 office a jar containing a Habu snake. They thought they had purloined a Det 1 prize. We had to tell them, that we had numerous jars with Habus in them and they could keep it if they wanted!

Former SR-71 pilot and last Det 1 Commander, Col. Lee Shelton (Ret), recalls the final flight from Okinawa on 21 January 1990.

The last sortie, sending the jet home, was an event shared by every-one. We did not advertise the mission outside the Det, but ensured everyone within the Det knew and was able to participate; all Det personnel and their families. The tail was decorated with chalk the day prior with a tomb-stone and RIP motif. The sortie generated and launched before dawn. It was perfect in every detail, and there was not a dry eye on the ramp. If the jet and the men who flew it ever had an ancestral home it was Kadena; not Burbank, not Edwards, Palmdale, or Beale. Kadena is where we began; it is fitting, it's where we ended.

Colonel Shelton decided it was appropriate to leave a permanent legacy on Okinawa of the aircraft and personnel who served their country with distinction for so many years. All of the Dets remaining "slush" fund money that everyone worked so hard to contribute towards was used to purchase a plaque from Korea, mounted on a stone pillar.

The chosen site to erect the plaque was "Habu Hill," a notorious viewing spot on Kadena where crowds of curious and avid aircraft watch-ers assembled to see the SR-71 takeoff and land. "Habu Hill" was located on a slight rise above the approach-end of runway 5R, allowing bystanders an excellent view from their cars. It was not uncommon to see 20 to 30 cars lined up on "Habu Hill" to watch our takeoffs, and we often joked among each other which crew could draw the largest crowd of onlookers. Friends of Habus were told to leave their headlights on for a "special" takeoff, just for them.

In the end, Lee wrote the following poignant words and had them inscribed on the plaque that resides on "Habu Hill":

This vantage point is dedicated to the magnificent SR-71 Blackbird, known worldwide as the Habu—an Okinawan cobra of black, sinister appearance, great stealth, and lightning fast strike. The first SR-71 arrived at Kadena Air Base on 9 March 1968, and the last aircraft depart-ed on 21 January 1990. Throughout those twenty-two years, the Habu roamed Pacific skies unchallenged, in war and peace, to ensure the freedom of the United States and her allies. Habu Hill stands as a memorial to the SR-71, the special men and women who sustained its strategic reconnais-sance mission, and to all people who gather here and know that jet noise is truly the sound of freedom. Sayonara Habu. Detachment One, Ninth Strategic Reconnaissance Wing 1968-1990.

CHAPTER TEN

RAF MILDENHALL, ENGLAND, (DET 4)

RAF Mildenhall is a small Air Force installation located just outside the village of Mildenhall in rural East Anglia, England. An SR-71 first landed at RAF Mildenhall in September of 1974 when it made its international debut at the Farnborough Air Show. It flew into Mildenhall to prepare for its return flight back to the United States. The plan was to establish a world speed record from London to Los Angeles. Captain "Buck" Adams and RSO Maj. Bill Machoreck flew the 5,645 mile trip in 3 hours and 47 minutes, setting the world record.

Many of the same reasons for choosing Okinawa as an SR-71 base (logistics, support, location, etc.) also held true for RAF Mildenhall. Furthermore, England was one of the few NATO countries willing to host the aircraft. Anywhere the SR-71 flew, or flew out of, was so sensitive politically that most foreign countries didn't want the pressure from either their own citizens, or other countries, concerning an American "spy" plane being based in their country.

The base was small and split in two basic areas: the secure side of the base had a single 9,000 foot runway (R/W 29 and 11) and housed all the flying operations and support; the other side was unsecured and housed the all the other base facilities. The U-2s were already flying out of Mildenhall as Det 4 when we first deployed there.

The first SR-71 operational deployment to Mildenhall occurred in April of 1976 when aircraft 972 was sent along with two crews and support personnel. Although two operational sorties were attempted into the Barents Sea area outside of Soviet airspace, they were never completed. Both missions had to be aborted and returned to Mildenhall when crews found themselves too low on fuel, due to significantly hotter than standard "temp devs" during the climb and cruise. On 6 September 1976, aircraft 962 arrived at Mildenhall, and Don and I completed the very first SR-71 operational sortie into the Barents Sea on 7 September 1976. Fortunately for us, the "temp devs" were cold enough during that time of the year, allowing us to finish the mission.

On our first visit to the Officers' Club, Don and I were sitting at the bar admiring all the unit stickers plastered on the mirrored walls behind the bar. It seemed as if every flying unit in the Air Force had their squadron sticker proudly displayed on the long mirrors when suddenly we both noticed a brilliant green bumper sticker that read, "SR-71 Crews do it Faster." It was a bumper sticker we had seen in 1974 at Beale, during the time the SR-71 flew to the Farnborough Air Show. We thought its message was appalling—it had to be removed! The next day we brought a razor blade and the "3+" sticker into the Officers' Club. We sneaked into the empty bar after lunch and went to work. In my haste to remove the bumper sticker before we were discovered, I inadvertently put the single edge razor blade against my right thumb and started to push it under the sticker to loosen it from the glass. With the first good shove my thumb split wide open and blood gushed everywhere behind the bar. Some cold water, a wet towel, and soon we were back in business removing the sticker—correctly this time! We proudly centered the "3+" sticker in a prominent place directly over the cash register and fled the scene. Everyone we talked with afterwards liked the "3+" replacement sticker much better.

Eleven more short-term deployments (ranging from 3 to 6 weeks each) to Mildenhall took place up through 1980, and in March of 1981 Habus deployed for two months with aircraft 972. On 12 August 1981, Majors "B.C." Thomas and Jay Reid flew aircraft 964 from Beale on what was to be a 10-1/2 hour mission into the Barents Sea and return. An oil pressure warning light caused them to divert into Bodo, Norway, where repairs could be made. Several days later a recovery team was in place and repaired the aircraft, permitting the crew to fly 964 subsonic to RAF Mildenhall. From Mildenhall the aircraft flew operational sorties into the Baltic Sea area and returned to Beale in November 1981.

Several days prior to an SR-71's arrival at Mildenhall, the 9th SRW deployed an advance party of about 30 personnel, including the SR-71 mobile crew, to establish and set up operations and maintenance facilities for the aircraft's arrival. As infrequently as we took the SR-71 to Mildenhall between 1976 and 1980 for short-term deployments, it became convenient for us to have the U-2 operation already there to provide us with basic support common to each aircraft, such as PSD personnel and facilities, high altitude weather data, communications, and security. Det 4 also provided us with administration support and helped to make each deployment run smoothly.

During our early deployments, we strictly ferried SR-71s to and from Mildenhall on "GLOWING HEAT" missions and flew reconnaissance sorties in support of annual NATO military exercises, such as

"COLD FIRE" and "REFORGER." Every time we deployed, it required over 100 military and civilian personnel, plus three to four KC-135Qs from Beale to support one SR-71.

Anytime there was a rumor of a deployment to Mildenhall, crews were "lining up their ducks" to go, especially knowing it meant you got to fly the SR-71 either over or back. I remember one Sunday afternoon getting a phone call from the Wing Commander to ask if Don and I wanted to deploy with the SR-71 to Mildenhall on Tuesday evening. Even though it was short notice, I knew what Don's answer would be, so I told him, "Snake and Nape were ready." We mission planned on Monday, launched on Tuesday, and landed in England on Wednesday. Surprisingly, even with such a short notice deployment, we saw our aircraft on British TV later that evening landing on runway 11 at Mildenhall. We weren't even allowed to tell our wives where we were going! I can only surmise that the British aircraft "spotters" saw our advance party land in a KC-135Q, and knew that an SR-71 must be following shortly.

It wasn't until the early 1980s that the ferry flights to and from Mildenhall were turned into operational sorties by adding an extra air refueling north of England and flying an operational reconnaissance leg prior to landing at Mildenhall or Beale. Former RSO and Det-4 Operations Officer, Col. Frank Stampf (Ret), talks about one deployment mission that didn't go quite as planned!

On 5 January 1982, after a year's absence from merry-olde England, it looked like Gil [pilot, Maj. Gil Bertelson] and I were finally going to get a chance to go to Mildenhall. Our mission was to depart across the Atlantic, make a operational pass in theater, then recover into Mildenhall. It was a high-priority sortie, so there was an airborne spare, which took off about thirty minutes behind us. The spare crew was none other than the infamous Neno and Geno [pilot Maj. Nevin Cunningham and RSO Maj. Geno Quist], who were no less anxious than I was to log some "pub time." If something extraordinary precluded either the primary or secondary crew from flying the ops portion of the sortie, there was still a high priority to get an airplane over to Mildenhall to provide the capability of flying follow-on sorties, since the political situation in theater was heating up.

Gil and I went through the mission preparation ritual and departed on schedule into the night sky while most of Northern California was engrossed in prime-time sitcoms. Not ten minutes after takeoff, on our way to the first tanker rendezvous, I discovered a malfunction with one of the primary electronic defensive (DEF) systems, required for the ops portion of the mission. Loss of that system meant a NO-GO for the operational mission. Needless to say, I was not a happy Habu!

I informed Gil of the problem, but pressed on with full intentions of going all the way to the preplanned subsonic abort point, just short of the Canadian border, before we would give up the sortie to our spare aircraft. On the way to the tanker, into our accel, and after level off at cruise Mach, I went through every procedure, technique, and trick I was taught to get that damn DEF system to work. That included a few subtle and highly technical techniques I invented on the spot, such as undoing my boot from the stirrup and kicking the stupid box for all I was worth!

It eventually became apparent that the DEF machine was a goner. We later found out that a circuit breaker down in one of the mission bays had popped, rendering the system hopelessly "inop." Therefore, I did the only honorable thing possible, I whispered the pre-determined abort code into the HF radio as quietly as I could, praying and hoping that the spare (and nobody else in the universe) would hear me and we'd be forced to press on without going through the sensitive area, just to get the aircraft to Mildenhall.

Being the conscientious Habu that I was, I continued mumbling the appropriate abort code (to the tune of "Amazing Grace") becoming more and more confident by the minute that I couldn't possibly be heard by anyone who cared outside of our own aircraft, and knowing that my reunion with my Smoke House friends would be 33 miles closer every minute!

There we were . . . barely three minutes from the Canadian border, our predetermined supersonic abort point beyond which we would be obliged to take the airplane directly to Mildenhall. I could almost taste the Bass Ale. Then I heard it! Through the always irritating static of the HF radio, I imagined I heard a faint voice calling, "Frankie . . . Frankie . . . are you guys OK?" I was sure it was my imagination as I anxiously watched the clock and our distance count down to our abort point

I started kicking the DEF box again in a last-minute frenzy to make us "ops capable," but by then I heard over the crackling, static-filled HF radio, the unmistakable voice of Geno calling, "Frankie . . . you there??" (So much for secure call signs, etc., they wanted to go as bad as we did!)

I waited until the very last second, hoping that the HF radio would die, along with that stupid DEF system, but I was finally forced to "answer the call," and said in a very short, distinct, professional, and irate tone of voice, "You got it, Geno." The rest is history. I was so perturbed for the remainder of the return flight to Beale that Gil probably would have been better off with ballast onboard than with me!

RSO Maj. Geno Quist tells his side of the story.

We were tasked to take an SR-71 to Mildenhall for a two week stay. Gil Bertelson and Frank Stampf were the primary crew, and Nevin and I were in 980 as a flying spare, taking off thirty minutes after them. Since Mildenhall wasn't a "normal" detachment at that time, we weren't allowed to tell our wives what was happening or where we were going, so I simply packed two bags and told her if somebody called and said send one bag, I was somewhere in the United States, and if they said send two bags, I was overseas.

Unfortunately for Gil and Frank, the DEF system was not working and required an abort at the GO/NO-GO point if it didn't correct itself. Within a minute of hitting the GO/NO-GO point, I heard Frank and responded, "We've got it!" I called the mobile crew and asked them to call my wife and tell her to send two bags—7.5 hours of Habu ecstasy!!

Once, Don and I ferried the aircraft over to Mildenhall. It was a routine night departure from Beale, refueling right after takeoff over Idaho, again over Goose Bay, Labrador, and finally landing mid-morning at Mildenhall, four hours later. As we taxied the aircraft to a stop outside the hangar, I spotted a large convoy of Air Force staff cars with General Officer flags flying from the front bumpers. I told Don I had never seen so many four-star flags and wasn't sure what was going on. We called the mobile crew, and they were equally puzzled. Don asked me, "What did we do wrong this time!"

Crawling out of the cockpit we spotted numerous Colonels, Generals, and three older gentlemen dressed in coats and ties, standing at the foot of the ladder obviously waiting for us to walk down from our perch. Little did we know that Air Force history was waiting to welcome us. They were Generals James Doolittle, Ira Eaker, and Curtis LeMay waiting to greet "Snake and Nape" and shake our hands! They were in England for an 8th Air Force reunion and got word of an SR-71 coming into Mildenhall. There's a group picture in the 1st SRS scrap book of all three of them meeting Don and I in our pressure suits at the foot of the ladder with the caption underneath reading, "Generals Doolittle, Acker, and LeMay arrive in England to greet 'Snake and Nape.'" Former RSO, Lt. Col. Doug Soifer, tells of a mission when he was also met on arrival back into Mildenhall.

Mike Smith and I were TDY for our first time to Mildenhall for our normal six week rotation. We went to the Det one morning to fly a routine six hour sortie—the Barents and the Baltic. During the preflight briefings the intelligence officer said a nuclear power site (Chernobyl) in the Soviet Union had an accident a few hours earlier. They had no other information on it yet. The weather briefing officer gave his normal briefing, but also mentioned they doubled checked with the weather service at Offutt AFB that we would not fly through any of the fall-out from Chernobyl. With the briefings done and no one concerned about our route of flight, we went to the jet and flew a normal mission.

The normal routine after an operational mission is to land and continue to taxi off the runway and directly into the hangar so they could download the mission take. But as we landed and turned off the runway we were told to stop way before the hangar. We both thought this was very strange and couldn't understand why we were stopping here. Then one person, and only one, dressed in very funny looking gear, came walking up to the plane. As he got closer we could seen he was

in full chemical gear and had a Geiger counter. After they had guaran-
teed Mike and I that we were in no danger of flying through radiation
from Chernobyl, they were checking the plane before any of THEM
would get close to us! Once he walked about the plane with the Geiger
counter we were allowed to continue to taxi into the hangar.

Rivalries and Habu Traditions

The U-2 crews were considerably more "tight lipped" over their presence at Mildenhall than we were. The first time Don and I arrived on Mildenhall we were thoroughly briefed by U-2 pilots, Captains Ken Stanford and Warren "Snake" Pierce that they had cover stories about what they do on Mildenhall (I seem to recall one was a plumber and the other a mechanic). They suggested that Don and I make up cover stories also and wear civilian clothes around the base rather than our bright orange flight suits. We actually thought they were trying to frag us with all these tales of "cover stories." As it turned out they were dead serious and became totally dumbfounded when they saw Don and I show up in our highly visible "orange bags" at Happy Hour. We were positive we would have been told something if that was the case for us and therefore totally disregarded their advice.

We kept the SR-71 in a large hangar on the far side of the runway and originally ran operations from an old abandoned fuel-supply facility. On those early deployments it was a come-as-you-are operation and had to bring everything we planned on using, from safes to typing paper. The U-2s operated and flew out of Building 538, a large hangar, conveniently located on the operations side of the runway. When it got down to the real flying mission, Det 4 supported us much as they could and intervened on our behalf whenever problems developed between us and base personnel. U-2 pilot, Lt. Col. Jerry West, was the first Det 4 Commander, creating an atmosphere for friendly rivalry between the U-2 and SR-71 units.

One day after a mission, we were taxiing back to our hangar and passed directly in front of a U-2 maintenance hangar. I could see something was brewing and told Don to look out his right window. There, in a perfect military line, were about 20 to 30 U-2 maintenance troops down on their knees and bowing with their hands extended over their heads as the SR-71 taxied in front of them. In unison they bowed up and down as if to mock their humility for the aircraft. It was a sight to behold!

On another occasion, our maintenance troops found out that a U-2 was going to take overhead pictures of Mildenhall at the end of its mission. The pictures were requested by SAC Headquarters to get an aerial layout of the base and location of our facilities. A four inch blanket of snow was covering the ground at the time and our maintenance troops wanted to send a message to SAC. About thirty of them (and some nameless Habus included) laid down head-to-foot with each other and spelled out a four letter word in the snow! The picture was taken and sent to SAC. A few weeks later we received a copy of the photo and could clearly see the word spelled out against the white background; however, because of the orientation of the picture you had to turn it upside down in order to read it.

Our first tour to Mildenhall was also the first occasion for Don and I to observe the U-2 flying operational sorties from one of its Dets. Watching the U-2 flying operation gave both of us a greater appreciation for our own program. By the time we launched our SR-71, a U-2 had already been airborne for 3 or 4 hours, and after we landed he still wasn't back on the ground for another 3 or 4 hours. That's a long day in anyone's book! Former U-2 Squadron Commander and pilot, Col. Willie Horton (Ret), recalls his experiences from the late 1960s.

I'd be on station for five hours, and I'd see a SR-71 contrail above me, coming in from the China Sea toward Thailand. An hour later I'd see a contrail going the other way. I'd know that pretty soon that S.O.B. would be in a bar having a cold beer and telling stories and I'd still have five more hours up there. You can imagine the feeling.

Habu traditions carried over to Det 4 as well. One Habu tradition was once introduced to old rivals—Soviet MiG pilots! SR Pilot, Capt. Steve "Griz" Grzebiniak, tells his story.

Jim [Maj. Jim Greenwood, his RSO] and I were TDY to Det 4 in June of 1989. The Det was tasked to send an SR-71 to the Paris Air Show. Lieutenant Colonel Tom Henichek was the Det 4 Commander at the time and became the Air Show deployment commander.

We flew a brief arrival show, landing in showery weather at Le Bourget airport for four days of static display. The big attraction at the '89 Paris Show was to be the unveiling of the Soviet SU-27 Flanker, for the first time on western soil. The SU-27 was an impressive example of the cutting edge of Eastern Bloc air superiority. It was a large fighter, with massive engines and silenced the crowds daily with its aerial demonstration. Victor Pugachev, the head test pilot for Sukhoi aircraft in the Soviet Union, and the inventor of the unbelievable "Cobra Maneuver" in which the fighter would make a slow speed, high angle pass at low altitude, then snatch its nose back beyond the vertical, and recover with AB's blazing, was there, along with an elite cadre of other Soviet pilots.

The Soviets were attracting a lot of attention and press coverage, as was anticipated. However, it seemed that a 25 year old aircraft, on display only a few hundred yards away was drawing an even bigger crowd each day. The air buzzed with tension each time Jim, myself, or Tom Henichek would approach the Soviet aircraft displays. We were finally granted a personal tour of the SU-27, and we reciprocated with an "up-close and personal introduction to our HABU." The Soviets were extremely interested in the tour Jim gave, and so was the foreign press. It seemed like every time the Soviet pilots got near us, there were cameras and microphones bristling everywhere. This seemed to unnerve the Eastern visitors, and all statements were made by the very flamboyant and eloquent speaking Victor Pugachev. He was obviously schooled in what we would call, "politically correct speech."

Jim and I decided we had to meet these pilots in a less formal manner. After all, they were flying some of the same aircraft, and indeed could have been the same pilots who regularly attempted high altitude intercepts against us in the Barents Sea! The day prior to our departure, after the final aerial demonstration of the afternoon, a note was passed to one of the Russian pilots reading, "Meet us at the base of the tower for a drink—the US pilots."

We avoided being seen in numbers together. We arranged to meet at the Hughes Aircraft chalet. No press was informed, in fact not even Hughes knew why we requested the use of their conference room. We all took round-about paths to the Hughes chalet to avoid being intercepted by the press.

There was no prior coordination between us and the Soviets, but it became apparent that they had the right idea from the beginning. One of our resourceful maintenance supervisors, Robby Butterfield, obtained two bottles of Cuervo Tequila from a source at the US Embassy. Once behind closed doors, we all introduced ourselves and told our Soviet guests that we invited them for a traditional HABU flyer's drink—a "Tequila Hooker" [also known as "Tequila Shooters"]! To our surprise, one of the Soviets produced two bottles of Russian vodka. They were prepared! We toasted our guests, showing them the proper "Tequila Hooker" technique, and they did the same for us with their native beverage.

They were acting very proper and cordial as Victor announced that they were ready to receive the "press" now. I told him there was, "no press, no cameras, no recorders, nobody knows we're here Vic!" At that announcement, the room erupted with revelry! Victor was no longer the "mouth piece" for the group. Everyone was eager to learn more about their "comrades" from across the ocean. Victor said to me, "Steve, the next time you are spying on us in the Barents Sea, please come up on my radio frequency so we can say hello." I jokingly said, "Vic, I'll be glad to do that, but if my voice sounds clear, its not because we are very near your border in the Barents Sea, I'm really far away on a training mission, but our radios are very powerful." We all had a good laugh, realizing that in a week, we would indeed be over the Barents, and we would see those tell-tale contrails of Soviet interceptors, hopelessly fluttering out of airspeed and ideas, far below us.

The spontaneous party lasted about an hour. We signed our bottle of Tequila, and our guests signed an unopened bottle of vodka, and we exchanged them as gifts. The following day, Jim and I departed Le Bouget with a series of afterburner passes. Our departure was to be the last aerial demonstration that day, immediately following the Soviets regular daily flying demo. All Soviet flying demos were mysteriously canceled that day. Could it have been the Tequila, or did they all want to be in place to see the HABU thunder past the crowd and disappear out of sight?

After returning to the Det, we placed the signed bottle of Russian vodka in a small glass case with a simple plaque reading, "GLASTNOST, Paris, '89."

Colonel Frank Stampf (RSO Ret), talks about other obstacles that had to be overcome at Mildenhall to keep Habu traditions going.

Habu "traditions" reflected what could be thought of as a singular, collective personality, comprised of bits and pieces formed from the individuals that flew and supported the mission over more than a quarter century. Deeply entrenched in those traditions is the music still being played whenever Habus gather. Memories are recalled, and still being made, to the tunes of David Allen Coe's "You Don't Have to Call Me By My Name", better known as "Darlin."

In contrast to the traditional country and western slant, one particular Habu commander made it almost mandatory for his crews to know the words to every song on Meatloaf's "Bat Out of Hell" album. You can be sure there aren't many Habus who haven't been awakened between the hours of midnight and three in the morning to the sound of "Would you offer your throat to the wolf with the red roses". . . the beginning of one of Mr. Loaf's more popular songs.

One pleasant English summer evening a group of Habus and associates were gathered for post-mission "hooks" in one of the second floor rooms in the Mildenhall BOQ. In the company of eight or ten other guests, all of whom were adorned with fashionable mustaches and goatees painted on with wine bottle corks, charred in candle flame. The crew dogs were leading a chorus of Meat Loaf's "Paradise By The Dashboard Light" at maximum volume. Being summer, all the windows were wide open to let the fresh air in and the 10,000 decibel stereo and vocal strains of Meat Loaf out!

It was somewhere between the deafening roar of "stop right there" and "let me sleep on it" that a "mystery Colonel" stormed into the room, demanding the music be turned off and all of us cease and desist from the God awful music. It seems he was the Deputy Base Commander, who happened to live in the base house right outside our room, and he wasn't nearly as interested in the story line of Mr. Loaf's poetry as the resident Habus and their guests were! After giving the assembled multitude a fire and brimstone sermon about respect for other people's rights to peace and quiet and chastising them for the sinful message of the song in question, the "mystery Colonel" left the room in a huff, quite sure that his message had been well delivered to and received by the renegade bunch of orange suited, mustached, bearded, non-conformists who dared to sing such lyrics in broad daylight.

After the Colonel's departure, the Habus, in absolute and sincere remorse, turned off the stereo, removed the cassette, the booze, and the other participants, and relocated to the room at the other end of the same hall where the lyrics were picked up at the point where she says, "I

139

gotta know right now ! ! !" The party continued well into the next morning. Log another successful "post-mission books" party.

Increased Activity

From 1980 onward the SR-71 was requested more and more in the European theater to provide a new intelligence capability for various agencies. Even though we had two aircraft permanently stationed at Det 4 from 1981, the British government had not yet approved it as a permanent location. It wasn't until 5 April 1984 that Prime Minister Thatcher formally announced SR-71s would be permanently based at RAF Mildenhall.

From around 1981 to 1982, Det 4 was in such a constant state of flux and build-up it created scheduling nightmares to keep both Dets fully manned. We only kept two crews at Det 4 because the number of sorties we flew each month were not as great as Det 1. Between the two Dets, the time away from home was starting to get excessive for Habus. A crew would literally be at Det 1 for six weeks, home at Beale for about two months, over to Det 4 for six weeks and then repeat the cycle going back to Beale for two months (or less). Knowing the lead time to choose and train an SR-71 aircrew could exceed a year, the decision was made to increase from nine combat ready crews to thirteen.

With an increasing demand for U-2 intelligence, the entire operation moved to RAF Alconbury, where it eventually became a Wing of U-2s and TR-1s, providing intelligence to European Commanders. After Lieutenant Colonel West departed with the U-2s, all succeeding Det 4 Commanders were former SR-71 aircrews.

When U-2 operations vacated building 538, SR-71 operations took over but continued to use the same hangar on the other side of the runway to house the aircraft. Eventually, hangar 538 housed all the Recce Tech processing vans and provided a large storage area for supplies. The front portion of 538 contained offices for the Det Commander, administration personnel, the Operations Officer, mission planners, and the briefing room. The rear of 538 housed PSD and supply offices.

After the announcement of Det 4 becoming permanent, it transformed from TDY personnel into a PCS assignment, except for our tanker crews, Habus, and PSD personnel. Lockheed put in a bid to perform the SR-71 aircraft maintenance, using civilians, at a lower cost than "blue suit" Air Force maintenance. It was accepted and proved to be an extremely good maintenance package. For the Det it provided a high degree of aircraft reliability at minimum costs.

In the mid-1980s, funds were secured to build two large SR-71 hangars, a maintenance and supply complex, and an engine test cell. Engine runs were previously limited to daytime only because of noise pollution to the surrounding community. The new engine test facility was a "hush house" that diffused and absorbed most of the engine noise, allowing 24 hour engine runs. The new maintenance complex was a real plus, providing a smooth operation and a quality working environment for maintenance personnel.

A similar living arrangement to Det 1 was worked out with base officials, setting aside designated BOQ rooms for Habus to live in. We ended up with four end rooms in a two story BOQ, within easy crawling distance of the Officers' Club. The rooms were pleasant and the furnishing comfortable, but soon Habu priorities turned to building bars for each room. It wasn't long before a car fund was started and each crew had their own vehicle. As long as someone knew where you were, we were permitted to travel anywhere in England that time allowed. For Habus that meant lots of trips to London and local pubs.

The sorties at Det 4 were more demanding than those flown from Okinawa; consequently, every new Habu flew their first operational tour at Det 1 before being sent to Det 4. They were more demanding for several reasons. Most of the tracks we flew provided little room for error. They were flown at maximum bank angles and into tight corners that took us very close to Soviet and Warsaw Pact airspace. Occasionally, we flew very complicated sorties into the Mediterranean. The winds we encountered flying from Det 4 were generally stronger at cruise altitude and required a greater degree of skill to stay on course. Det 4's routine operational sorties consisted of flying any combination (or all three) of the following geographical regions: Barents Sea/Kola peninsula area, the Baltic Sea, and the perimeter of West Germany. The choice of emergency alternates for diverting were generally not the best of airfields and usually had lousy weather associated with them year round.

Mildenhall itself had very changeable weather. Former Habus, Col. Tom Alison (Ret) and Lt. Col. Joseph T. "JT" Vida (Ret), were up flying a mission in January of 1977. Our Wing Commander at the time, Col. John Storrie was in the mobile car with Don and I because he wanted to meet a VIP arriving on the tanker from Beale. The tanker was due to land just before the SR-71, so we planned to do both chores from the mobile car. After the tanker landed in a light snow shower, we followed it to its parking spot to meet the VIP. Arriving earlier than we anticipated, Tom and JT were on final, flying a precision radar approach to runway 29. The visibility was suddenly reduced to about 1/8 of a mile in heavy snow showers. For some unknown reason, the Mildenhall radar equipment suddenly failed, and they had to do a go-around at the last minute. We never saw the aircraft but heard it roar past the runway.

By now, the snow was coming down so hard you couldn't even find the runway if it weren't for the lights showing the outline. Low on fuel, they had enough gas for one more approach, and then they would have to divert to another base. We couldn't launch the strip alert tanker because the weather was well below their takeoff minimums. We waited intently at the edge of the runway as they began their ILS approach. All eyes in the mobile car were staring in the direction of final approach, searching for the SR about to land, or at least that's what we hoped. For the longest time we never saw anything through the blinding snowfall when suddenly we spotted his landing light just as he touched down on what we assumed was the runway. As his tires hit the runway, fresh powered snow swirled up and seemed to surround the entire aircraft. We raced down the runway, slipping and sliding, as we chased after the aircraft. Passing Tom and JT in the aircraft we all gave them a "thumbs up"—glad to see them on the ground!

At certain times of the year, the Barents Sea missions had "temp devs" considerably warmer than standard (up to 30 degrees warmer!), requiring Habus to use all of their "skill and cunning" just to stay on the fuel profile. When we first flew out of Mildenhall it wasn't uncommon to be 5,000 pounds below Bingo fuel for the air refueling because of warmer temperatures during the accel and cruise. Although we didn't like to be that low on fuel, it became a matter of having to get your gas in order to get home.

Soon we obtained new computers at Mildenhall that allowed our mission planners to program for forecast "temp devs" on our flight plans. With the new computer capability, a policy decision was made that we wouldn't fly the mission if the flight plan predicted us below Bingo fuel at the ARCP. As it turned out, there were times at Det 4 when we had to cancel the mission because the flight plan predicted us arriving at the air refueling well below Bingo. Even when the flight plan predicted you to be right on the fuel curve, Habus had to monitor fuel consumption closely, because forecasting high altitude "temp devs" was not an exact science.

Former RSO and Det 4 Commander, Col. Barry MacKean (Ret), recalls problems caused by extreme "temp devs" in the European theater.

As with all operational missions flown by the SR-71, fuel was critical. The mission planners' task was to collect as much intelligence data with each mission as possible; therefore, the "black line" was extended to its maximum as a function of fuel remaining. I recall a sortie out of Mildenhall one Spring being forecast for higher than normal temperatures in both the climb and cruise, when traditionally the temperatures in the Barents Sea area were relatively cool. We discussed with the crew the normal precautions of closely monitoring the fuel curve and for them to use their good judgment for aborting the mission if they felt they would not be able to return to their last refueling point with the prescribed "bingo" fuel. As fate would have it that particular day, the temperatures were indeed warmer than usual and even slightly higher than forecast, so the crew made the correct decision at the appropriate point in flight and aborted the mission early, went to their last refueling point early, refueled, and returned safely to Mildenhall to fly another day.

Anytime there is a deviation to a PARPRO mission, the reason and result get briefed at all levels (wing, headquarters, Pentagon, and higher as the mission dictates). Most of our wing personnel understood the phenomenon, but at both the SRC and the JRC the reason needed a little more than normal explanation. Fortunately the SR program had wisely chosen former crew members for placement in some of the these key intermediate positions to manage and protect the program from naysayers and the uninformed. They did their jobs well and explained a logical occurrence of high temperatures causing increased fuel consumption and the need to abort the mission.

Only a week later an even more rare phenomena occurred that really tasked the ability of our intermediate managers to explain a PARPRO deviation. The weather forecaster briefed both the Barents Sea and Baltic Sea high-altitude temperatures would be extremely colder than normal. The up-side of this condition is that the plane can fly higher and faster than normal and consume much less fuel. The down side was since we could normally only fly at Mach 2.8 because of the closer land masses in the Baltic Sea area, the colder temperatures might prevent the crew from being able to maintain 2.8. Any speed greater than that would risk overflight of denied territory. We again discussed the options the crew had and confidently launched them.

The temperatures they encountered were exactly as cold as briefed, so they did indeed go faster than desired in the Barents area, but because the landmass was not so constrictive, they were able to continue. However, as they entered the Baltic area after refueling, they determined there was no way they would be able to keep their airspeed low enough to prevent an overflight condition, so they aborted the mission. Can't you imagine what puzzled looks and comments our friends at SRC and JRC encountered when only a week before we aborted a mission because the temperatures were too hot, and now they explained we had to abort another mission because the temperatures were too cold!! Fortunately, they were all very knowledgeable about the SR-71 performance capabilities and equally as quick on their feet, so they were able to fend any questions put forth.

One crew became very famous among us for a comment made while flying an operational sortie from Det 4. They were flying a clockwise loop inside the perimeter of West Germany when their ANS slowly started to degrade without their knowledge. The ANS was navigating the SR through its final turn, rolling out north so they could start the decel. Although cockpit indications were normal, the ANS rolled the aircraft out heading westerly instead. While in the decel they realized they weren't where they were supposed to be, but couldn't be sure where they were due to bad navigational systems and clouds below. During the decel, the pilot suddenly spotted a coastline through a break in the clouds and told the RSO in a calm, reassuring voice, "Sure looks like England to me."

For a while they thought they were home free when suddenly the UHF radios started screaming in French accents, "Unidentified aircraft flying in French airspace identify yourself!" They knew where they were now, but still needed to get back to Mildenhall. Fortunately, the KC-135Q tanker they were due to refuel with overheard the radio conversations and realized they were in trouble. The tanker headed directly towards the SR-71, made a successful rendezvous, where the SR took on fuel and followed the tanker back to Mildenhall. Had the tanker crew not taken the initiative to go after the SR-71, they would have had to land in France, which could have been politically sensitive. The tanker crew received Air Force awards for their actions. Every time we see the crew at the Blackbird Reunions we all get a laugh when someone says, "Sure looks like England to me!"

After several years of getting established at Det 4, Habus were soon living a comfortable existence. Now we had the best of both worlds—flying operational missions in the Orient and in Europe.

CHAPTER ELEVEN

FLYING THE SR-71 ON AN OPERATIONAL SORTIE

When aviators ask, "What's it like flying the SR-71?", I usually tell them it's not like any other aircraft they might have ever flown. In normal military and civilian worlds of flying, a pilot doesn't have to concentrate and focus his attention on his aircraft's operating parameters. He concentrates on whatever his primary mission is (dropping bombs, firing missiles, transporting cargo, instructing students, flying instruments, etc.) and assumes his aircraft will fly satisfactory to allow him to accomplish that mission. Flying the SR-71 was just the opposite. You devoted so much of your concentration and flying skills to keep the aircraft running at peak efficiency, that the primary mission of reconnaissance felt very secondary.

With the SR-71, your primary goal is to get the aircraft from a subsonic speed up to Mach 3 cruise (or above). During the accel the pilot has to concentrate intently on aircraft performance and watch for any abnormal signs that might develop. The entire time the pilot is in the accel, the aircraft's engine and inlet performance is constantly changing. In an instant, Habus had to be able to react to sudden, abnormal changes and know immediately what all their options, alternatives, and back-up modes of operating were. Most of the time, military and civilian pilots fly their aircraft well within its operating parameters and don't even come close to its actual limits. Practically every time Habus took to the skies they were pushing the SR-71 to its limits—that's where the aircraft flew best, and that's the way they liked it. Until the SR-71 was leveled off at cruise you couldn't begin to think about relaxing, and then the aircraft seemed to sense when you were at ease and gave a wake up call.

This chapter was written to give the reader some insight to the amount of detail that went into the preparation and execution of every mission. It's a crew member's perspective of what was involved in flying the SR-71 from start to finish. I will distinguish between Det 1 (Kadena) and Det 4 (Mildenhall) procedures whenever differences existed. The reader must also understand what was considered standard procedure during my time was slightly different before and after, however, the basics remain the same. The sortie will be a typical operational mission with two refuelings and two "Hot" (supersonic) legs flown from one of the Dets. The mission will not require a spare SR-71.

Mission Planning

Once it was your turn on the "ladder" to fly, mission planning began in earnest the day before the flight. The primary and back-up crew met in Operations to go over the details with our mission planners. They were a dedicated staff of personnel, experts in areas such as: SR-71 navigation, enemy defenses, sensor operations, Air Traffic Control, and other associated operational flying criteria.

The pilot and RSO discussed the flight profile to familiarize themselves with any changes or problems they might have encountered the last time they flew that particular sortie. Critical items discussed between the pilot and RSO during mission planning included: the air refueling tracks, fuel offloads, bank angles, Mach numbers, fuel minimums, threat areas, SAM missile sites, the Closest Point of Approach (CPA) to unfriendly airspace, abort scenarios, alternate bases, and weather forecasts. For a routine sortie, mission planning took about 30 minutes for an experienced crew and about one and a half to two hours for a new crew. New and more complicated sorties could take several days to plan effectively.

After mission planning was finished to everyone's satisfaction, crews stored their classified materials back in the safe and were free to do as they pleased until crew rest time came around—the standard Air Force 8 hours of uninterrupted sleep. However, since our wake-up time was usually about 3 hours before takeoff, Habus had to get to bed much earlier. The times scheduled for all the events prior to takeoff could be adjusted slightly to meet the experience levels of different crews, but typically followed the schedule below for a 0800 takeoff:

2100 - Sleep (if you could)
0500 - Wake up (the hard part), shower, dress
0530 - Eat high protein/low residue meal
0615 - Formal mission briefing start
0645 - Physical exam and suit up
0715 - Arrive at aircraft
0730 - Start Engines (depending on taxi distance)
0800 - Takeoff

Most crews wanted to relax the day before their mission. Since the mobile crew also performed as backup fliers, they had to meet the same crew rest requirements. Replacement crews arriving at the Dets were not allowed to fly for 48 hours to allow for their bodies to adjust to the new time zone. During training we were screened for usage of specific drugs to help us sleep or stay alert. We could request a limited number of "downers" to aid in sleeping before a mission, and "uppers" to help stay awake during the mission. Few Habus ever took the pills.

Preflight Procedures

The pilot and RSO decided among themselves what time to meet each other in the BOQ before driving to eat their preflight meals. The mess halls at Kadena and Mildenhall were set up to provide our preflight meals, however most crews opted to eat elsewhere. Some Habus liked to cook their own meals while others went to Officers' Clubs, Base Exchange cafeterias, and even to Mickey's Tea Bar on Mildenhall to have their preflight meals. By the time we were eating, mission planners were already busy preparing for the briefing. Maintenance began their preparations on the aircraft long before we went to sleep.

After eating, the mobile crew and the fliers drove to Det Operations for the mission briefing. The first thing the fliers did was retrieve their classified checklists, route maps, and flight plans from the safe. Since the fliers and mobile crew had already prepared and knew the mission by heart, the real purpose of the briefing was to apprise the Det Commander of the mission being flown and to make sure everyone involved in the mission was "singing from the same sheet of music." It was extremely important for everyone in the briefing to know precisely what the mission entailed since our operational missions were conducted in radio silence to the maximum extent possible. The SR-71 program *always* worked under the concept "no news is good news"—as long as everything was proceeding normally with a mission, there was no need to communicate—everyone knew precisely what to do. Using this concept provided an extra measure of communication security for our operational sorties.

We had one mission where the Det Commander was not quite aware of what was going on. The mission was a non-operational "DEBBIE," to check out the aircraft after having extensive maintenance work completed. Former RSO, Col. Roger Jacks, tells the story:

> During the mission briefing, the senior SR-71 crew suggested we abort our scheduled route of flight around the island and fly over Okinawa creating a sonic boom. Further, they said if we dumped fuel as we crossed the island, the airplane's tremendous speed would be visible in the sky. In fact, they would get all the maintenance troops out to watch the amazing spectacle also. We quickly saw ourselves as modern day heroes, and here was our chance to share a thrill with the maintenance troops with just a simple reprogramming of the SR-71's ANS.
>
> The decision was made, and since the Det commander was in the room while all this was being discussed, we assumed this met with

his approval also. The flyover was done with flair and complete success. What we didn't know was that maintenance had planned a special test of the Side Looking Radar (SLR) on the mission before flying it on an operational sortie. Since they couldn't find the data that was supposed to have been collected, they had to assume the system had failed to operate. I was called back down to the Det to confirm the SLR's operation.

When I proudly told the commander what we had done, he went ballistic! He proceeded to chew me out by calling me every name in the book. I tried to tell him our senior crew came up with the idea and that he was there when we discussed it. He just looked at me and screamed, "Damn it, just because I am in the room doesn't mean I know what is going on!" He finished the 15 minute butt-chewing by telling me he was sending me home immediately and that I was nothing but a no-good "God damn navigator!" I called Joe [pilot, Maj. Joe Kinego] on the phone and told him the Det commander wanted to see him immediately. When Joe went in to see the commander, I hid just outside the door to listen. The thing that had hurt the most was being labeled just a "God damn navigator!" My feelings were somewhat soothed when Joe was told he was just another "God damn pilot!" and would be going home on the next KC-135 with me. It turned out the SLR data was usable, and we weren't sent back to Beal; however, we learned a valuable lesson on communications.

Personnel required to attend the mission briefing were: the Det Commander, his Operations Officer, the fliers, the mobile crew, a mission planner, and the maintenance supervisor (an Air Force Officer at Kadena and Lockheed civilian at Mildenhall). Everyone was seated, waiting to be called to "ATTENTION!" when the Det Commander walked into the room. After everyone was seated, the briefer started out with the following, "Colonel Cunningham, gentlemen, I'm Lt. Col. Randy Crook, briefing "GIANT SCALE" Mission number 1040. In 20 seconds the time will be 2300 Zulu (GMT)." After the time hack he briefed the specific sortie objectives, including which sensors would be used to cover the targets.

Through a series of about 10 to 15 slides the briefer went over the route, highlighting air refueling tracks, fuel offloads, tanker call signs, steep bank angle turns, cruise Mach numbers, high threat areas, CPA to foreign airspace, alternates, and any Notices to Airmen (NOTAMs) important to the mission. A communications slide listed all the UHF frequencies and call signs for the tankers and classified HF call signs for other ground and airborne assets.

Every operational mission we flew had a period of time in which the SR-71 could take off late and still complete the sortie. This was called the takeoff "window" and varied from a few minutes to several hours depending on a variety of factors such as: the SR-71's fuel load, number of tankers and their available fuel, spare aircraft availability, sun angles, and Germany's sonic boom quiet hours, etc. The takeoff "window" was briefed as well as the limiting factor(s) leading up to the last available takeoff time.

Weather was briefed next, followed by maintenance slides showing the aircraft's previous discrepancies and maintenance corrective actions. After the formal briefing, crews were asked if they had any questions about the mission, followed by the Commanders comments.

Every Det Commander used this time in different ways. Some Commanders used it to ask the fliers "what if" scenarios along their intended route of flight. If the weather was lousy, Commanders usually discussed playing it cautiously, telling us to be alert for a possible weather recall message. Others used the time to emphasize to the fliers that no mission warranted risking an SR-71 over, and that we could always try again another day if things were going wrong. Most crews wanted to hear their Det Commander say they would back them if they reached their "comfort level" and decided to abort the mission. Habus needed the Det Commander to be a buffer in the chain of command between them and SAC Headquarters, who would "second guess" whatever decision they made. Without exception, every Det Commander backed his crews' decisions 100 percent! After the Commander was done, everyone rose to "ATTENTION!" as he departed the room.

The crew chief waited for the briefing to end and then went over the aircraft's maintenance forms, start-engine procedures, and engine run-up at the end of the runway. The mobile crew stayed around to listen in case there was anything they needed to know and to offer advice. There was generally 15 to 20 minutes remaining before going to suit up. Since it was *mandatory* to fly operational sorties as a formed crew, it was imperative that both crew members stay healthy. If one of the fliers thought he was verging on being too sick to fly, we had him take his preflight physical exam before the briefing, so we knew as soon as possible who the actual fliers were going to be. The mobile crew gathered up all their classified material, the "brick," mobile kit bag, and departed for the hangar in the mobile car to preflight the aircraft. The mobile kit bag contained a wealth of classified information such as the Dash-1, local operating instructions, phone numbers, frequencies, and a variety of other procedures, readily available if needed for an emergency.

In fact, the classified kit bag got one mobile crew into trouble at Kadena. They had just finished launching the SR and headed to a temporary Officers' Club, called the Banyon Tree, for lunch. Most Habus locked the car and hid the kit bag under the seat, so it couldn't be seen by anyone looking in the windows. As it happened, they didn't, and our friendly RC-135 reconnaissance rivals parked beside the mobile car and saw the bright red classified "SECRET" stickers all over the kit bag. They knew exactly who the kit bag belonged to and thought it would be cute to call the Security Police and report a classified bag in the back of a military vehicle. Sure enough, the police arrived and after an extensive security investigation lasting several weeks, the crew was chastised. From then on, Habus were not to let the classified kit bag out of their sight.

The mobile crew also had a copy of the mission flight plan and map, so they could tell precisely where along the route the fliers were at any given moment. The mobile crew was free to go wherever they wanted while the SR-71 was airborne but had to be able to respond quickly in case the aircraft returned with an emergency. If anything happened to the SR, the mobile crew would be alerted on the "brick."

At Kadena, about the same time as the SR-71 briefing was taking place, the KC-135Q mission was also being briefed, depending on the air refueling locations. At Mildenhall, the tankers usually had briefed and took off several hours prior to the SR-71 in order to get to their assigned air refueling tracks in time to meet the SR at the ARCT. At both Dets the operational flying atmosphere between Habus and tanker crews was very open and allowed a free exchange of ideas with only one goal in mind—whatever it took to get the mission accomplished.

The mobile crew arrived at the aircraft about the time the fliers were starting their preflight physicals. In each cockpit, the mobile crew went through their respective preflight checks, stopping at the "STARTING ENGINES" checklist. If the mobile crew found anything wrong with the aircraft during their preflight that could jeopardize the mission, the crew chief was the first to be notified. After their physicals and suit-up, the fliers arrived at the hangar in the PSD van. The mobile crew went inside the van to brief them on the status of their airplane and pass along any last minute thoughts. PSD technicians departed the van and prepared each cockpit to receive the crew.

About now, a lot was happening elsewhere. The tankers were getting ready to start their engines, already taxiing, or well on their way to the refueling point. For long missions, into areas such as the Mediterranean Sea or Persian Gulf, tankers would have been pre-positioned at forward bases around the globe, days in advance, with the precious JP-7 onboard.

A mission planner, designated as the "Mission Monitor" for the flight, was responsible for following the aircraft's route of flight based on timing and to monitor the HF radio for the SR-71's coded "Ops Normal" call or a possible abort call from the RSO. If the crew was aborting, the mission monitor was the first to know and had an extensive notification checklist to follow. His first step was to get the base telephone operator to page everyone on a conference call network with their portable "bricks," so he could advise everyone of the crew's intentions with an estimated landing time. When the operator paged everyone on the VHF network, each "brick" sounded off with a five-second, ear piercing, high frequency squeal—you knew instinctively something had gone wrong. If they were aborting to another location, everyone rushed to the Det to find out the details and get organized for the recovery operation.

Back to the normal mission routine. After the mission briefing was finished, the Operations Officer had just enough time to wrap up any loose ends and depart for the airfield tower with his "brick." At Kadena and Mildenhall (or anywhere else the SR-71 flew from, other than Beale) the Operations Officer had an additional duty to perform as the "Tower Officer." His job in the tower was to be another set of eyes and ears for the mobile crew and fliers from a vantage point high above the field. At Kadena, he first stopped at the radar control facility to give the senior controller the unclassified flight plan and call sign of the SR-71 for the mission. At Mildenhall the mission monitor made secure phone calls, passing along to British air traffic controllers the SR-71's unclassified route of flight. On every operational mission we flew, the unclassified flight plan stopped at 60,000 feet. As far as the air traffic controllers knew, we fell off the face of the earth at that point. No one outside of the SR-71 community (SENIOR CROWN access) knew the classified supersonic flight track above FL 600. The same rule applied during the decel, picking up radio and radar contact as we descended through FL 600.

The Tower Officer's primary job was to insure there were no taxi conflicts and that the SR-71 was cleared onto the runway a minimum of one minute prior to the scheduled takeoff time. A UHF radio was available for him to listen and talk to the fliers if needed. At Kadena, he also monitored tower personnel for the correct arming and disarming procedures of the BAK-11/12 barrier.

For many years we used standard UHF radio calls for taxi, takeoff, and climbout to the air refueling track. In the late 1970s we received feedback from the National Security Agency (NSA) that we were compromising our mission security by using standard UHF radio calls. Soviet "fishing trawlers," with an elaborate array of antennas and other snooping devices, were just off the west coast of Okinawa and in the vicinity of our air refueling tracks, listening in on our radio conversations. NSA recommended we change to radio silent launch procedures. Through a series of lightgun signals from the tower to the aircraft and mobile, radio-silent launches soon became routine. The Tower Officer told the tower controllers when to flash which light signal.

It was comforting as a flier to know the tower was always manned by another SR-71 crew member who knew both the aircraft and aircrew capabilities. It was not unusual for Habus to radio into mobile they were "low on gas" or had a "minor malfunction," requiring expeditious handling on arrival. Once the Tower Officer heard the call, he knew instinctively what the problem was and informed approach control and tower personnel to give landing priority to the SR-71. All the controllers were excellent at giving our aircraft priority when we asked for it; we never abused the request. The Tower Officer had direct access to a world of communications and emergency equipment if needed. From his vantage point high above the field, he could closely monitor rapidly changing weather conditions and airfield status.

Back at the hanger, after the PSD technicians gave a "thumbs up" signal from atop the ladder, the fliers exited the back of the van, climbed the steps, and crawled into their cockpits. Before sitting down in their cockpit seats, they pushed down on each of their flight boot stirrups to lock them into the ejection system retraction cable. The rest of the pressure suit hook-up was left to PSD. After they were finished mating us to the seat and cockpit, one PSD technician read a challenge-and-response checklist while the other technician pulled and tugged on each connection called out, verbally responding back. It was in our best interest to listen carefully and feel for the appropriate tugs while they went through the checklist.

After PSD completed their checklist, each crew member started their individual INTERIOR COCKPIT checklist. The crew chief put on his headset and plugged his communication cord into the nose wheel-well receptacle. The crew chief checked in with the pilot to let him know everything was ready down below for engine start.

Engine Start

The Det Commander drove to the hangar about the time the crews were getting into their cockpits and joined the mobile crew in their car, so he could monitor the UHF radios. The mobile crew aimed the car directly at the aircraft in the hangar, so they could monitor maintenance actions and know precisely how far along the crew was with their checklist.

A few minutes before the crew was ready to start engines, they went through their STARTING ENGINES checklist. The interphone system was checked between each cockpit, and the pilot activated the bailout light switch to see if the RSO's corresponding ALERT and BAILOUT lights illuminated in his cockpit. Their TDIs were checked against each other for proper Mach, KEAS, and altitude readings. Individual fuel tank quantities were checked next. The RSO used a CG computer wheel to enter the fuel readings of each tank and calculated a manually computed CG setting for the aircraft. The cockpit CG reading had to agree within 0.5 percent of the manually computed CG.

By now the hangar probably had 15 to 20 maintenance personnel and "Tech Reps" waiting for the engine start. One minute before starting engines, the crew lowered and locked their Bailer Bars to start the flow of 100 percent oxygen to begin the de-nitrification process on their bodies. As the pilot turned on the retractable anti-collision lights, the bright red lights swirled around the hangar walls, signaling to everyone the start of engines in one minute. Like a dragster revving up at the starting line, you could hear the souped-up "Buicks" idling rough as their exhaust echoed throughout the hangar.

When the pilot was ready for engine start he queried the crew chief over the interphone, "Intakes and exhaust clear, fire guard posted, chocks installed?" After the crew chief replied the pilot called out, "I'll take rotation." At that point the crew chief signaled back under the wing to his assistants to open full throttle on the "Buicks." Their exhaust noise was deafening, but to a Habu, it was sweet music. At the first sign of engine rotation on the RPM gauge the pilot brought the throttle out of cutoff, to the idle position. As the rpm and noise from the "Buicks" steadily increased, the J-58 rotated faster and faster until the TEB ignited the fuel and the engine was started. The pilot called out, "Disconnect rotation," when he saw 3200 rpm on the gauge. A quick check of the engine gauges for normal idle parameters: RPM (3975, -/+ 50 rpm), EGT (350-565°C), fuel flow (4600-6300 lb/hr), oil pressure (35 psi min), hydraulic pressure (3000-3500 psi), and CIP (slightly below ambient). The engine was started.

After waiting two minutes for the hydraulic fluid to thoroughly circulate throughout the aircraft, a flight control check was made by the pilot and verified by the crew chief, watching for the rudders and elevons to move appropriately. After the single hydraulic system checked satisfactorily, the second engine was started in the same manner.

After both engines were started, the left and right generators were turned ON, taking over from the external electrical power. The pilot thoroughly checked the fuel system to make sure all the boost pumps were operative, the crossfeed valve opened and closed, and manual selection of each fuel tank's boost pumps worked. When the crew chief was in position to check the brakes, the pilot pumped them while the crew chief confirmed brake actuation. To check out the primary and back-up hydraulic systems used for steering and braking, the pilot applied moderate brake pressure on the rudder pedals, then moved the brake switch between the NORMAL and ALT STEER & BRAKES systems. If both brake systems were working satisfactory he felt a slight "thump" in the pedal pressure as he switched from one system to the other. The absence of a "thump" indicated only one braking system was available.

Before Taxi

The BEFORE TAXI checklist was next. All six SAS channels were engaged, and the pitch and roll switches of the autopilot were turned on. The stick grip trigger was squeezed to check the autopilot for immediate disengagement. Next, re-engage the pitch and roll autopilot and activate the DAFICS test switch to run a thorough test of all components, taking one minute to complete. Navigation systems and radios were checked thoroughly. The RSO established secure radio contact with "MAMA Control" to check the ranging and bearing features of the ARC-50 radios. "MAMA Control" was the call sign given to the ARC-50 ground radio station maintenance used to check our radio against. Pitch, roll, and yaw trim switches were checked and confirmed for proper movement, as well as checking the Right Hand Rudder Synchronizer moving the right rudder correctly.

Next, the pilot tested the fuel derich system by increasing idle rpm slightly (400 rpm) and reaching back along the left console to actuate the derich test switch. Holding the test switch in the left or right position increased the respective EGT gauge to 860°C, creating an artificial over-temperature situation, and thus deriching the engine. Observing and hearing each engine's rpm decrease during the derich confirmed it was operating OK.

While the derich check was being accomplished, the crew chief walked up the stairs and into position to check out the air refueling system. He verified the air refueling door and the boom latching mechanism were all working satisfactory. Now in position to look down the fuselage, he confirmed to the pilot that the "drag chute doors closed." All the time these checks were being completed by the pilot, the RSO was busy checking out the ANS for navigational accuracy.

When PSD saw the crew chief going up the ladder for the air refueling checks, they got out of their van and waited at the foot of the ladder. The crew chief motioned for them to come up after he confirmed the drag chute doors were closed. PSD technicians reached in each cockpit and pulled the primary and alternate ejection seat pin, the canopy T-handle safety pin, and the parachute gun safety cap, arming all the ejection systems. They held up three safety pins and a red cover, displaying them prominently to each crew member, who returned a "thumbs up" signal acknowledging they were removed. After PSD started down the stairs, the crew chief pulled out the canopy locking bar and lowered the pilot's canopy, pushing down on it until the pilot moved the canopy locking lever forward and turned the canopy seal switch ON. Next, the RSO's canopy was closed.

The crew chief walked down the stairs and with the help of his assistants, rolled both ladders to the sides of the hangar. The pilot turned ON the left and right air refrigeration switches to supply the aircraft's cooling needs, and the crew chief asked permission to disconnect the ground cooling air supply hose. The pilot checked the periscope for proper operation and engaged the nosewheel steering to check for slight left and right movements of the aircraft. A final check with the crew chief that all panels and gear pins were "secured and removed," and he was cleared by the pilot to disconnect his interphone. Most Habus gave their crew chief a few words of "thanks" before disconnecting.

Taxi

The crew chief walked smartly about 150 feet out in front of the aircraft and stood at "Parade Rest" waiting for a flash of the taxi light. During these final minutes the mobile crew had been watching tower for the flashing green "cleared to taxi" light signal. When it was received, the mobile car started onto the taxiway to lead the SR-71 out. A quick flash of the taxi light signaled the crew chief for his assistants to remove the chocks. With "taxi" hand signals from the crew chief, the pilot added a small amount of power and gracefully taxied out of the hangar.

Following behind the taxiing SR-71 was a caravan of anywhere between two to six maintenance vehicles, depending on how many personnel wanted to watch the takeoff. Most of them were going out to watch the fruits of their labor—the impressive takeoff and climbout—others to make sure their particular aircraft systems passed their final checks. The one maintenance vehicle that was required to follow us out was a large, six-man military pickup truck, modified to drive up to the cockpits of the SR-71 and provide a means for the crew to exit the aircraft quickly if the need arose. Unlike most other aircraft, SR-71 crews had no means of getting up or down from their cockpits without outside stairs.

During taxi the only check was to test the brakes on the individual hydraulic systems. After disengaging the nosewheel steering, the pilot braked slightly in both directions on the L and R hydraulic systems, checking for the proper brake responses and a possible dragging brake. A quick glance at the SAS panel to make sure the pitch, roll, and yaw sensor lights remained out completed the TAXI checklist. Sometime during taxi, the RSO switched the ANS from the "INERTIAL ONLY" mode and placed it into the "ASTRO INERTIAL" mode of navigation. The ANS easily achieved star tracking while taxiing out, even on hazy days.

At the departure end of the runway, the crew chief jumped out of his van and walked into position on the taxiway to help line the aircraft up for the BEFORE TAKEOFF checks. He had to insure nothing was behind the aircraft because the engine run was accomplished at full military power. Once the crew chief gave the signal for the "chocks installed," the pilot and RSO coordinated the navigation systems to be used on the departure and checked them over for accuracy. Next came the engine run.

The pilot and crew chief used visual hand signals for the engine run and other checks. The engine run involved a rather lengthy checkout of all engine parameters, one engine at a time. During the run-up, engine gauges were checked for their proper values, the EGT trimming system was checked, and IGV shifting was confirmed. The pilot remained at full military power on each engine a minimum of 30 seconds to allow the MRS to record stable engine parameters for maintenance.

After both engine runs were complete, another flight control check was accomplished with the crew chief, and the pilot rechecked all his flight control trim settings to make sure they were at zero. By now fuel should have decreased sufficiently out of tank-3, and the pilot checked the tank to insure decrease. If the CG shifted aft of 22 percent, the pilot had to forward transfer fuel to get the CG below the 22 percent takeoff limit. The pilot and RSO confirmed both oxygen switches were ON and that their Baylor bars were down and locked. The pilot set the brake switch for DRY or WET, depending on runway condition. One final review of the takeoff data with the RSO: acceleration check speed, refusal speed, rotation speed, takeoff speed, and single-engine speed. The crew chief gave the signal to turn the pitot heat ON and felt it for warmth.

While the pilot held the brakes, the crew chief signaled his assistants to remove the chocks. After the engine run, the chocks were usually wedged so tight between the tires and the concrete they couldn't be pulled out and required his assistants to use sledge hammers to pound them free. To me it always seemed so ironic to have a sophisticated, technologically-advanced aircraft like the SR-71 having to be freed up to taxi by two maintenance personnel slugging away beneath the aircraft with sledge hammers!

After the pilot gave his final "thumbs up," the crew chief responded back with a salute and walked back to his maintenance truck to wait for takeoff. We tried to finish all the checks and have about five minutes remaining before the departure time. As soon as the Tower Officer saw through his binoculars that the crew was ready and the runway was free, he asked tower personnel to give the steady green "cleared for takeoff" light. Mobile led the aircraft onto the runway and continued down the full length of his takeoff roll, looking for anything that could possibly damage the engines or tires.

If we were pressed for time, or the taxiway too slippery or too narrow, occasionally we bypassed the engine run on the taxiway and went straight onto the runway along with the crew chief and his truck. In position for takeoff, the crew chief quickly checked the flight controls and pitot heat, then departed the runway while mobile finished checking the runway in front. Holding brakes tightly, the pilot and RSO accomplished the individual engine run checks and the remainder of the BEFORE TAKEOFF checklist. At Mildenhall, the runway was frequently utilized for the engine run because of limited space on the taxiways leading up to the runway. A story from former RSO Maj. Gene "Geno" Quist reminds us of England's dreaded "black ice" on taxiways:

> On 13 December 1984, we were flying 974 on a sortie out of Mildenhall. The weather had been typical England winter weather, and some snow and ice were on the roads and taxiways. We were taxiing to the end of the runway when we tried to stop for the engine run-up checks, and the airplane wouldn't stop. We were on pure "black ice!" I had just seen and heard another aircraft taxi onto the active runway at the other end, so I immediately called the tower to say we may be unable to hold short—please stop the other aircraft. At the same time some of our maintenance troops were running from their vehicles to try to stop us by throwing chocks under the tires. I saw one of them fall down as his feet literally slipped out from underneath him. We finally stopped. Needless to say, the engine run-up checks were done during the takeoff roll. Bottom line—mission accomplished!

The mobile vehicles at both Dets were generally run-down. Every Det Commander had to fight with the rest of the base just to get any vehicle, and when the motor pool finally allocated one, it was usually the "lemon" of their fleet. An example of how unreliable they were occurred one hot summer day at Kadena, with Don and I on mobile duty and the Commander, Col. Abe Kardong (Ret), sitting in the back seat. We led the SR-71 onto the runway and got about 3,000 feet down the up-sloped runway 5R when the car suddenly died on us. The SR-71 had about 3 minutes remaining before its takeoff time. Don continued to steer the Ford station wagon while Colonel Kardong and I pushed it down the runway to the nearest taxiway, about 1,000 feet away. Huffing, puffing, and sweating profusely, we cleared the runway just in time as the SR-71 roared by us. Fortunately, our maintenance troops saw our dilemma and came to the rescue, giving us a ride back to the Det and eventually towing the mobile car back to the hangars where they repaired it themselves.

Takeoff

Lined up on the runway, the TAKEOFF checks began. They consisted of turning ON the IFF transponder, engaging all SAS channels, insuring all warning and caution lights were out, circuit breakers checked in, compass headings checked, nosewheel steering engaged, and tank-4 boost pumps turned ON. Tank-4 pumps were on to insure a positive fuel supply at high pitch attitudes and high fuel-consumption rates at low altitude. The total fuel flow for both engines at max AB on takeoff was around 80,000 pounds per hour! After the mobile car was clear of the runway, tower gave the crew another "cleared for takeoff" light signal with about a minute to go. Habus took pride on releasing brakes at the precise takeoff time, using the RSO's ANS clock for an accurate countdown.

As the throttles were slowly advanced, the pilot released brakes when the IGV shift lights illuminated. After reaching full military power (all the way to the throttle stops) it was a quick glance at the RPM, EGT, ENP, and oil pressure gauges to see appropriate values. An exact readout of each gauge was too time consuming during the rapid takeoff, so Habus were taught to merely anticipate where the gauge needles should be pointing and checked them quickly against a clock position. After pausing very briefly at full military power, the pilot lifted both throttles up and moved them forward into the mid-AB range for ignition, then smoothly advanced them to max afterburner once they lit. Seldom did the ABs light simultaneously, creating individual left and right "kicks" of the aircraft. At max AB, the pilot made another quick scan of his engine gauges to make sure the needles were pointing to their new clock positions.

At 3,000 feet down the runway (later changed to 2,000 feet) we made our acceleration speed check. It was a comparison of our pre-computed airspeed to our indicated airspeed at the 3,000 foot runway marker to let the pilot know whether he was getting proper thrust from the engines. A typical acceleration-check airspeed at the 3,000 foot marker, at a gross weight of 120,000 pounds and 86°F, was 156 knots, and the total takeoff distance was 4,800 feet. Any airspeed significantly less than the acceleration check speed was cause for an abort.

The takeoff acceleration was rapid, and the pilot had to be ready to start bringing the nose off the ground at 180 knots (207mph). Slowly, but steadily pulling back on the stick the nose traveled upward to about 10 degrees of pitch allowing the aircraft to break ground around 210 knots (242 mph). Once airborne, the pilot had to relax back pressure on the stick to stop the nose up pitch rate.

Rapid pitch rates during a climb has placed Habus into difficult situations not thoroughly covered by our Dash-1. If an experienced SR-71 pilot knew the hazards associated with high pitch rates, he could take you aside and brief you on things to be aware of. Otherwise, you found out on your own! A crew flying the 1976 Andrews AFB Open House departure on Sunday afternoon did just that. Their fuel reserves and prior coordination with air traffic control allowed them to perform their last high-speed pass over the field with an unrestricted climb to 25,000 feet. It was a magnificent high speed pass as Don, myself, the 9th SRW Commander, and a host of others watched in awe. As the pilot began to pull the nose up sharply, you could see the aft profile of the aircraft rapidly change to a full length profile. Visible moisture was streaming off the chines and wingtips as the pilot increased the upward rate of pitch rotation.

With the nose pointing upward, at what appeared to be completely vertical, all the fuel once resting on the bottom of the six fuselage tanks had now moved aft, rapidly increasing the aft CG. Try balancing a pencil on your finger and then slowly rotating your finger so the pointed end of the pencil moves upward. As the CG shifts aft, it doesn't take long until the pointed end of the pencil pitches up beyond your control and falls off. The SR-71 in this predicament was no different. Once you rapidly started the nose up, it wanted to continue moving up on its own as the CG shifted aft and the control stick pressure suddenly becomes very light in your hand. Depending on how quickly you pulled the nose up, it sometimes required a very forceful forward stick movement to arrest the nose from continuing upward.

To further complicate the crew's situation, at high angles of attack, adequate airflow to supply the hungry engines was being blocked out by the inlets and fuselage, and the engines began to compressor stall on them. Watching from the ground we had no idea what was going on at the time. To those of us who flew the aircraft, it was an extremely impressive maneuver. I made a mental note to myself to be sure and ask the pilot when we returned to Beale how he accomplished it.

All we saw from the ground was an SR-71 going practically straight up, followed immediately by the aircraft lurching over as the pilot pushed the stick forward rapidly. Pulling negative "Gs" during the maneuver, fuel streamed profusely from the dump mast as the aircraft arced over. As the aircraft disappeared from view, over a large, billowy white cloud, the Wing Commander looked at Don and I and said, "What the hell was that?" We didn't know either, but told him it looked as if the pilot was trying to get over the clouds building up off the end of the runway. He didn't buy our story. We called the crew up on the UHF radio and asked what had happened. They mumbled something about compressor stalls and that everything was OK now and they were proceeding on to the first refueling. Talking to the crew afterwards revealed that it took *full* forward stick input from the pilot to get the nose started back down to level flight. Colonel Roger Jacks (RSO) tells what it was like from the rear cockpit.

> *We had heard many stories on how tough the aircraft was and how on some occasions it had surpassed design limits and survived. On a fateful day in July of 1976, [pilot] Joe Kinego and I found out how tough the SR-71 really was. We had been part of a SR-71 static display at an Andrews AFB Open House celebrating the country's 200th anniversary. Now it was time to fly the aircraft back to Beale AFB. We had been selected to fly the aircraft home but not before a fly-by and a maximum performance climb to 25,000 feet. The fly-by went well and as we started the performance climb, all seemed to be going well.*
>
> *As we passed 8,000 feet we unknowingly entered an area of moderate to severe turbulence. The SR-71, reacting to the turbulence, began pitching up, and I thought it was going over on its back. Joe was able to stop the pitch-up by moving the control stick full forward and holding it there. As the pitch-up stopped, the aircraft briefly hung in space and then pitched down. As we floated over the top, the approach plate books came out of their storage bins and crashed into my helmet, cracking the protective visor. One of my legs floated up and wedged itself in a console panel. As I struggled to get into an ejection position, I saw the airspeed rapidly increasing.*
>
> *As Joe put it, we were on a runaway shopping cart heading down the hills of San Francisco. Joe was fighting to pull the aircraft out of the dive as the airspeed climbed toward the maximum design limit for that altitude [500 KEAS]. We leveled off around 4,000 feet, ran through checklists, and headed back to California. Nervous laughter broke out between the two of us when discussing the unbelievable air-show we must have put on for the airplane's fans. Observers to the event said they had never seen a SR-71 go almost straight up and straight down in a matter of seconds.*

Back to the takeoff. The first priority for the pilot after getting airborne was to get the gear up and then quickly scan the engine instruments. As the aircraft passed through 0.5 Mach the SURFACE LIMITER caution light came on, telling the pilot to rotate and engage the surface limiter T-handle located on the center pedestal between his two knees. Engaged, the surface limiter restricted roll and rudder movement at higher airspeeds to preclude over stressing the aircraft. During climbout, the pilot switched his attitude reference gyro source from INS to ANS while the RSO switched his reference source from ANS to INS. We never flew with both crew members on the same attitude gyro reference source in case one of them failed.

We climbed out at 400 KEAS until reaching 0.9 Mach, then held the Mach constant until reaching our subsonic cruise altitude. During the climb, fuel tank-4 was released, the altimeters reset to 29.92 passing through 18,000 feet, and the RSO tuned the HF radio, and checked out the DEF systems. The climb pitch attitude was initially around 35-40 degrees (depending on the fuel load) and decreased to about 25 degrees as we approached our subsonic level-off altitude. The climb rate of the SR-71 with a 45,000 pound fuel load was around 10,000 feet/minute, taking about 3 minutes to reach 30,000 feet. Whenever we cruised subsonic at the higher altitudes it was always at 0.9 Mach.

After level off at 25,000 feet enroute to the tanker, we checked out the autopilot and the ANS's ability to navigate the aircraft. Most all of our operational sorties started off with a refueling right after takeoff. Infrequently, we flew a "hot" leg immediately after takeoff to check out an aircraft's performance at Mach 3 before going on a high priority mission. The key to checking out the SR-71's systems was to fly it long enough at Mach 3 to get the entire aircraft warmed up, so any problems associated with heating would have time to manifest themselves. If an SR flew well on its first "hot" leg, you were *generally* assured it would be a good aircraft on subsequent "hot" legs.

"Cold" Air Refueling Rendezvous

The climbout and departures were radio silent—we spoke to no one! The monitoring radar control facility identified the SR-71 by our IFF (Identification Friend or Foe) code appearing on their radar screen. Air traffic controllers cleared the airspace around us so there was no need for radio transmissions. If they had to call us or give emergency instructions, we acknowledged by pushing the identification feature of the IFF rather than making a UHF radio call.

With no weather radar on the SR-71, most crews were anxious to establish secure radio contact with the tankers. All our tankers were required to be established in the air refueling track 30 minutes prior to the ARCT (Air Refueling Control Time—our time of arrival over the ARCP) to evaluate the weather and determine if the track needed to be moved. Soon after takeoff, the RSO began to establish ranging and bearing on the tanker with the ARC-50 radio. Both tanker and SR-71 crews had the same information on their classified air refueling cards showing: call signs, track locations, refueling altitudes, onload fuel, bingo fuel, and the external codes used to link up the ARC-50 radios with each aircraft in order to get range, bearing, and secure communication with each other.

The rendezvous was basically left up to the lead tanker crew to accomplish—we merely flew on course, straight towards the ARCP at 0.9 Mach, and monitored his progress during the final stages of the rendezvous. The lead tanker navigator used special SR-71 rendezvous charts to determine the length of his final racetrack orbit that would hopefully place him in front of the SR-71 by three to four miles when they rolled out of their final turn over the ARCP.

Closing in on the lead tanker, the pilot and RSO began their REFUELING checklist. Fuel was transferred forward to get the CG as far forward as possible since it moved aft naturally, as the tanks filled up during the refueling process. An aft CG during refueling made the SR-71 less stable and more difficult to handle on the boom. To complete the checklist, the air refueling door was opened, fuel tank-4 pressed ON, interphone panels set to communicate on boom interphone, pilot's seat lowered, radio frequencies dialed in, and exterior lights set.

After sighting the lead tanker visually, we maneuvered the SR-71 to what is called the "pre-contact" position, about 50 feet behind and 10 feet low of the tanker's boom nozzle. Stabilized in the pre-contact position, with no rapid forward movement, the boom operator moved his boom fore and aft rapidly several times, telling the SR-71 pilot he was cleared into the "contact" position for a hook up.

Air Refueling

Adding a small amount of power, the SR-71 slowly moved forward to the contact position. The pilot slowly maneuvered the SR to place the end of the air refueling boom about three feet outside his front window. Even in turbulence, an experienced boom operator could plug into your aircraft immediately without missed attempts, whereas you could feel and hear a new "boomer" banging the end of his nozzle all around your air refuel receptacle before finally hooking up. Once the boom nozzle was locked into the receptacle, a Habu's favorite words from the boom operator were, "you're taking gas." As long as we were hooked up with the tanker's nozzle we communicated with each other over the boom interphone.

Refueling the SR was easy as long as everything was going smoothly. It was very stable on the boom and responded quickly to small throttle movements. Connected to the boom, you tended to get a springboard effect in turbulent air. You could feel turbulence ripple throughout the aircraft fuselage and watch the boom move in and out in response to turbulence. Former SR pilot Lt. Col. Les Dyer (Ret), talks about his refueling experiences:

> One would be remiss as a Habu not to mention air refueling. Aside from white-knuckle monitoring of the "beast" throughout the sensitive area, nothing was more demanding than the process of getting a pressure disconnect with full tanks. This was a full-team effort, and the parts played by tanker and RSO can't be sufficiently lauded. These thoughts are a front seat memory merely because that's about all this 46 year old mind can recall with anything approaching clarity.
>
> Even a day VFR refueling over northern Nevada was potentially an aircraft handling exercise to physically drain the best pilot. Given night and weather in heavy thunderstorms over the South China Sea, and you had the recipe for an exercise which frequently left one weak in both body and mind for a considerable time. Alternatively,

though the adrenaline was probably already present, nothing could beat the thrill of successfully getting the offload in the midst of crackling St. Elmo's Fire, turbulence to rival a series of your best "unstarts," and lightning which left you three-quarters blind. Throw in a Star Wars kaleidoscope of reflected lights from the cockpit and a 1960s out-of-body experience would not have been beyond the realm of possibility. But then from the back seat, "Hey, no problem pilot, you're upside down, but wings are level and almost full tanks!"

While you were in the final stages of refueling with the lead tanker, the second tanker was slowly maneuvering into his position, ready to receive the SR-71. By now, the second tanker was 1,000 feet above and line abreast of the lead tanker, clearly visible to the SR-71 pilot. When the lead tanker advised, "you have your offload," the SR pilot squeezed the trigger to disconnect the nozzle and dropped down and back slightly.

He then maneuvered the SR up into the pre-contact position and repeated the previous procedures for another hook up. Once you were satisfied the second tanker was capable of transferring fuel, you could disconnect and fly formation with him if extra time remained to the EAR point. Your other option was to just remain hooked up and not transfer any fuel. Don and I always planned to start our final transfer with about 5,000 pounds to go and 10 minutes remaining. The idea was to pressure disconnect from the boom precisely at the EAR with a full load of gas.

The final stages of filling up were controlled by the RSO telling the tanker how many fuel transfer pumps to use as we approached the EAR point. Normal fuel transfer was accomplished with four of their fuel pumps operating, and by reducing the number down to three, two, or one pump, the rate of fuel transfer would slow down accordingly. If you weren't scheduled for a full load of gas, now was the time to beg for a few extra thousand pounds of gas for insurance. Even though the tanker crews were briefed previously, we reminded them before disconnecting which direction the accel started out and told them on which side the SR-71 would clear them after refueling.

When you were about 3,000 pounds from a full load of gas (80,000 pounds full) the aircraft started to become thrust limited on warmer than standard days. Pilots could sense this happening because their throttles began touching the military stops more and more frequently. We needed the additional thrust from one AB in order to stay hooked to the boom. To light the AB, the "book" answer was to disconnect from the boom, drop back to the precontact position, light the AB, trim the aircraft up, and move back into the contact position. Forget all that.

Habus learned to safely light the AB still hooked to the boom, so they were always getting their gas. I used a technique of slowly letting my aircraft drift back until I saw the bright red "go forward" light illuminate on the belly of the tanker. That way, when the left AB ignited and the SR lurched forward on the tanker, it was easy to control the rate of forward movement by immediately retarding the right throttle. Once you got the hang of timing the two throttles, the SR slowly moved forward, back into perfect position. By using the same AB each time, Habus could anticipate the same yawing motion and put in about 15 degrees of bank to compensate for the yaw. Although you flew the aircraft cross-controlled during those last few thousand pounds of fuel, it was not an uncomfortable feeling from the front seat.

Hopefully you got a pressure disconnect right at EAR and cleared the tanker down and back slightly. Once clear of the tankers, the pilot selected roll autopilot and "AUTO NAV" to start the aircraft heading on course to begin the accel. The POST-AIR REFUELING checklist consisted of monitoring airspeeds so you didn't get too slow with a maximum gross weight aircraft, closing the air refueling door, releasing fuel tank-4 boost pumps, setting up the exterior lights, and raising the seat.

The Accel

The trans-sonic acceleration called for a climb-and-descent maneuver we called the "Dipsey Doodle." The maneuver accelerated the SR-71 to supersonic speeds as rapidly as possible to minimize the time spent between Mach 1.05 and 1.15, an area of excessive drag on the aircraft. Most Habus hand flew the maneuver and engaged the pitch autopilot after they intercepted the final climb schedule. The "Dipsey Doodle" started out by lighting both ABs to their minimum setting and climbing at 0.9 Mach. As you passed through 30,000 feet, the throttles were advanced to max AB, continuing the climb to 33,000 feet and slowly increasing the airspeed to 0.95 Mach.

Approaching 33,000 feet, Habus nosed the aircraft over gently and began a descent of 2,500–3,000 feet/min. For optimum acceleration, it was important to exceed Mach 1.05 early in the descent and to avoid any turning until the climb was established. Going through Mach 1 in the SR-71 behaved no different than any other aircraft—the pitot/static instruments jumped momentarily, then settled down after passing through the sound barrier. Approaching 420-430 KEAS, the pilot started to bring the nose up slowly, so as to capture and hold 450 KEAS while climbing. Stabilized at 450 KEAS, he engaged the pitch autopilot and the "KEAS HOLD" function. For the remainder of the accel the autopilot held 450 KEAS until the KEAS bleed schedule was reached at Mach 2.6.

Pilots watched for the forward bypass doors to begin opening up at around Mach 1.4. The SUPERSONIC ACCELERATION checklist began at Mach 1.7. There, the pilot began to monitor the spike and forward bypass door positions, along with inlet pressure (CIP) for the remainder of the accel. Our checklists contained a chart that showed for any given Mach number, precisely how many inches aft into the inlet the spike should be, and what the CIP should read. Once the forward doors started to open up more than desired, the aft bypass doors were opened to the "A" position.

The next checklist was initiated after the IGV's shifted. Between Mach 1.7 and 2.3, individual IGV shifting could be felt as the aircraft lurched into fifth-gear. The respective IGV switches were placed into the "LOCKOUT" position and the aft bypass control opened to the "B" position, to again close down the forward bypass doors.

The forward doors began to close down tighter and tighter and required constant monitoring as the aircraft accelerated. The exterior lights were turned OFF to reduce the chances of being seen visually and the pitot heat turned OFF. Above 50,000 feet the RSO set the DEF systems up, and above 60,000 feet he turned the IFF off. Throughout the accel there was considerable pilot technique and finesse involved in managing the inlets. Pilots didn't automatically shift the aft bypass doors at specific Mach numbers, unless their inlet parameters said they should.

At Mach 2.6, or when the forward doors closed down to about 5 percent open, the aft bypass controls were closed back to the "A" position to open the forward doors slightly. The KEAS bleed schedule began at Mach 2.6 and called for the pilot to monitor the decreasing KEAS for the remainder of the accel. Throughout the accel, the pilot and RSO were constantly cross-checking the Mach, KEAS, and altitude relationship from charts in their checklist to ensure no discrepancies existed.

Around Mach 2.95 the pilot disengaged the KEAS HOLD function of the autopilot and began to control pitch by rotating the pitch wheel forward with his right index finger to achieve a smooth level off. He slowly lowered the nose of the aircraft until the pitch steering bar on the ADI barely touched the miniature aircraft while retarding the throttles from full AB to the approximate fuel flow readings for Mach 3 cruise.

The first thing the pilot had to decide at level off was whether to cruise with the aft bypass doors in the "A" or "CLOSE" position. He decided by watching the individual forward bypass doors to see how far they were modulating open. If the pilot felt either forward door was too far open at cruise, he left the aft bypass door(s) in "A", and if they were too tight, he set the door(s) to "CLOSE." If the mission profile called for accelerating above Mach 3.05, the aft bypass doors were generally placed in the "CLOSE" position.

If he ran the forward doors too far open (conservative) he lost aircraft performance (fuel), and if he ran them too tight he increased his risk of unstarts occurring. Throughout the mission, the pilot had to monitor forward door positioning and set the aft bypass doors accordingly to minimize drag. This is where experience in the SR-71 really paid off, knowing how (and when) to optimize the forward bypass door positions. An experienced Habu knew instinctively how to position the forward and aft bypass doors for maximum efficiency. During many of our turns, as the forward door biased more open, an experienced pilot knew he could save precious fuel by shifting his aft bypass open during the turn.

High Mach Cruise

Above 60,000 feet the airspace was all ours! On the rare occasion there was more than one SR airborne at a time, or a possible U-2 conflict existed, we coordinated our altitude separation with each other. Since there were no other aircraft to concern ourselves with above 60,000 feet, we flew the SR-71 in what is called a cruise/climb maneuver for maximum efficiency. Because of the tremendous rate of fuel consumption in afterburner cruise (around 44,000 pounds per hour initially), we flew continuously at the optimum cruise altitude for the aircraft as our gross weight decreased. That worked out to about a 100 to 150 foot/minute rate of climb for the aircraft. With a full load of gas from the tanker, Habus typically (standard day) started off a mission with an initial level-off altitude of around 71,000 feet, and by the time they were ready to descend, they were cruising up around 78,000 feet.

Soon after level-off was a good time to look in the periscope to see if the rudders were centered and trim them out if necessary. Habus kept the CG as close to the supersonic aft limit (25 percent) as possible to minimize drag caused by elevon deflection. Although the automatic fuel sequencing was designed to keep the CG aft, during the later stage of cruise, the pilot had to manually control the fuel sequencing, transferring fuel as necessary to keep the CG close to 25 percent. We generally flew the Mach programmed on the flight plan as long as "temp devs" were not a factor. Often, because of warmer temperatures, we flew slightly faster to keep the forward bypass doors running tighter. For example, if the forward bypass doors were opened more than desired at Mach 3 cruise, you could fly at Mach 3.04 to keep them closed down further.

The SR-71's cruise performance was not like other jet aircraft. In other jets, if you wanted to fly considerably faster, it cost you more fuel to do so. The SR-71 was just the opposite; the faster you flew, the more fuel you saved. For example, the specific range charts show for a standard day temperature (-69°F), a 100,000 pound gross-weight SR-71 flying at 3.0 Mach maximum range cruise has a total fuel flow of 38,000 pounds per hour. Accelerate to 3.15 Mach, and the total fuel flow drops down to 36,000 pounds per hour.

Temperature deviations (shortened to "temp devs") from the standard day would either aid or hinder us dramatically. The biggest influence on aircraft performance were the "temp devs" during the climb and acceleration. As the outside air temperatures increased you could actually feel the SR slow down its rate of climb and acceleration. At hotter-than-standard day temperatures, the inlets were not as efficient because the forward bypass doors opened more and slowed down our rate of climb during the acceleration, and required more thrust during cruise.

To illustrate the effect of temperature on the climb we'll assume the SR-71 has just air refueled to full tanks and used about 5,000 pounds of fuel for the subsonic climb and transonic acceleration maneuver, leaving a gross weight of approximately 135,000 pounds to begin its acceleration to Mach 3. Taking a 135,000 gross weight aircraft from 1.25 Mach at 30,000 feet, to 3.0 Mach at 70,000 feet with a +10°C temperature deviation from standard burns around 28,000 pounds of fuel. Under the same parameters, but with the "temp dev" now at -10°C, it burns around 16,000 pounds of fuel. That's 12,000 pounds of fuel difference from a 20°C temperature spread!

At cruise, "temp devs" from standard had a similar effect on our performance, although not as degrading as the climb performance. For example, a 100,000 pound aircraft at Mach 3 and a "temp dev" of -10°C had a total fuel flow of around 35,000 pounds per hour. With a "temp dev" of +10°C the total fuel flow jumps to around 44,000 pounds per hour. That adds up to a total fuel flow increase of about 9,000 pounds per hour for a temperature change of 20°C.

As you flew from one air refueling track to another, climb "temp devs" could change dramatically at each location. In many flying locations it was next to impossible for the weather forecaster to obtain accurate "temp devs." Cruise temperatures also changed as you hit pockets of hot and cold air masses. The CIT indicator was the pilot's only gage of ambient temperatures. We had a chart in our checklist that compared Mach number with CIT and ambient temperatures. For instance, if the CIT gauge read 328°C at Mach 3.0, the chart told us the outside air temperature had to be around -56°C. Needless to say, Habus were constantly monitoring CIT temperatures and fuel consumption, and then trying every trick in the book to stay up with the fuel curve if they found themselves up against hotter than standard day "temp devs."

Although the SR-71's cruise fuel flows are quite large, the maximum range of the aircraft compares favorably with modern day commercial jet airliners. At Mach 3.2 and standard day temperatures, the maximum specific range of the SR-71 at a gross weight of 90,000 pounds is 54.1 nm/1,000 pounds of fuel at an altitude of 78,700 feet. By way of comparison, a McDonnell Douglas DC-10 cruising at 41,000 feet at .84 Mach, at an average gross weight, has a specific range factor of 38.4 nm/1,000 pounds of fuel. A McDonnell Douglas Super 80, cruising at 37,000 feet at .76 Mach, has a specific range factor of 79 nm/1,000 pounds of fuel.

The design Mach of the SR-71 was Mach 3.2. However, when authorized by the Commander, speeds up to Mach 3.3 could be flown as long as the CIT limit of 427°C was not exceeded. The maximum altitude limit was 85,000 feet unless specifically authorized higher. There were times Habus either had to, or inadvertently, exceed the Mach and altitude limits. Former RSO Col. Roger Jacks flew to the limits on his very first flight.

My first ride was with Maj. Ty Judkins, a "throw caution to the wind" pilot who embraced a work-hard, play-hard philosophy. We had just climbed above 80,000 feet and were cruising in excess of Mach 3 when Ty said, "You want to see how high and fast she'll go?" I said hesitantly, "OK." I remembered from my B-52 flying days another pilot once reaching that aircraft's maximum airspeed and how it shook so violently I thought it was going to come apart. I was waiting for the same thing to happen in the SR-71 and thinking to myself, this is going to be one hell of a free fall down to 14,000 feet if we have to eject. To my surprise the aircraft was smooth and rock-solid as it reached its maximum airspeed and altitude[Mach 3.2 at 85,000 ft.]. In fact, it was clear to me the aircraft wanted to go higher and faster. Ty proudly announced, "well, here we are!" I managed a slowly spoken and in awe, "ya."

Former RSO, Col. Frank Stampf (Ret), explains how exceptional aircraft performance can get you into trouble you never thought of.

Extreme temperatures at altitude could affect the SR in more ways than one. In addition to much warmer than standard temperatures causing Habu crews lots of problems by robbing them of precious JP-7, significantly colder than standard temperatures gave us a whole different set of challenges.

Gil [pilot, Maj. Gil Bertelson] and I were flying a "routine" sortie out of Mildenhall into the Barents Sea. I don't remember being briefed about any specific weather problems for the track. Our mission was right out of the textbook as we broke off from our tankers and started the accel that would take us "round the bend" of the Kola Peninsula. The fact that things were going so smoothly up to that point should have made us suspect that something out of the ordinary was probably about to happen!

Not long into the accel, both Gil and I remarked that the airplane was climbing like the proverbial "Bat Out of Hell." The outside temperatures were quite a bit colder than anticipated, and that always made a difference in performance—the colder the temperatures, the "hotter" the performance. I don't think either of us were expecting quite as "hot" a ride as we were about to get. Gil started to ease the throttles back to level off at Mach 3.0. However, although we were ready to level off, the airplane wasn't! The outside temperatures were running 29 degrees below standard, almost twice as cold as either of us had ever experienced in our relatively-short Habu flying careers. The result was that the airplane just wanted to keep climbing and accelerating past Mach 3.0 and 80,000 feet.

To most aircrews flying more "normal" aircraft, that probably sounds pretty neat. Unfortunately, it put us in a bit of a predicament. If Gil let the airplane continue its climb on its own, we'd soon bump up against the minimum-allowable airspeed of 310 KEAS—

avoiding it was critical to providing aerodynamic controllability—and we were losing speed as rapidly as our altitude was increasing . If we leveled off to maintain minimum allowable KEAS, the resultant higher-than-planned Mach number would more than likely force us outside of our preplanned turn radius, and off the sacred "black line."

Our CPA tolerances were close enough without that kind of help! Since aborting the mission because the airplane was performing better than we'd expected seemed a bit embarrassing, we accepted the higher Mach, and Gil manually increased our bank angles to keep us on our planned track through the sensitive area. The mission was successful, and we learned yet another lesson about just how many different ways the SR could surprise us!

After the SR-71 cruised for about 15 to 20 minutes, the entire aircraft had heated up to cruise temperatures. This ranged from around 500-600°F on all the leading edges to 1,100°F at the exhaust nozzle area. There was very little weather (as aviators normally think of weather) to contend with above 60,000 feet, only winds and "temp devs" to consider. As a general rule, if the aircraft performed satisfactorily up to this point, it typically remained so. However, just about the time you thought the aircraft was running perfectly, it would turn around and bite you if you weren't paying attention. Shortly after level-off with everything squared away was the first time you could relax (slightly) and take in the sights of Mach 3 cruise at 72,000 feet.

At our cruising altitudes, there is very little sensation of traveling at 2,200 mph. I always had a greater sensation of speed over the ground flying a T-38 on one of our low level navigation routes at 360 knots (415 mph) at 1,000 feet. The only sense of speed at that altitude was watching the DME click off at 33 miles per minute. More than a speed sensation, Habus gained a greater appreciation of time and distance relationships. To be able to fly from California to England in only four hours, or Japan in five hours, was a remarkable feat for any aircraft!

Above 80,000 feet the horizon-to-horizon view of the ground beneath was tremendous, providing a pronounced view of the curvature of the earth. Colors in the sky were deeper and more vivid, and the sun was so brilliant that it washed out cockpit instrumentation as it moved across the panel in turns. During the day the horizon was a deep blue color, slowly changing to the black of night as you looked higher and higher above the horizon. Peering upward into the dark sky you could see stars in the daytime. Colonel Roger Jacks (Ret) remembers the first time he went to maximum speed and altitude.

I was amazed how quiet, smooth, and graceful the aircraft performed. What a feeling as an SR-71 crew member to fly so high above the earth, be awed by the beauty, and the peacefulness. It was as comforting as sitting in a movie theater seat and mentally being rocketed through space while glued to a Star Trek movie. The view outside the aircraft window above 80,000 feet was breathtaking. Below the air-

craft, the sky was a light, almost baby blue; clouds were far below and looked like small clusters of white cotton. Looking out to the horizon, the curvature of the earth could clearly be seen. At the aircraft's altitude the sky was a dark blue, and as I swept my eyes upward, the color darkened to a deep purple hue. Aerodynamically, the aircraft was so well designed that it was very difficult to slow down for a turn programmed at a slower airspeed. I quickly decided the airplane was indeed born to be a "high flyer."

One of my most memorable sights was during an SR flight to Mildenhall. We finished our refueling over Goose Bay and had leveled off at Mach 3 heading out over the North Atlantic. It was pitch black outside when the sun began to rise rapidly off the nose of the aircraft. Watching a spectacular sunrise in front of the aircraft, I peeked in the periscope just in time to see a brilliant full moon behind me, centered precisely between the two blue afterburner exhausts with their associated concentric shock waves inside. If there were only some way to capture that fleeting picture—a true Kodak moment!

Some of the most notable sights were at night crossing the North Atlantic Ocean enroute to RAF Mildenhall. The northern lights, viewed from 75,000 feet on a clear night, were a spectacle of vivid green and blue colors, moving and dancing out the left and right windows. They surrounded the aircraft in what appeared to be colorful sheets and stayed with us forever, then rapidly disappeared as the sun began to rise in the east. Former SR pilot Col. Tom Alison (Ret) explains his experiences with the northern lights:

> *One vivid memory that I have, and JT [Lt. Col. Joseph T. "JT" Vida, his RSO] and I talked about, was the experience of seeing the northern lights during the night sortie flown from Beale to Mildenhall. The route went so far north that at altitude during the cruise legs, the northern lights were also south of us. It gave the illusion of flying down a dark corridor at Mach 3 with the greenish colored lights rising like a wall above us on both sides.*

SR pilot Col. Joe Kinego (Ret) gives his version of the Northern Lights:

> *One of the most interesting flights I flew was an operational deployment flight from Beale AFB to RAF Mildenhall. The flight was scheduled to go over the North Pole, into the Barents Sea from the backside and recover at Mildenhall. My RSO was Col. Larry Elliot for this flight. We departed Beale about 2200 hours. The mission called for a "hot" departure, so we immediately accelerated and climbed above 80,000 feet and headed straight north into Canada. It was a clear, cold night, so the sky appeared as one giant Milky Way with stars everywhere. As we got further north into Canada, we started to pick up the Northern Lights. Our first air refueling was scheduled over Canada,*

and as we descended into the tanker, the Northern Lights were so bright that I thought they would hamper the refueling. I remember telling my RSO that as we were descending and decelerating it was becoming increasingly more difficult for me to remain oriented due to the brightness of the lights. I put my seat all the way down, turned up my instrument lights, and put up the "bat wings" to keep from becoming too distracted by the lights.

Depending on the time of day and which direction you were flying, most Habus could experience multiple sunsets or sunrises on one flight. Colonel Alison tells of two such occasions.

In the area of "sun chasing," several stories come to mind. The first would be the experience of seeing the sun come up in the West. The first time we saw it happen was during a night training sortie from Beale. As often as we could, we would take off just after sunset while there was still a little light at altitude. By the time we had completed air refueling, usually heading in a northeasterly direction, it had gotten dark. As we accelerated to "speed and altitude" we would eventually turn southbound and then westbound and would actually catch up to the sun on its westward journey. The experience in the cockpit, at altitudes of 70,000 feet or more, was one of seeing the horizon begin to lighten and then as we caught up with the sun, seeing it appear to rise on the western horizon.

I remember another mission when JT and I were coming back to Beale from Mildenhall. It was early in the year, probably Jan/Feb of 1977. We had gotten airborne sometime around midmorning, and it was light (the days are rather short in the UK in the winter). After our first air refueling, we headed across the North Atlantic toward our next refueling near Goose Bay, Labrador. As we headed west at Mach 3, we began to outrun the sun, and for us it "set" in the east. That made our air refueling rendezvous a night effort and it was completely dark as we got on the boom. During the refueling, the sun caught up with us, and it began to get light again. Then when we completed the refueling and again accelerated to Mach 3 cruise, we again began to outrun the sun, flying into darkness, experiencing the second sunset in about 3 hours.

SR pilot, Lt. Col. Rod Dyckman (Ret) tells how Habus could produce their own sights.

If you were brave enough to turn all cockpit lights off at night in a turn, you would get the most spectacular sight imaginable. It appeared as though you were looking at a 3-D picture of the stars. Some actually appeared closer than others—truly an incredible sight.

Habus had to anticipate every turn with a power increase. If you didn't, the Mach dropped off rapidly, possibly requiring a descent to get the speed back. A small decrease in Mach, from 3.0 to around 2.95 in a turn, could normally be regained by increasing power to maximum AB, depending on the bank angle and how far open the forward bypass doors were. A larger decrease in Mach at a constant altitude caused the aircraft to become thrust limited, sometimes requiring a descent of several thousand feet to re-establish the desired Mach.

As they entered each turn, Habus increased each throttle to about 3,000 pounds/hour on each engine's fuel flow gauge to hold the Mach steady. Constant altitude turns of up to 35 degrees of bank could normally be made at maximum-range cruise altitude by adding power. Once established in the turn, very small throttle movements held the Mach constant. During steep bank turns (more than 35 degrees), it was not always possible to maintain your cruise altitude. Whenever the aircraft became power-limited during a steep bank turn, it was better to lose altitude to maintain the Mach than to lose Mach and maintain altitude. Pilots anticipated making a descent before a 45 degree bank turn was coming up, particularly if outside temperatures were hotter than standard. To help anticipate each turn, the pilot followed along his moving map display, showing the bank angle, altitude, and airspeed for each turn.

Flying in hostile areas, Habus had a higher set of limits they could follow in an emergency, called the "tactical limits." If they found the normal operating restrictions unacceptable because of a hostile environment (threat to the aircraft), the pilot was authorized to use the tactical limits spelled out in our Dash-1. The margin of safety provided by the tactical limits was substantially reduced, and exposure to these limits had to be as brief as possible. They were to be used *only* when adherence to normal or emergency restrictions would place the aircraft in a more hazardous situation because of probable hostile actions. By applying the tactical limits, the crew could exit a hostile area at high Mach and altitude for a brief time.

On all operational missions we had to monitor a specific "Giant Talk" HF radio frequency in case someone was trying to reach us with important information. On a few occasions, an SR-71 had to be recalled back to the Det because of impending or rapidly deteriorating weather conditions. If other "National Reconnaissance Systems" thought we were straying off course, we were issued a coded HF warning message, telling us to recheck our navigation systems for accuracy. If the coded message authenticated properly and all our navigational systems checked out OK, we pressed on.

Other than the HF crackling away, the only communication was between the pilot and RSO. For Don and I, that consisted primarily of keeping each other informed of upcoming turns, so we could monitor our position around the turn and increase or decrease speed as necessary. If the True Air Speed (TAS) was too high for the turn, Don would tell me how many knots too fast we were, and I translated that into a Mach decrease. Flying the SR-71 as a formed crew was paramount for good crew coordination. If something unusual came up, or if we had an emergency, I hardly had to speak because Don could tell by the tone of my voice the seriousness of the situation. Fortunately, like most Habus, Don and I were both "go" oriented and instinctively knew neither one of us would abort a mission unless it was absolutely necessary.

The RSO made a required "Ops Normal" call on the HF radio after exiting the "sensitive area" to let everyone know the mission was successful thus far. RSO, Maj. Randy Shelhorse, recalls a special "Ops Normal" call he once made.

> On Christmas Eve, 24 Dec 1988, Maj. Warren "Mac" McKendree and I flew our 42nd operational sortie. The sortie designation was "GIANT REACH" 104I, and the area of operation was the Barents Sea, near the North Pole. After an uneventful flight through the "sensitive area" and while descending for the tanker rendezvous, I was required to make an inflight report, detailing the effectiveness of the "take." During this time, I transmitted an additional "PIREP" (pilot report) to a monitoring station in Keflavik, Iceland. I reported seeing a fat, bearded man dressed in red in a sleigh being pulled by reindeer just south of the North Pole. The female controller assured me that she would pass on this special sighting.

The Decel

The SR-71's decel was a maneuver that left little room for error. Unlike most other jet aircraft, Habus didn't have the latitude to change throttle settings at random or add and subtract drag devices to modify their rate of descent. Once the throttles were brought out of AB at 78,000 feet, the bottom-out point of our decel was basically set. The SR-71's engines and inlets had to be managed during the decel in a precise configuration to preclude unstarts, compressor stalls, and engine flameouts.

Prior to starting down, the RSO established ranging with the tanker to make sure he was there waiting for us. We continued to monitor the ARC-50 radio in case the tanker had something important to tell us or had to move the ARCP because of bad weather. As we approached our descent point, Don made some last minute calculations and adjusted our start descent point earlier or later, depending on his interpretation of the descent winds and how they would effect us. Our checklist chart showed that a 350 KEAS normal descent profile from 78,000 feet to 25,000 feet (tankers altitude) required around 170 nm and about 10 minutes to complete.

When the aircraft arrived at the computed start-descent point, the pilot slowly retarded both throttles to min AB, paused momentarily, and pulled them back further to drop into the full military position. As the KEAS began to decrease, the pilot slowly rolled the pitch wheel forward, and intercepted a speed between 350-365 KEAS for the decel. Since 350 KEAS was the minimum airspeed, most Habus wanted an extra margin of safety and descended at 365 KEAS to reduce the probability of an "unstart," engine stall, or flameout(s). As airspeed approached 365 KEAS the "KEAS HOLD" function on the autopilot was engaged. Airspeed was now controlled with pitch attitude. The descent profile required us to keep the throttles between full military power and 720°C on the EGT gauge.

At Mach 2.5 the checklist called for the throttles to be pulled back slowly and set at 6900 rpm. Passing through 60,000 feet, the RSO turned on the IFF and set the DEF systems as required. Below Mach 1.7, the fuel-forward transfer switch was turned ON to obtain a subsonic CG forward of 22 percent and the pitot heat and exterior lights turned ON. Below Mach 1.3, the inlet controls were checked in their proper positions, the spike full forward, and the bypass doors closed. The IGV switches were placed in "NORM," so they could shift normally.

After Mach 1.3, the throttles could be placed anywhere to adjust the descent profile as necessary. Once the aircraft was subsonic, we maintained 0.9 Mach, disengaged "KEAS HOLD," and leveled off with either the pitch wheel or the control stick. The descent was fairly steep by now and required about a 2,000 foot lead point to level off at the air refueling altitude. Colonel Roger Jacks recalls the steep descent.

> With the aircraft in the "AUTO NAV" mode, and about the time the aircraft reached 38,000 feet in the descent, it would all-of-a-sudden increase its pitch attitude until I started to believe it was going to bury itself and us about 100 feet into good old mother earth. I was really proud of myself one day while in this descent situation I quipped to my pilot, Joe Kinego, "What is a nice guy like you doing in a dive like this!"

Fuel tank pressure had to be monitored closely during the descent to make sure the minimum (-0.5psi) was not exceeded. If the descent was too fast, or the nitrogen supply in the fuel tanks was too low, negative fuel tank pressure readings below -0.5psi could possibly cause a tank to collapse. If the tank pressure was low, it required the pilot to level off for a while and allow the pressure to equalize.

If you were ever to have an engine flameout, it would most likely occur during the decel. Even holding the decel parameters perfectly, the engines would occasionally compressor stall and flameout for no apparent reason. A few select Habus have the distinction of logging "glider" time in the SR-71 by having both engines flame out during the decel. In most instances they were not successful in obtaining air starts for the engines at high altitudes and high Mach numbers. They usually got both engines started somewhere below Mach 1.7 and landed uneventfully. With both engines windmilling (no power), the SR-71 glide distance and time from 80,000 feet at Mach 3.2, down to 10,000 feet was 102 nm and took slightly over 6 minutes at a 375 KEAS descent. That works out to around 11,600 feet per minute rate of descent—about like a rock!

"Hot" Air Refueling Rendezvous

We leveled off from the decel 40 nm from the ARCP and 2,000 feet below the air refueling altitude, continuing to close at 0.9 Mach. Once the lead tanker was ranging on us, they began timing and controlling the length of their racetrack orbit legs, planning to end up at a precise point (abeam the ARCP) when the SR was about 15 miles out from the ARCP. The tanker navigator used timing charts, based on the distance between the two aircraft, to help him compute when to make the final turn for join up.

When the time was right, the lead tanker navigator had his pilot begin their final left-hand turn, planning to roll out about three to four miles in front of us. With ARC-50 giving us range and bearing we were allowed by "the book" to rendezvous down to one mile in the weather before we had to visually sight the tankers. To get their gas, many Habus joined up on the tankers with visibilities well below one mile. Former RSO, Lt. Col. John Manzi, describes one such important rendezvous.

Take the Blackbird's speed, add crew endurance and lots of in-flight refueling, and you get the makings of a remarkable flight. On 9 August 1987, [pilot, Lt. Col.] Terry Pappas and I reached out 6,000 miles from Kadena Air Base and touched someone. Lasting a little over 11 hours, the 12,000 mile round trip was easily the longest and most challenging of our Habu careers.

Shortly before takeoff, we entered a briefing room nearly filled with 50 or more tanker pilots, navigators, and boom operators. A fairly routine procedure, in-flight refueling was nonetheless critical to the SR-71's operation. The Blackbird needed to drink every 2,000 miles or so. We would have to rendezvous with our tanker friends five times on this mission. The weather was looking a little shaky for a couple of the planned refuelings.

Weather in the target area was cloud free, so we were certain our cameras were full of high quality images. All we had to do now was retrace our steps, find our tankers, and set the jet back on the ground at Kadena for the mission to be a success. As luck would have it, Murphy's Law took over on our fifth refueling, almost ruining our day.

Rendezvous with a tanker in bad weather demands the smoothest possible coordination between a pilot and his RSO. The RSO uses his instrumentation to guide the pilot to a position one mile behind the tanker. Nine hours into the flight, with night falling, and Kadena still about 3,000 miles away, Terry and I found ourselves facing a worst-case refueling rendezvous. We and our tankers were enveloped in featureless white clouds, thick as pea soup. We strained our eyes in a futile attempt to see the fuel-laden KC-10s holding a mile ahead of us. With our own fuel running low and safe haven a thousand miles away, we had no choice but to creep closer. We had to see the tanker to complete the rendezvous.

Moving to within a mile of tankers we couldn't see was risky business. The maneuver required the utmost discipline from all involved. *The tankers had to maintain precise altitude and speed control while we carefully closed in on them. Terry had to alternate his visual scan between his flight instruments and the dull white clouds outside his window searching for the huge tankers. Terry also had to listen as I verbalized what the "bearing needle" and "distance to go" were telling me about the tankers' positions. We approached to the point where our instruments became too sensitive to tell us anything more. We held what we had, still blind and hoping for a break. The ocean below us stretched for hundreds of miles in all directions.*

Miraculously, in-flight visibility improved just enough for Terry to slide us into the contact position. We expressed our mutual relief when the KC-10's air refueling boom "clunked" reassuringly into our refueling receptacle. We weren't able to relax for long, however, for the pea soup clouds suddenly enveloped the KC-10 once again. At times we were riding on the KC-10's boom with its big white fuselage just barely visible. Terry's smooth hand kept us well inside the refueling envelope while I ensured we took on fuel as quickly as possible without upsetting our center of gravity.

With our tanks topped off, Terry and I gratefully bid our tanker friends farewell and accelerated ahead of them on the last leg of our incredible journey. Though drained of energy and with eyes painfully dried by nearly eleven hours exposure to pure oxygen, we couldn't help enjoy the show occurring far below us as lightning danced across the thunderclouds hanging over the moonlit South Pacific Ocean.

Lieutenant Colonel Terry Pappas (Ret) recalls encountering problems on the same mission.

Every SR-71 pilot and RSO has a particular mission that he flew which ranks at the top of his list of memorable Blackbird experiences. For RSO, Maj. John Manzi, and this "nose gunner," it was easily our 11-plus hour mission flown out of Okinawa, during the Iran-Iraq war. We had 25 tankers, mostly KC-10s, plus several of our own KC-135Qs, supporting our five air refuelings. Four of our five refuelings had to be accomplished in the worst instrument weather conditions I ever had to deal with in air refuelings. Of the five hours we flew in air refueling tracks, I spent three and a half hours flying on the boom!

That grueling mission, which had us in our pressure suits for nearly 13 hours and on 100 percent oxygen for 12 hours, required John and I to use every trick we had ever learned, plus a few new ones. The relatively small confines of the mission's target area required that we fly slower, permitting tighter turns. Our speed of 2.67 Mach in the target area meant a correspondingly lower altitude was necessary to make the Blackbird's inlet system run smoothly, and allow for enough aircraft turn performance to stay on the black line. Lower and slower is not what Habus prefer, especially in close proximity to enemy fighters and surface-to-air missiles.

I remember one critical turn point in the take area vividly. We had just rolled out of a high banked turn and were racing straight at a hostile country's coastline. With 20 seconds to go before turn initiation, John quickly informed me that we had tail winds 60 knots above forecast. This meant that a higher ground speed could sling us wide on the turn, causing us to miss some vital intelligence. We had planned this turn within 2 degrees of maximum allowable bank angle for control of the aircraft. I selected minimum afterburner on both engines, but she didn't want to slow down. I knew that coming out of burner would mean a descent—wrong time, wrong place for that. I remembered a technique that I'd heard recently from one of the old heads, Lt. Col. B.C. Thomas. I quickly took the EGT controls for each engine from AUTO to MANUAL and down-trimmed each one about 50 degrees. Painfully, the Blackbird relinquished some of her excess thrust and slowed just enough for us to make the turn.

John did a masterful job of navigating us through those winding turns, out of the sensitive area, and into our third air refueling. He had no idea what was going on when I said, "Man, what a beautiful sight." I described to him the three KC-10s waiting to give us gas, with Navy F-14 Tomcats flying escort. We were still dangerously close to the bad guys to be "low and slow" on the boom of a tanker. That day I became a genuine supporter of the US Navy.

Hours later, after the fifth and last air refueling, we were cruising the last hot leg of that unbelievable mission. John and I were exhausted. Our bodies must have been on a metabolic roller coaster that matched the climbs and descents of our aircraft. We had focused so hard for so long. Just an hour and a half to go until I could pull it out of burner for the final descent into Okinawa and a night landing.

Suddenly, I couldn't read cockpit instruments. Everything was blurred. I could see the round dials and gauges but couldn't READ them. My mind was racing, and I'm sure my pulse was too. I didn't say a word to John. I was in near panic, trying to think of some way to recover my vision. I considered opening up the helmet faceplate but remembered that could prove fatal if we lost cabin pressure while it was open. Finally, I tried squinting, hard. I kept trying, for what seemed like minutes, but must have been only seconds, until finally I was able to squeeze out a tear into each eye. Miraculously, the moisture brought back my vision. Apparently, the long exposure to 100 percent oxygen and helmet faceplate heat had dried my eyes completely.

With over two hours to go still, I knew my body was in bad shape at that moment. I could feel it. I had been unable to urinate for hours. I could feel my body trying to come down from the adrenaline high that I had hit several times already on the flight. I fought hard to keep my level of concentration up and the shakes to a minimum. The Det called us to say that we could cut the arrival short and land on the opposite runway if we wanted, I told them, "No thanks." I didn't want to make any changes to our planned and briefed recovery unless they

*were absolutely necessary. I knew my body was running on fumes, and
I had to get this machine on the ground safely, and soon!*

*When we taxied into the hangar that night at Kadena, there
must have been 150 members of the detachment waiting for us, cheering and clapping. Many of them had been up over 24 hours to make
this mission work. You should have seen the pride on their faces as they
celebrated that moment. It wasn't just the aircraft, or the aircrew, or
any one member of our team. They were celebrating the magic and
spirit of the Blackbird program. I don't think there has ever been anything quite like it in the Air Force, and I doubt there ever will.*

If everything proceeded normally during the rendezvous, the
tanker cell initiated their "descend and accelerate" maneuver when
the SR-71 was one mile behind them and closing fast. The maneuver
called for the tanker cell to add power, descend 1,000 feet, and accelerate to 310 knots. We remained at our altitude (now 1,000 feet below
the tankers) until sighting the tankers visually, then slowly closed in,
and up to the pre-contact position. Normal refueling altitudes were
anywhere between 25,000 and 28,000 feet.

Not every rendezvous went smoothly. If the SR-71 crew initiated their decel too late from 78,000 feet, or the tanker crew made
their final turn too late, it was possible to end up with what was called
an "overrun". In an overrun situation it was highly probable that the
SR-71 would end up in front of the tankers, rather than behind them.
If an overrun was called out over the radio by either the tanker or SR-
71 crew, the procedure was for the tanker to descend and accelerate
immediately and the SR-71 to slow down as much, and as quickly as
possible. Often we did S-turns to help increase the distance between
us and the tankers. In any case, we eventually sorted ourselves out and
completed the rendezvous.

During a "hot" rendezvous we sometimes arrived at the ARCP
with only 10,000 to 12,000 pounds of fuel remaining, depending on
the proximity of the nearest alternate base. Once the rejoin was
accomplished there is no difference between a "hot" rendezvous and
the "cold" rendezvous previously described. The second refueling,
accel, and cruise were flown the same as described previously, except
that they generally took place in a different geographical location.

On the final descent for home, the RSO gave his last "Ops
Normal" call on the HF radio and then made a quick call to "MAMA
CONTROL" on the ARC-50 radio to give the Det the status of the aircraft
and to also find out what the current weather conditions were like. If the
mission had not gone normally, the RSO transmitted a series of coded
letters over the HF radio to alert everyone monitoring the frequency.
About 30 to 45 minutes prior to planned arrival, the Tower Officer drove
back to the tower for the recovery while the mobile crew stopped by
Operations to pick up the Det Commander on their way out to the landing runway. They positioned the mobile car on a taxiway that allowed
them to accelerate and catch up with the SR during its landing roll.

Subsonic Recovery

The final decel began as close to the Dets as possible. At Kadena that meant one continuous descent from cruise altitude to landing while at Mildenhall we had to be subsonic prior to crossing the English landmass. On the final return leg we stopped using radio-silent procedures and made normal radio calls to Air Traffic Control agencies as we descended through 60,000 feet. A courtesy radio call was made to the mobile crew about 30 minutes out from landing to advise them of any needs. Prior to starting the subsonic descent, the RSO checked that his DEF and sensor switches were OFF. The pilot changed his navigation display mode from ANS to TACAN or ILS, depending on the type of approach he planned on making. Generally, we received radar vectors to a precision final approach. With power back at idle, the SR-71's subsonic descent rate was over 6,000 feet/min.

During the subsonic DESCENT checklist, the fuel crossfeed was opened to insure adequate fuel supply to both engines during landing and go-around operations. If the runway was wet or slippery the pilot placed the brake switch to the "WET" position. Slowing down through 0.5 Mach the surface limiter light came on again, reminding the pilot to pull and rotate the handle to regain full flight control movement. In high humidity conditions the defog switch had to be held in the OPEN position for several seconds, providing hot air to dissipate any fogging that might have occurred during the descent. Lastly, the landing light was turned ON so we could be seen by the tower and the mobile crew, once the landing gear was down. Passing through 10,000 feet, most Habus couldn't wait to unlock the Baylor Bar and raise their face plate to get their first breath of fresh air after sucking on dry, 100 percent oxygen for so long. The cool cockpit air blowing over your face felt very refreshing.

The BEFORE LANDING checklist required you to compute final approach and landing speeds. The basic airspeeds were 175 KIAS and 155 KIAS, respectively, with 10,000 pounds of fuel remaining. For each additional 1,000 pounds of fuel remaining you added one knot extra to each airspeed. Whenever possible, our Dash-1 recommended we make our full stop landing with no more than 10,000 pounds of fuel remaining. For a short or wet runway, we could reduce our landing speed by 10 KIAS and our fuel to 5,000 pounds for a maximum performance landing requiring a minimum ground roll after touchdown. Fuel was transferred forward to obtain a CG between 17-22 percent for subsonic operation.

We entered the VFR traffic pattern at 300 KIAS and 1,500 feet above the ground. Flying directly over the runway, we "pitched out" by rolling into a 60 degree bank. After turning a 180 degrees, the airspeed was reduced sufficiently to lower the gear at 250 KIAS on the downwind leg. Before turning base leg the pilot quickly scanned the landing gear lights, hydraulic pressure gauges, and the annunciator panel for proper indications. Coming off the downwind leg, the base turn was a gradual 180 degree descending turn, slowing to 230 KIAS with the power close to idle. Rolling out on final approach, about one mile from the end of the runway and 500 feet, the power remained near idle as the pilot slowed the aircraft to its computed final approach speed. If a go-around was necessary, the engines accelerated quickly from idle power as the throttles were advanced to either the military or AB position.

The final approach pitch attitude was relatively steep, somewhere around 10 degrees nose up. Forward visibility during landing was good although the long nose and chines blocked out runway references beneath and to the sides of the aircraft. Normally the aircraft was flown directly to touchdown rather than attempting to hold it off the runway. The large delta wing and chine area created a large amount of "ground effect," allowing the SR-71 to float, and cushioned the landing for a smooth touchdown.

After the main gear touched down, your first action was to reach forward with your left hand and pull the drag chute handle out, deploying all three chutes. As the main chute blossomed, the pilot slowly lowered the nosewheel onto the runway by releasing back pressure on the stick. After the nosewheel was on the runway, the steering was engaged, and the brakes were checked for normal operation before jettisoning the drag chute. At or above 55 KIAS, the drag chute T-handle was pushed in to jettison the main chute onto the runway. If the crosswind was greater than 12 knots or the braking action unsatisfactory, the pilot retained the drag chute.

Practice touch-and-go landings were permitted once the fuel was below 25,000 pounds. After the aircraft touched down for a touch-and-go landing, Habus maintained the same aircraft pitch attitude and smoothly added power to full military. As the thrust started to increase rapidly, the nose had to be lowered slightly in order to let the aircraft fly off the runway smoothly at 210 KIAS. When you were ready for the full stop landing, you informed the tower in plenty of time, so they could arm the BAK-11/12 barrier, and mobile could position the car, ready for their chase down the runway.

As the aircraft passed mobile, they floored the car onto the runway, chasing after the SR-71. Racing down the runway they watched for blown tires on touchdown and a good drag chute deployment. If anything was abnormal during the landing rollout, the mobile crew advised the fliers over the radio. The mobile car caught up with the aircraft just about the time the drag chute was jettisoned, then passed along side the SR-71 to lead him back to the hangar. Clearance for the SR-71 to taxi was also clearance for the mobile car.

By now the Tower Officer was thanking everyone in the tower for their good work and started back to Operations. The mission monitor was busy making all the necessary classified notifications and filling out reports, then headed back to Operations. Some of the tanker crews were already on the ground, busy debriefing how the mission went from their viewpoint and what could be done to make it better the next time. The aircraft's crew chief had been making arrival preparations in the hangar while "Tech Reps" and others maintenance personnel started to gather awaiting the SR-71's arrival.

After Landing

The AFTER LANDING checklist consisted of disengaging the SAS channels, turning the landing light OFF, turning the right refrigeration system and the cockpit air shutoff handle ON, and turning OFF the HF radio and IFF transponder. When clear of the runway, the pitot heat was turned OFF, the fuel crossfeed closed, EGT trim switches placed in the HOLD position, periscope stowed, and RSO's viewsight turned OFF.

For all operational sorties, we taxied directly into the hangar so maintenance could download the sensors expeditiously. The mobile car preceded the SR right up to the hangar and then parked off to the side while the aircraft continued into the hangar. It was about this time Don pulled out his bright red "FOR SALE" and "ROOM FOR LET" signs and placed them over his two side windows. I could always tell when he put them up because everyone in the hangar was pointing up at the aircraft and laughing.

We followed the crew chief's hand signals, guiding us safely into the tight confines of the hangar until signaled to stop. After he gave the "chocks installed" signal, the pilot released the brakes, disengaged the nosewheel steering, and transferred fuel forward to a CG of 17 percent to facilitate downloading of sensor equipment. The crew chief's assistants were busy placing the brake cooling fans around each main landing gear. A post-flight DAFICS check was accomplished by engaging the test switch. Next we turned OFF the exterior lights, the TACAN, ILS, PVD, and the canopy seal.

After all our loose items in the cockpit were secured, we opened the canopies and locked them up. By this time the crew chief already had the ladder in place for PSD to come up to install safety pins to secure the ejection seat. The remainder of the SHUTDOWN checklist had us verifying the electrical and hydraulic back-up systems. The crew chief had been on the intercom headset as soon as the chocks were installed and cleared the pilot to shut down the engines.

The first person to greet you during engine shutdown was PSD. They reached in the cockpits and inserted the ejection seat and canopy safety pins. After the seats were safely pinned, we unlocked our pressure suit helmets and handed them to PSD, followed by the gloves, checklist, and other mission materials. Once you disconnected the parachute harness, lap belt, survival kit straps, the stirrups, both oxygen hoses, the manual parachute D-ring, communications cord, and cooling air supply hose, you were free to exit the cockpit. Most Habus waited for each other at the top of the ladder before stepping down to the hangar floor.

Debriefings

As soon as the last engine was shut down maintenance personnel immediately swarmed all over the aircraft, like bees on honey, each with a specific job to do. It was a sight to behold, watching everyone working on the aircraft in perfect orchestration. Highest priority was to download the sensors from the chine bays as quickly as possible and rush them to our Mobile Processing Center (MPC) for film development, computer processing, and analysis. The MPC consisted of around fifteen large portable vans, interconnected to each other, where all of our intelligence "take" was processed, analyzed, and disseminated to the user. After our photo interpreters first looked over the film, they immediately put out the Initial Photo Interpretation Report (IPIR), letting everyone know the success or failure of the intelligence we were sent to gather.

At the foot of the ladder, waiting for the crew to descend, was the Det Commander, the maintenance supervisor, mobile crew, and the aircraft's crew chief. Everyone was interested to hear what the pilot and RSO had to say about how everything ran. It was a quick debriefing, lasting about five minutes or so, depending on how many maintenance problems the crew had with the aircraft. Often, by the time we had debriefed at the aircraft, the sensors were already downloaded and well on their way to being processed.

After everyone finished asking questions, we jumped into the PSD van for the drive back to de-suit, and the Det Commander and mobile crew drove immediately back to Operations to get ready for the debriefing. During the drive back, our stirrups were taken off and boots unzipped to ready us for the de-suiting process. PSD recorded several routine questions about the flight and asked if we had any problems with the suit that needed fixing. Once inside PSD, it took a few minutes to remove the boots and peel the suit off. Out of the sweaty long underwear and off to the shower. We changed back into our flight suits, gathered up all our classified materials, and were off to debrief the mission.

Crews attended the operations debriefing session first. The Det Commander, Operations Officer, fliers, mobile crew, weather personnel, and mission planners attended the debriefing to ask a series of routine questions. The mission planners wanted to know if there were any unusual sightings, any problems with the route, how well the aircraft flew the track, refueling procedures, sensor operations, target area weather, and HF radio calls. Weather personnel were especially interested in "temp devs" during the climb and cruise, winds during cruise, and any other significant weather conditions. The Operations Officer wanted to know how everything went from his vantage point in the tower, and the mobile crew wanted to know if there was anything they could have done better to make the operation run smoother.

At the end of each debriefing, the Det Commander usually had a few words of praise if everything went smoothly. If it didn't, we discussed our problems and came up with ways to improve the operation next time. When the Commander stood up to leave, everyone came to "ATTENTION!", and we departed for the maintenance debriefing session. Everyone else went back to their office and began filling in classified reports that had to be sent to various agencies.

At Kadena, we stored our classified materials back in the safes and drove our Habu car to the maintenance complex for their debriefing on the second floor. At Mildenhall, maintenance personnel were waiting outside the same room and merely switched personnel after the operations debriefing was completed. All major aircraft systems (engines, inlets, electrical, fuel, hydraulics, communications, avionics, SAS, DAFICS, etc.) were represented with maintenance experts around the table.

The RSO had filled out a pre-printed maintenance form, ready to hand over to the maintenance supervisor who conducted the debriefing session. To begin the debriefing, the supervisor read from the form all the pertinent data the RSO had supplied (time above certain Mach numbers, maximum Mach, maximum altitude, CG settings, air refueling off loads, aircraft discrepancies, etc.). After the supervisor finished reading data from the form, each representative asked questions about their specific aircraft system. Once the formal debriefing was concluded, crews remained to discuss any problem areas in greater detail. Between a thorough debriefing from the aircrews and a reading of the MRS tapes afterwards, maintenance could trouble-shoot and correct discrepancies quite accurately.

Night Flying

The SR-71 was not originally envisioned to be a night flying reconnaissance aircraft. For many years its primary sensor was a basic camera system, requiring daylight and high sun angles (minimum shadows) for good photography. Our night flying training was basically an orientation in flying the aircraft at night. It wasn't until a radar imaging system was developed for the SR-71 that we could advertise a "day/night/all-weather" reconnaissance capability.

If I had to give credit to the start of our aggressive entry into operational reconnaissance sorties at night, it was through the works of Lt. Col. Bob Cunningham, one of our Det 1 Commanders in the late 70s. He had the foresight and vision necessary to keep the SR-71 viable for the future, knowing someday we would have to compete with other national reconnaissance systems that were starting to gather intelligence 24 hours a day. Bob's thinking and probing was exactly what the program needed at the time. He tried to get our minds away from the traditional ways of employing the SR-71 and to stimulate new thoughts and ideas. As radical as his ideas seemed at times, he was always thinking about what was best for the program.

Habus were not overjoyed about operational night flying with the SR. We resisted Lieutenant Colonel Cunningham's initiatives towards night flying by trying to show how dangerous it was. Cockpit visibility with the pressure suit helmet on was minimal at best. Add to that the lack of any horizon at 75,000 feet at night, the criticality of bank angles over 35 degrees, and the ever-present possibility of unstarts occurring were all real concerns to the aircrews. Former SR-71 pilot, 1st SRS Commander, and 9th SRW Commander, Maj. Gen. Pat Halloran (Ret), discusses problems with night flying the aircraft in the early days.

> *I recall that when [pilot, Major] Roy St. Martin and [RSO, Captain] John Carnahan had to bail out of their bird at night over the Nevada desert following a failure of the flight director system on descent, we had a great deal of discussion on how to best handle such an emergency, pending a fix, and just how difficult night malfunctions were in the aircraft.*
>
> *I remember Mort Jarvis and I were on a night training mission shortly after Roy's accident when we encountered severe, repeated "unstarts" on one of the inlets. That was before there were spike/door indicators, sympathetic "unstarts" systems, or automatic restart features. We had one hell of a time keeping the aircraft under control in the pitch black environment, and the next morning we were asked by Col. Bill Hayes, the 9th Commander then, to brief the full staff at the daily "stand up" briefing as to our opinions on the necessity for inlet and flight instrumentation improvements. We had plenty!*

Some of the most challenging (and rewarding) SR-71 flying for me was air refueling at night over the East China Sea. The typical scenario goes something like this: It's pitch black outside the cockpit, and you're in thick, pea-soup weather, encountering moderate turbulence with St. Elmo's fire dancing all over your windshield. Lightning is flashing all around you. The tanker's in a 30 degree banked turn, and you're having to use an AB just to stay on the boom, and to top it off, you need every drop of gas at the EAR to complete the mission. That scenario was not too uncommon, and for me, created the worst case of vertigo I ever experienced in my Air Force career—I'm positive that's when my hair started graying! However, as Lt. Col. Bob Cunningham predicted, operational night flying was to become a routine part of our worldwide reconnaissance collection capability, and we had better get accustomed to it.

Habus were convinced that the next SR-71 incident or accident would involve operational night flying. As crews we talked openly about the inherent dangers of flying the SR-71 at night and started to develop night time simulator training missions to make everyone aware of the dangers. It wasn't until several crews reported reaching bank angles well over 45 degrees at night that we started to look for help. We described our problem to Lockheed "Tech Reps," and soon they had a solution with a prototype for us to evaluate. The engineers developed a gyro stabilized horizon line that superimposed itself over the entire front cockpit panel. The bright red horizon line was projected by a laser light beam. They mounted a prototype between the seats of a T-37 and had several SR-71 crews evaluate its effectiveness during night flying. The simulator was next. The artificial horizon was well received by the crews and finally installed on the right side of the front cockpit canopy sill during the early 1980s.

The final product was called the Peripheral Vision Device (PVD), a laser beam projecting a thin horizon line that could be adjusted in brightness, thickness, and vertical position across the front instrument panel. As the aircraft pitched and rolled the red laser line also pitched and rolled across the instrument panel and gave the pilot instant orientation to the horizon. The red horizon light flashed to warn the pilot when the pitch angle exceeded 35 degrees nose up or 15 degrees nose down.

CHAPTER TWELVE

THE 1ST STRATEGIC RECONNAISSANCE SQUADRON (1ST SRS)

The SR-71 squadron's numerical designation (1st) was, and still is, the oldest in the Air Force. It was first organized as the 1st Provisional Aero Squadron in 1913 at Texas City, Texas, flying the Wright "B" Pusher. In 1966, the unit assumed its current mission of strategic reconnaissance at Beale AFB as the 1st Strategic Reconnaissance Squadron (1st SRS).

At its very peak, the 9th SRW had approximately 50 SR-71 aviators, consisting of two squadrons, the 1st SRS and the 99th SRS. Both squadrons were activated in January 1966 and with a slow, constant decrease in aircrews, the 99th SRS was deactivated on 1 April 1971. On that date, the 99th SRS Commander, Lt. Col. Harlon Hain, then assumed command of the 1st SRS.

The squadron was a humble place, located on the second floor, at the south end of a huge, sprawling flight line building numbered and referred to as "1086." The 1st SRS consisted of individual offices for the Squadron Commander, Operations Officer, administration, and crew pre-flight mission planning. A crew lounge in the squadron had a large bar at one end of the room, surrounded by SR-71 pictures and paintings. One entire wall was devoted to pictures of each SR-71 crew, posing in their pressure suits beside the airplane. The opposite wall had a picture board of the current SR-71 crews. Centered on the floor of the lounge was a large tile replica of the "Mach 3+" patch Habus wore on their flight suits. An inscription beneath the patch read, "He will buy the house a round, who steps upon this hallowed ground." That was the squadron's way of keeping the tiles clean!

A large briefing room, containing theater seats and a raised podium, was used for our squadron aircrew meetings. Once a month we set aside an entire day to get everyone available together and discussed flying safety of our SR-71s and T-38s, presented awards and decorations, and "hangar flew" the afternoon away at the squadron bar. One wall of the briefing room contained a pictorial history of the 1st SRS, tracing its earliest days of flying reconnaissance balloons in the Spanish-American War to flying the SR-71. Another wall contained chronological pictures of all the VIPs who received their "token" flight in the SR-71.

It's hard to come from a normal sized Air Force flying squadron and grasp how few SR-71 crew members actually comprised the squadron. When I arrived I thought the squadron was a ghost town, there were only nine SR-71 crews considered Combat Ready (CR) and eligible to go TDY anywhere in the world. Three of these crews were always TDY to Kadena, leaving six back at Beale. There was at least one crew on military leave and quite often another crew was TDY somewhere in the states, leaving four crews remaining in the squadron. With an instructor crew in the simulator all day and another crew flying the SR-71 on a training sortie, plus the "mobile crew," there weren't many crews hanging around the squadron.

The standard TDY tour length for crews at Kadena was six weeks at a time. Having only nine crews total, and three of them always at Kadena, it meant you could count on being gone from Beale a minimum of 120 days a year. In the early '80s, when Mildenhall became a full-time operation, we had many crews away from home in excess of 200 days.

In late 1978, Don and I were in the TOP SECRET "vault," mission planning for a high priority sortie the next day, when one of the planners told me I had a phone call from the Wing Commander's office. I had no reason at all to expect a call from his office. When his secretary, Mrs. Mary Ulmer, told me Col. Dave Young (Ret) wanted to see me in his office the next morning at 0700, I was stunned. I told Don about the phone conversation and began pondering what I (or we) might have done wrong this time. We continued our mission planning when one of the "old head" planners, Lt. Col. "Red" Winters, who overheard our conversation said, "I'll bet you've been promoted." I was a year away from even being considered for Lieutenant Colonel and never followed when promotion boards were in session. I thought to myself, "No way," but Don kept insisting that had to be the reason.

Well, as luck had it, I was promoted to Lieutenant Colonel, and that began a sequence of events which has to be a classic case of the military axiom, "timing is everything." I had been on the Intermediate Service School list when I arrived at Beale four years earlier and was deferred each year from attending because we were short of SR-71 crews. My last year (mandatory) to attend school was in the summer of 1980. I had the world's best job and didn't want to go to school any more than a man-in-the-moon but faced the grim reality that I would be replacing my cockpit for textbooks in the summer of 1980. Guess what. Because of the promotion to Lieutenant Colonel, I automatically became ineligible to attend school!

More important than the promotion, I got to stay on the crew force another year and a half flying the SR-71. I pinned on Lieutenant Colonel in November of 1979 and shortly thereafter was selected to be the next 1st SRS Commander, replacing Lt. Col. Randy Hertzog in January of

1980. Although I knew the position meant my days of flying the SR-71 were over, I already had an extra year and a half flying the Blackbird and considered myself very fortunate. I was extremely proud to be able to command the best flying squadron in the Air Force and work closely with a program to which I was deeply committed for the rest of my Air Force career.

When I first took over the 1st SRS, there was no Operations Officer, so I asked Lt. Col. Bruce Liebman to be the acting Operations Officer until one could be permanently assigned. Don and I worked well flying together, and I didn't want to split up the "Snake and Nape" team, so I asked Col. Young if Don could be my Operations Officer. He got it approved at SAC Headquarters, and we were a team once again, and Don became SAC's first navigator to hold a Squadron Operations Officer position.

For over a year, until Lt. Col. Jay Murphy was selected as the permanent Mildenhall Commander, Don and I replaced each other as the TDY Commander. When I was at Mildenhall, Don was back at Beale performing Squadron Commander duties. We barely ever saw each other and had to do most of our communicating either over the phone or with notes left behind for each other at Beale and Mildenhall. We both despised the volume of paperwork and multitude of meetings to attend back at Beale, and consequently, both enjoyed going TDY, where the "real" SR-71 missions were being flown, and life was unencumbered by bureaucracy.

One of the most fascinating stories ever to come out of the 1st SRS was that of the Airman Bruce Ott spy case. Ott was an enlisted administrative clerk assigned to the 1st SRS under the command of Lt. Col. Joe Kinego. Joe tells the following story:

> One morning I was called by the Wing Vice Commander and told to come over to his office and bring my hat. When I arrived at his office, he told me that coming to his office was just a cover story and that I really had an appointment with the base Staff Judge Advocate (SJA) at the legal office in two hours. He could not tell me what the appointment was about, but I was not to go back to my squadron before the appointment. So I spent the next two hours driving around the base wondering what was going on.
>
> When I arrived at the legal office, I went into SJA's office as directed. He proceeded to tell me that we could not talk until the "counterintelligence" people arrived and I signed my nondisclosure statement. Needless to say, this really peaked my interest. The agents finally arrived, I signed the necessary documents, and they proceeded to tell me that they believed one of my squadron members was trying to sell SR-71 secrets to the Soviets. This really shocked me, especially when they told me who it was. I was not convinced at first, but after they showed me pictures of Ott meeting a "Soviet Agent" (he was really an OSI operative—code named "Ivan") at the Davis, California, McDonald's and also let me hear the tape (Ivan was wired) of Ott offering to sell secrets, I became a believer.
>
> The next few weeks were very busy for me. I was working with the OSI to help complete the "sting" that would catch Ott in the act of passing

secrets to Ivan whom Ott thought was an actual Soviet agent. I spent hours in a motel in Yuba City meeting with agents going over plans for my squadron building, so they could identify areas where they could place video and listening devices. In the evenings at about 1800 when the squadron was empty of my aircrews, I would meet "civil engineers" (really OSI agents) who would come to the squadron to set up their monitoring devices. They always pretended to be working on the air conditioner as a cover story for their real purpose. After several nights, they finally completed their project, having installed two cameras behind a wall directly across from the safes and listening devices throughout the squadron. The goal here was to actually catch Ott taking secrets from the safe. This was very tiring for me since I would work all day and then spend several hours at night working with the agents. My family was really concerned as to why I was gone so much. I was the only one within the squadron who was aware of what was going on, and that also made life tough. I did have to tell my Operations Officer that I was working on a "special project" and to cover for me at various meetings. Other than that, it was just me and the agents and Lieutenant Colonel Swanson who were aware of what was going on.

While all this was occurring, Ott was still contacting Ivan, discussing money, and telling him how valuable he would be to the Soviets as a "deep cover mole." He planned to deliver some good SR secrets to prove his worth. A post office box was established in Marysville between Ott and Ivan where information drops were made. On one occasion they actually met in Marysville because Ott's car needed repair and Ivan had to pass some money to him for the repairs.

Finally, one night Ott came to the squadron to get secrets from the safe to pass to Ivan. Ivan had told Ott to bring the information to a motel in Davis, California, that night. The cameras recorded Ott taking the SR-71 secret documents from the safe, and agents watching from the parking lot followed Ott to Davis. Unknown to Ott, the room where he and Ivan were to meet had been refurnished by the OSI to include furniture that contained cameras and sound recorders. Additionally, agents were waiting and watching from the next room.

Ott arrived at the motel and began his meeting with Ivan. After several minutes, the OSI felt they had enough information and they broke into the room and arrested Ott, Ivan, and his "comrades." They did this to continue Ivan's cover. Ott immediately broke down and began confessing to everything even before the agents could finish reading him his rights. The whole episode was on tape.

Back at Beale, I was called after dinner to come to the legal office because the operation was "going down" that night. I remember we all sat there eating pizza awaiting the call that the arrest had been made. Finally we got the call, and we knew that Ott was heading back to Beale, not as a rich man who had completed a successful information pass, but as a prisoner. I was excited because this ended a very busy time for me.

Later that night I had to do something that was very difficult for me. In spite of the fact that Ott was trying to sell our squadron out, and in spite of the fact that his actions could have eventually cost us an aircraft *and possibly crew members, I was still his commander, and I had to meet with him and be sure all his needs were being met. I met with him briefly and told him exactly what I thought of his actions. The case went to trial several months later. I was a key witness and spent many hours on the witness stand. The final resolution was very satisfactory to me when the judge sent Ott "up the river" for 25 years in Leavenworth.*

With only 20 to 25 crew members in the squadron, and because of their senior rank, it was probably the easiest squadron in the Air Force to lead and manage. Very few crews had to be told twice, and everyone knew precisely what was expected of them. Because of the 1,500 hour minimum flying time requirement to apply for the SR-71 program, it was a very senior squadron compared to a typical Air Force squadron. Just to be competitive with other applicants, most crews had over 3,000 hours of flying before applying. Where a regular Air Force flying squadron was comprised chiefly of Lieutenants and Captains, the 1st SRS had Majors and Lieutenant Colonels as aircrews. Most of my contemporaries arrived at Beale as senior Captains and were promoted to Major and Lieutenant Colonel as SR-71 crew members.

In my new position I soon discovered that as long as everything went smoothly with the SR-71 program, General Officers at higher head-quarters willingly took the praise. However, the crews were always under a microscope, and one little screw up and the entire squadron was in serious trouble. The single most important Habu rule I tried to instill in new crews was to never, *ever*, put the SR-71 program in jeopardy by doing something stupid. We couldn't afford it because the visibility of our program was at such a high level already, there were always General Officers that would love to see our program terminated for any reason. I was always concerned that some Habu's ego would eventually get the better of him, and he'd end up placing the entire SR-71 program in jeopardy by doing something stupid.

One such incident took place later on in my career when I was the 9th SRW Vice Wing Commander. The crew was returning from a routine night training sortie when they planned to fly the SR-71 over the pilot's neighborhood, allowing friends on the ground to see the afterburners at night. They departed the standard traffic pattern and flew low over his neighborhood for better effects. What they hadn't planned on was other neighbors calling the Beale Command Post to report an aircraft flying low over their houses with afterburners lit, creating a tremendous noise. Many of the callers thought the aircraft was in trouble and about to crash. At the time, the SR-71 was the only aircraft airborne in the vicinity of Beale, so the Command Post called the SR-71 crew on the radio and asked them if any-thing was wrong with their aircraft. They reported some problems and decided to make a full stop landing before they got into more trouble. While flying their last traffic pattern, the pilot and RSO began to fabricate their story.

The story they made up about their aircraft problems sounded suspicious but believable. Soon after the incident, the pilot was at Kadena and began bragging to other Habus about his exploits with the aircraft that night. When the "word" filtered its way back to the squadron commander, he knew he had a problem on his hands. A few days later the Wing Commander, Col. Dave Pinsky, called me into his office and told me about the incident and asked the Squadron Commander to review the MRS tapes from the flight and report back. After reconstructing the aircraft's flight path (heading, altitude, airspeed, etc.) from the MRS data and listening to the voice tape, the Squadron Commander reported back to Colonel Pinsky. All three of us listened to the tape in his office. I was totally stunned by what I heard from the two Habus in the cockpit. Distinctly, you heard them concoct a story about having mechanical problems in order to justify their low level afterburner passes.

Colonel Pinsky wasn't a Habu and asked me for my opinion. After what I had just heard I deliberated for about two seconds. My recommendation was to immediately remove both of them from the SR-71 crew force. The crew had committed the ultimate sin of the SR-71 program—putting their own ego and vanity above the program. What they had done, and attempted to cover up, ran against everything I had been taught by Habus before me and what I tried to teach others.

The Wing Commander went along with the recommendation and immediately removed both the pilot and RSO from the SR-71 crew force. In defense of the RSO, it was obvious from hearing the tapes, he only went along with the deception because he was intimidated into supporting his pilot's story. Colonel Pinsky was able to keep the incident from going further up the chain of command by taking direct and positive action at Beale. Fortunately, stories like this were rare.

I could no longer avoid going to school, and in July of 1981 I turned the 1st SRS over to the able command of Lt. Col. Al Joersz (now Maj. Gen.). I was off to Air War College for a year at Maxwell AFB, Montgomery, Alabama. After school, in July of 1982, I was assigned to the Air Staff in the Pentagon, Washington, D.C.

CHAPTER THIRTEEN

THE PENTAGON

A short primer on the Pentagon helps to understand how things get done inside the building. For each and every program in the Air Force there was an officer somewhere in the halls of the Pentagon responsible for maintaining its budget. He was called the Program Element Monitor (PEM, pronounced "pim"). The PEM was *the* Pentagon expert on his program and held the purse strings tightly, looking years down the road to ensure sufficient funding. Jokingly, yet in a serious vain, the way some PEMs bartered to fund their programs, we changed their nicknames from PEMs to pimps!

Highly classified programs within the Defense Department are financed under a special funding category called the "Black World," protecting them from public scrutiny. This provides them with a relatively stabilized funding level that doesn't have to struggle and compete with the rest of the DoD budget. "Black World" funding also permits a high-risk, technologically advanced program to emerge from the research and test phase, into the developmental and prototype stage without all of the problems and scrutiny plaguing "White World" programs. Originally, the SR-71 program's funding was contained in the "Black World" budgets of the Pentagon. The Air Staff office responsible for the SR-71's "Black World" funding was located in the Research and Development directorate (office symbol RDPJ).

I quickly learned that two things were important in the Pentagon to be successful—money and knowledge! Those who could garner the greatest support for their program (money) and gain the upper hand by knowing more than anyone else (knowledge) were generally successful. I saw time and time again in various meetings the Secretary of the Air Force being swayed by a General Officer having information that others did not have. In the halls of the Pentagon, knowledge equaled power!

In the mid-1970s, SR-71 funding was moved out of the "Black World" and into the "White World." Now, for the first time, the SR-71 program had to compete for its funding along with the rest of the DoD budget. When SR-71 funds entered the "White World," responsibility for the program transferred from RDPJ to another office in the basement of the Pentagon (office symbol XOORZ), becoming its only advocate and spokesperson, fully responsible for its annual budget. Through every budget cycle, XOORZ action officers had to justify, defend, and compete the SR-71's requirements against SAC's other needs, the Air Force's needs, and the intelligence communities needs. They were competing against SAC's need to conclude its greatest modernization effort and upgrade program of all time. At the same time, the Air Force was also trying to increase its conventional warfighting capability, and the national intelligence community was placing increasing reliance on its satellite programs. Each budget cycle was an annual frenzy—full of sharks and pitfalls!

While assigned to the Air Staff (June 1982 to June 1986), I worked my first two years in a Pentagon office (symbol PRPFS) that handled SAC's portion of the Air Force budget. The programs I financially managed were the B-1 bombers, the Air Launched Cruise Missiles (ALCMs), B-52 modifications, and the KC-10 tanker. Each year our office received SAC's budget request, and it became our job to "scrub" their financial data for accuracy. As budget programmers, it was our responsibility to make sure the funds requested by SAC were not only accurate, but with the money they requested each program could accomplish its stated goal.

The mainstream of SAC, and logically their highest financial priority, were the two legs of the nuclear triad, its nuclear ICBMs and B-52 bombers. Shortly after the SR-71 funding entered the "White World," SAC's nuclear ICBMs and B-52s were beginning to age and in need of upgrades and replacements. New ICBMs and the B-1 bomber were trying to make their entry into SAC's inventory during the late 1970s and early-'80s and thus received a high priority on SAC's funding list. Competition for funding various programs was getting tough, as SAC began a major modernization of its ICBMs, B-52s, and adding B-1s to its inventory.

It was obvious SAC's interest in the SR-71 was slowly waning; it had higher priority programs to fund. The intelligence community, believing overhead satellites were the way of the future, became more vocal in comparing the SR-71's high operating costs to that of satellites. During my four years at the Pentagon, it became increasingly obvious that defending and justifying the SR-71 program was becoming more difficult. Talking daily to the XOORZ SR-71 action officers, Cols. Emmons and Shelton, it was obvious that SR-71 support within the DoD, the Air Force, SAC, and the intelligence community was slowly disappearing.

I've always believed the SR-71 program would have been better served if it had been under the command of an intelligence organization such as the CIA or NSA. At the very least they would have been more receptive than SAC to updating the aircraft with state-of-the-art intelligence sensors, enabling it to fly well into the 21st Century. The SR-71 never had a legitimate place in SAC—our entire program was always considered their "step-child."

During my last two years in the Pentagon, I worked for the Assistant Secretary of the Air Force, The Honorable Mr. Tidal McCoy, in the office of Manpower, Installations, and Reserve Affairs (symbol

SAF/MI). As his Air Force budget expert, Mr. McCoy and I attended various meetings with the two other Assistant Secretaries, the Secretary of the Air Force (Mr. Vern Orr and later Mr. Russell Rourke and Mr. Edward "Pete" Aldridge), and a host of other three and four-star General Officers in attendance. After two years of attending these meetings, I was able to predict with reasonable accuracy who was supporting which Air Force programs and who wasn't. Behind every successful program in the Pentagon was a General Officer(s) who supported and believed in it for the good of the Air Force. I was quick to learn from these meetings that the greater advocacy a program garnered, the greater its chances of being successful.

One of the more subtle (albeit, highly important) reasons the SR-71 program became increasingly "under the gun" was its decreasing General Officer sponsorship. The first seven 9th SRW Commanders (Jan 1966 to Sept 1977) were all SR-71 pilots and went on in their Air Force careers to become General Officers. As they moved on to more responsible positions throughout the Air Force, they still supported the SR-71 program because they truly understood it. Just like the "Fighter Mafia" within the Air Force, that promotes newer and better manned fighter aircraft, the SR-71 also had its sponsors and supporters early on.

The most noted advocate of all was General Jerome "Jerry" F. O'Malley, who flew the very first SR-71 operational sortie from Okinawa in March of 1968 and later became a 9th Wing Commander. He was the Vice Chief of Staff of the Air Force until October of 1983, and from the Pentagon became the four-star Commander of Pacific Forces (PACAF), and finally took over the highly coveted job as Commander of the Tactical Air Command (TAC). Having completed all the necessary requisites, there was no doubt among senior Pentagon officers that General O'Malley was destined to become the next Chief of Staff of the Air Force, replacing the then current Chief, General Gabriel (interestingly, in 1971 when I was stationed at Udorn Royal Thai AFB in Thailand, then Colonel O'Malley was Vice Wing Commander for then Colonel Gabriel, the 366th Tactical Fighter Wing Commander). Sadly though, while flying to attend a speaking engagement in Pennsylvania, General O'Malley and his wife were killed in a tragic T-39 crash on 20 April 1985. The Air Force lost one of its greatest leaders of all time, and the SR-71 program its greatest supporter.

When I first arrived in the Pentagon, the Directorate I worked under was called Programs and Resources (PR) and was led by Lt. Gen. Bill Campbell (Ret), former SR-71 pilot. Basically, he was responsible for formulating the entire Air Force budget for the DoD Five Year Defense Plan (FYDP) and had a *major* influence on which programs lived and which ones died. About the same time another former SR-71 pilot and 9th SRW Commander, Maj. Gen. John Storrie (Ret), was working in the Space Division of the Air Force Plans Directorate (XOS). Major General Pat Halloran (Ret), former SR-71 pilot, 1st SRS Commander and 9th SRW Commander, was at SAC Headquarters as the Inspector General. Former SR-71 pilot, Col. Willie Lawson (Ret), was the boss of RDPJ, where the SR-71's "Black World" funding was once maintained. Colonel Ken Collins (Ret), A-12 pilot and 1st SRS Commander, worked at 15th Air Force, March AFB, California.

In 1983, Colonel Collins visited my office in the Pentagon and said he was going to introduce me to a Habu I never heard of before. We walked down to "E" ring (called "General's row" because of the outside window view) and entered an office belonging to Maj. Gen. Mel Vojvodich (Ret). Ken walked in as if it were his home and introduced me to another A-12 pilot. I was meeting the pilot that flew the first A-12 (937) to Okinawa in May of 1967 and also flew the first "Black Shield" mission on 31 May 1967. They chatted informally about the "old days" and then talked about the future of the SR-71. I couldn't believe his office was right down the hall and I never knew it! Habus were everywhere throughout the Air Force and at all levels of command.

I'm not suggesting all these former Habus were out actively campaigning to champion the SR-71 program, but I can state with assurance other General Officers who wanted to see the SR-71 program canceled remained silent as long as these former Habus were in positions of power and influence. Unfortunately, by 1986 practically all former Habu General Officers had retired, and the SR-71 program was now left with very little support. In hindsight, it was just a matter of time before a new generation of Generals would soon be scrutinizing the SR-71 program closely, looking for means to fund their own pet programs.

Over the years our "customers" were also our vocal advocates. They included agencies such as the Central Intelligence Agency (CIA), Defense Intelligence Agency (DIA), National Security Agency (NSA), Foreign Technology Division (FTD), the military departments, theater commanders (PACAF and USAFE), and several foreign countries. Many of the intelligence agencies were instrumental in keeping the program strong during its early days but later favored satellites and other "technical means" of gathering intelligence. Colonel Lee Shelton (Ret) adds his insights to the SR-71 program's shortcomings.

> *In hindsight, our program probably contributed to its own demise by being too secretive and too aloof. Additionally, we became complacent; we did not think ahead until the mid-'80s; very little was done to establish a circle of influential "friends." We did not market the airplane or its capabilities, but stayed too long "behind the green door." When we did begin to work with the Hill and aggressively fight for improvements to the jet, we made real progress. I am convinced it was only the aggressive education program during the program's last five to seven years, with key members and committees of Congress, that fueled the debate and eventually delayed our planned shutdown in 1988.*

Surprisingly, however, during the struggling 1980s, the US Navy was probably the greatest advocate of our SR-71 missions with the

Barents and Baltic Sea sorties flown out of Mildenhall. Our ability to locate and track nuclear submarines for the Navy, in certain regions of Europe, could not be accomplished by satellites. To provide the Navy expertise on the SR-71's capabilities, an experienced Habu was permanently assigned to CINCLANT Headquarters in Norfolk, Virginia. Each branch of the military service is extremely protective of their individual "roles and missions," so it seemed ironic to me that the SR-71 program's chief advocate, in its later years, was the US Navy.

I was never comfortable with a subtle shift in mission emphasis that occurred over several years, changing from our Peacetime Aerial Reconnaissance Program (PARPRO) missions to SAC's post-SIOP use of the aircraft. When I left the 9th Wing in 1981, PARPRO was our "bread and butter" mission, and anyone who thought seriously about our Post-SIOP role of nuclear Bomb Damage Assessment (BDA) after all the "nukes" had gone off was foolish. Few Habus were ever convinced the SR-71 would survive a nuclear attack on the United States, even with all the intricate survivability and reconstitution plans SAC had created. When the SR-71 had a Quick Reaction checklist developed to get it off the ground quickly, all we were doing was falling into the mainstream of SAC's alert philosophy. I was always troubled with anything SAC mandated that changed our mode of operations into their way of thinking. They had their way of doing business, and so did we.

I always believe PARPRO was the SR-71's main purpose in life, being highly effective in "keeping the other guy honest" around the world. When I returned to Beale in 1986, the emphasis had shifted to the post-SIOP role, and PARPRO seemed to take a back seat. I was extremely surprised at the amount of planning and money that SAC had poured into the survivability and reconstitution of the SR-71 fleet in the event of a nuclear attack on the United States. If that same level of support, effort, and funding had been used to develop our PARPRO capabilities rather than post-SIOP, I believe the aircraft would not have been retired. I felt that the further we got into SAC's Post-SIOP mission of nuclear BDA, the more we distanced the aircraft from its primary function.

In the very beginning, getting the SR-71 into SAC's post-SIOP role was not out of genuine concern for the aircraft's future. In the early 1970s, SAC wanted to justify the need for a larger tanker aircraft, using the SR-71's new post-SIOP role as a requirement that needed to be filled. This led to testing an SR-71 (as well as other aircraft) on a modified Boeing 747 in July of 1972. SAC generals used the SR-71 post-SIOP requirement in order to promote their need for a new, larger tanker fleet. The result of that effort was the KC-10 program which began in the early 1980s and turned out to be one of the aircraft I budgeted and programmed for in the Pentagon in 1982.

CHAPTER FOURTEEN

BACK TO BEALE—THE FINAL DAYS

In July of 1986 I left the Pentagon and returned to Beale as the 9th SRW Vice Wing Commander. In July of 1987 I was fortunate enough to be selected to command the 9th SRW. By the time I took over the Wing, rumors were already buzzing around the halls of the Pentagon (and elsewhere) about closing down the SR-71 program. After four years in the Pentagon, I came away with the distinct impression that the SR-71 program was definitely going to see darker days ahead. At first I didn't think the program would end as soon as it did, but through my new position I began to gather a greater insight into SAC's senior leadership's thoughts, ideas, and plans for reconnaissance assets in general, and the SR-71 specifically.

The head of SAC intelligence (office SAC/IN) favored satellites over the SR-71 and wouldn't stand in the way of his boss, General Chain, who wanted to terminate the program entirely. Between 1986 and 1988 I attended several classified briefings at Offutt AFB given by the SAC intelligence community, emphasizing the future of satellites and the lack of responsiveness of the SR-71 to the theater commander. Lieutenant Colonel "Geno" Quist recalls an occasion when the SAC leadership didn't even know what the SR-71 did!

> In 1988 I was representing my office (XOORZ) in the Pentagon at a reconnaissance conference at SAC Headquarters. Upon arrival, I gave a call to our mutual Habu friends to see if we could get together for "Happy Hour." They said there was a briefing on the SR-71 at 1400 and asked if would I like to attend. I accepted their offer and attended the briefing given by Lockheed on other possible applications for the SR-71. At the end of the briefing, during a question and answer session, General Doyle, the SAC Chief of Intelligence, found out I was in the audience. He immediately turned to me, ignoring the rest of the audience and the presentation, and asked, "What is the

requirement for the SR-71?" I was so dumbfounded, I couldn't answer. If the head of SAC Intelligence has no clue what he needs an airplane for, how could I possibly have an answer. The man obviously had no idea of the value of pictures to the men and women who risk their lives to drop bombs on target.

Having worked at SAC Headquarters, Col. Lee Shelton adds his perspective.

SAC Intelligence, under General Doyle and Colonel Tanner, mounted an aggressive campaign to derail the program. They were personally responsible for significant overruns in time and money of the ASARS program. They demanded features and capabilities be present in the sensor that were unnecessary or far exceeded the requirement or capability of the intelligence community. Even after the sensor was fielded, they continued to be obstructive and to negatively influence the intelligence community on the value and application of the SR-71.

About the time I took over the 9th Wing, the ASARS was in the final stages of being fully developed. We wanted to get it up and running as quickly as possible to help stave off rumors by showing a new capability of the SR-71. The ASARS radar nose and associated ground processing equipment was sent to Det 4 and put into operational use immediately. It took several months to work all the bugs out of the airborne sensor and ground processing equipment, but the final product was a highly detailed radar image (approximating a grainy black and white photograph), giving the SR-71 improved day/night, all-weather capability. The Navy loved our ASARS imagery, but by now they were a lone voice in a sea of wolves, nipping at the heals of our program.

Friends and Enemies

During these trying times, many of us would have given anything to have General O'Malley back in the Pentagon. Everyone was scrambling to find a friend of the program—someone with high visibility who knew the intelligence value of keeping the SR-71 flying. XOORZ looked for help outside the building and finally found a congressional staffer on the Hill who worked on the Senate Select Committee on Intelligence. His name was Larry Kettlewell, and was directly responsible for the oversight of all air breathing reconnaissance programs for Congress. He was familiar with our program and firmly believed in the need for a flexible, manned, national reconnaissance system that could be sent anywhere in the world. Larry willingly accepted the challenge to fight SAC and the Air Force, in their attempt to retire the SR-71.

Larry got smart quickly by visiting Beale, Det 1, Det 4, and Det 6 so he could talk with authority about our SR-71 program. Habus assigned throughout the Air Force resisted the program's demise, but like all good soldiers we had to eventually respond to higher authority by taking actions that affected all of us very profoundly. Larry was our "White Knight" because he didn't have to follow orders and soon became our closest ally, friend, and in our hearts—every bit a Habu!

In XOORZ, Habus were being reassigned to other jobs. Lieutenant Colonels "Geno" Quist and Curt Osterheld were the last Habus assigned to XOORZ and quickly took up the difficult and lonely task of defending the program. They in particular, as well as other Habus working closely with the SR-71 program, were in a very precarious situation. As much as Habus everywhere would "die on their sword" to save the program, they also had a higher allegiance as professional military officers in the Air Force. Larry Kettlewell worked closely with everyone in an attempt to fund the SR-71 program over the strong objections of the Air Force. Colonel Lee Shelton talks about the unsung heroes.

> No history of our program would be complete or responsible without acknowledging the significant contribution made by John Latta, Mike Syracuse, Anna Hogan and the gifted staff of Adroit Systems, Inc. For the last decade of our program, these people were the genuine "force multipliers" and "phantom PEMs" responsible for the conceptualization, analysis, presentation, and integration of the major system enhancements and mission advancements we blue-suiters took credit for. If the Air Staff was the villain, these troops must be the heroes.

A vocal DoD official who expressed displeasure with the SR-71 was the Assistant Secretary for Defense for Command, Control and Communications (symbol ASD/C3), Mr. Duane Andrews. As his Pentagon title would suggest, he was an avid supporter of increased reliance on satellites to gather intelligence and used his Pentagon influence to keep the SR-71 from being a viable reconnaissance aircraft. Whenever funding support for needed upgrades to the aircraft were sought, he used his connections on the House Permanent Select Committee on Intelligence (where he once served as a staff member) to disapprove the request. Lieutenant Colonel "Geno" Quist remembers briefing Mr. Andrews when he was a Congressional staffer.

> One day in 1985, I was summoned over to the "Hill" to talk to some Congressional staffers on the SR-71 program. The two that I talked to eventually became "somebody" in the Bush administration— Mr. Duane Andrews and Mr. Marty Faga. In a closed room, these two advocates of space-based assets tried to give me their solution to all of the problems of military reconnaissance. Their idea was to "mothball" the entire SR-71 fleet but have it ready to respond to any needs the nation may see in the future. I tried to explain in vain that you needed the SR-71 support, aircrews, and infrastructure in existence before you could fly the aircraft. The fact that I had experience flying the SR had no effect on their ideas, and it soon became obvious their only answer to future reconnaissance systems was going to be spaced-based. It was just a mat-

ter of time before they were in a position to make things happen. Mr. Faga went on to become an Assistant Secretary of the Air Force (in fact he was the head of the National Reconnaissance Office) and Mr. Andrews worked in the Office of the Secretary of Defense.

Two key Air Force players instrumental in retiring the SR-71 were Generals Larry Welch and John Chain. By now there were no longer any Habu General officers standing in their way. Both individuals had different reasons for not wanting the SR-71 program around. From 1 July 1986 to 31 January 1991, General Chain was the Commander In Chief of SAC (CINCSAC) and, consequently, directly responsible for funding SAC's needs—conventional and nuclear B-52s, the B-1 bombers, and ICBM upgrades. SAC saw the annual $300 million dollar budget (varied between $300-350 million, depending on what dollars were included) of the SR-71 program as an easy place to make some trades. Consequently, what little support there was for the SR-71 program at SAC Headquarters soon turned negative.

It's important to note that General Larry Welch replaced former SR-71 pilot, Lt. Gen. Bill Campbell, as head of the Air Force's Programs and Resources (PR) directorate. General Welch first recognized the SR-71's vulnerability to being terminated when I worked for him in PRPFS. From there he went to Offutt AFB as the four-star Commander of SAC (1 August 1985 to 30 June 1986) and began laying the ground work at SAC Headquarters for the program's demise. After his brief tour at SAC, he came back to the Pentagon as the Chief of Staff of the Air Force (1 July 1986 to 30 June 1990), a position of power and influence that allowed him to complete his task of terminating the SR-71 program. Over the next four years, Generals Welch and Chain were in a position to orchestrate the demise of the SR-71.

When asked during a 12 September 1990 interview with *ABC News* about why he terminated the SR-71 program, General Welch stated it was, "too expensive, vulnerable to enemy defenses, and duplicated overhead systems." ABC news in Dallas called me later that day to ask if I would respond to General Welch's comments on the SR-71. They taped an interview the next day but unfortunately didn't report on *ABC News* that evening what I thought were the relevant issues against retiring the SR-71.

Many experts contend it would be easier to render a predictable satellite out of commission than to shoot down an SR-71. During my 15 year association with the SR-71 program I had the necessary security clearances, giving me access to many classified reports and analyses both at SAC Headquarters and in the Pentagon, concerning the vulnerability of the SR-71 to the latest Soviet defenses. Many of these studies were computer generated scenarios pitting the SR-71 against the latest thoughts on enemy tactics. My own conclusion is that the air-to-air threat to the SR-71 is nonexistent, and the Soviet SA-5 and SA-10 Surface-to-Air Missiles (SAMs) pose a minimal threat to the aircraft. However, no matter how many studies I read or had briefings on, I always came away with the same conclusion (and still do today), that it would take "a Golden B-B" to down an SR-71.

One of the primary reasons the senior Air Force leadership gave for closing down the SR-71 program was that it was an aging aircraft, becoming more and more difficult to maintain. Nothing could be further from the truth. After DAFICS was installed, aircraft reliability and maintainability increased dramatically. The supply system had sufficient spare parts and more spare J-58 engines than ever in the history of the program. The aircraft were running better than they ever had before—like a good bottle of wine, the SR-71 fleet got better with time!

Once the senior leadership of the Pentagon made their feelings known about the fate of the SR-71 program, it was easy for others to join the "band wagon" and participate in its demise. Lieutenant Colonel "Geno" Quist recalls the events at one particular Pentagon meeting.

> During the budget cycle at the Pentagon things can get rather hectic to say the least. At one point in 1988, things had gotten to the point where we had a Budget Review Board (BRB) meeting on a Saturday. We all showed up in "civvies"—kind of a relaxed atmosphere. The senior officer of this BRB was General Leo Smith. We (the various program managers) each briefed our programs, and questions were asked as necessary. As I finished my briefing, the "proposal" was made at the head of the table that the Air Force would fund the program at a level that would not include Palmdale. I was at the other end of the room from the head table and made the comment, "Without Palmdale, we will not be able to run the program, nor will we be able to bring it back, if directed." General Smith looked me directly in the eye and said, "We don't want you to be able to bring back the program." In some degree of defense for Air Force leadership, General Bracken, in AF Logistics at the time, did point up to General Smith that closing Palmdale was in effect making a "hollow and unsafe" program. However, his comments had no effect. "Geno" also had problems in his own Pentagon office, XOORZ.
>
> Shortly after I got into XOORZ, I was tasked to answer some questions we had received from Congressional staffers. I prepared my response, let Curt Osterheld read it, then gave it to our office Deputy, Lt. Col. Lou Campbell, a former U-2 pilot. Lou read through it and gave it back unchanged saying, "Looks great to me—good job!" Then I passed it to Col. John Woody, our Chief of XOORZ. He came back to my desk a while later, literally shaking with rage, threw the red-inked paper on my desk saying, "We can't send this out of here. It doesn't say what they want to hear." I told him, "The paper has only facts and truths, and I will not change it, just to speak the party line."
>
> One of the references he questioned was the fact I referred to a letter signed by President Reagan, supporting the SR-71 program. He said, "Who do you think wrote that letter? Probably (Col. Lee) Shelton and (Lt. Col. Bob) Coats from this very office, so it doesn't mean a

thing." I tried to explain that everything a President signs is probably written by someone else, but when a paper has his signature on the bottom it's an excellent indicator he believes in it. Additionally, nothing was ever received in the Pentagon, to the best of my knowledge, indicating President Reagan never changed his mind. So now we have an Air Force Colonel actually questioning the President of the United States because he wants to support General Welch and his merry band of yahoo generals. My reply to this whole scene was, "I quit! I will not compromise my integrity for the sake of general officers manipulating the system to get themselves promoted." Later, I was told Colonel Woody made the statement, "I've never heard of anybody just quitting an Air Force job. I don't know what to do." In the end, I think the paper was left much as I had written it, but I suspect there were many other changes made as it made its way back to the staffers.

Other Pentagon offices had also joined the "band wagon" as "Geno" recalls.

I was coordinating a paper I had written on defending the continuation of the SR-71 program. It was classified at the SCI level since it had "overhead" information in it, so I had to hand-carry it everywhere. When I got to General Fogleman's office (PR), he would not let me in his office but made me give the paper to his executive officer (probably against regulations but I had to do it). General Fogleman changed the bottom line (conclusion) of the paper into a false statement, then gave it to his "exec" to bring back to me and send me on my merry way.

I reviewed it prior to departing his office, noticed the falsehood, and asked the "exec" if I could go in and talk to the General about it. I was told, "No, that's what the General wants to say." Basically, his change said the United States could actually launch a satellite earlier than scheduled (and, of course this would preclude the need for the SR-71)—something that has never been done and probably will never happen. The tough part of all of this was my name stayed on the paper as the author. I took the paper to one of my bosses, General Craft, who finally called General Fogleman, and we got the paper changed to at least a bit of the truth.

In the late 70s and early 80s, the buzz words running around the intelligence community were having a reconnaissance system capable of transmitting "real-time imagery directly to the theater commanders." Real-time imagery is possible with electro-optical cameras and various other imaging sensors. However, when an all-weather, day or night, radar imaging sensor is used, it requires a slight delay to process the digital imagery and transmit it directly to a theater commander. In the intelligence world this is called "near real-time" imagery.

Habus realized early on that a major drawback of the SR-71 was having to land and have its sensors downloaded, processed, and finally disseminated to the user. Photographic imagery could be ready in about two hours after the SR-71 landed, and a dedicated courier air-craft flew the pictures directly to the user. It was a time-consuming process. On the other hand, our ELINT intelligence could be sent out quickly via secure electronic communications, directly to the user.

Satellites were being developed with the ability to receive and transmit secure digital images anywhere in the world. In the late 70s, a program called "SENIOR KING" was developed for the SR-71. It would have modified the aircraft with computers, digital processors, and a long conformal antenna down the top of the fuselage, enabling it to uplink via satellites "near real-time" digital radar imagery to a the-ater commander. This was our *key* opportunity to obtain the flexibili-ty we needed and be able to compete with satellites.

Unfortunately, SAC did not think the "SENIOR KING" modi-fication, at a cost of $10 million per aircraft, was justified, and the pro-gram was never funded. This short-sightedness on the part of SAC and the Air Force in the late '70s was the very beginning of the SR-71's struggle to compete in a new era of world-wide intelligence gathering capability. Later on, a downlink antenna was tested out on the belly of the fuselage to transmit digital radar imagery to a ground receiving station for processing into pictures. Likewise, it was not funded. Colonel Shelton reflects on the "SENIOR KING" program.

The SR-71 with ASARS and "SENIOR KING" would have been one of the most potent air-breathing collectors ever. SAC was not in the datalink architecture business until our program proposed one. When we did, however, our datalink architecture did not conform to what General Doyle suddenly wanted (a SAC-owned and operated, Omaha-based network paid for by our development effort). He then campaigned against this technology as aggressively as he had against ASARS.

The U-2 and the SR-71 were considered to complement each other by having their own unique intelligence gathering capabilities. While the U-2 is used as a standoff reconnaissance platform from a high threat area, it has a distinct advantage in its ability to loiter in an area of interest in excess of 10 hours or more. On the other hand, the SR-71 can directly overfly a high threat area, and because of its tremen-dous speed, its time to gather intelligence is relatively short. Compared to the SR-71, U-2 aircraft are cheap to operate. Lieutenant Colonel "Geno" Quist recalls a conversation he had in the Pentagon, compar-ing the SR-71 and U-2.

I knew from USAF Academy days the executive officer to an Assistant Secretary of the Air Force at the time. The executive, Col. Don Rakestraw, once finding out I was the Program Manager for the SR-71, would call me directly whenever any questions came up. More than once I literally ran up from the basement location of XOORZ to the "hallowed" fourth floor on E-ring. The Assistant Secretary was Mr. Jim

McGovern, and he was in many ways "clueless" on the SR-71, or recce in general, so when he had problems, he needed help! Once when I was beckoned to his office, he was on the phone to the Secretary of Defense at a breakfast meeting. Every time SECDEF asked him a question about the SR, he would cover the mouthpiece and ask me the answer! What a zoo that was!!

Curt Osterheld and I were called up to Mr. McGovern's office (at this particular time he was Acting Secretary of the Air Force) to discuss the program and its possible cancellation. He asked, "Why should I support the continuation of the SR-71 program?" Curt and I gave our normal, fact-based reasons, one of which being the virtual invulnerability of the SR and the complimentary capabilities of the U-2. He said, "Why can't the U-2 do everything, it's high altitude and cheaper?" We explained how in an overflight situation, with surface-to-air missile threats, the U-2 could get shot down. His response was, "Well, we'll just have to send a U-2 to do the job, and when it gets shot down, we'll have a excuse to go in with our fighters and bombers."

During the SR-71's troubled years, the 9th Wing's U-2 aircraft were being modified and updated with highly sophisticated sensors as part of its continuing upgrade program. Advances in electro-optical capability, digital radar sensors, and secure global satellites gave U-2 missions increased emphasis around the world. Although the SR-71 and U-2s were part of a total reconnaissance package, one could logically conclude that having the U-2 perform so well did not help the SR-71's cause.

Between 1987 and 1988, "Geno" and Curt working in XOORZ developed numerous funding proposals for both SAC and the Air Force, showing various levels of retaining the SR-71 in the inventory. It was a gamble, but if they could sway the senior leadership that a reduced number of SR-71s, flying at a lower sortie rate, could cover the globe at a cheaper cost, they might be able to fend off those who wanted the program completely terminated. One of their proposals had two aircraft stationed at Det 1 and Det 4, and three SR-71s at Beale including the "B" model, for a cost of $155 million a year.

Another proposal they developed had five SR-71s flying at Beale and the two Dets closed down to a caretaker status. The idea was for SR-71s to deploy from Beale to either Det and gather intelligence where ever "hot spots" developed around the world, keeping our civilian and military leadership thoroughly informed. The costs for that proposal was somewhere around $100 million a year. General Welch wouldn't hear of it and didn't want anything short of complete termination of the program, so the reduced SR-71 options died quickly.

To put all those proposals into perspective, the recent Heavy Bomber Force Study performed by the Pentagon estimates that the cost of *one* B-2 bomber is sure to exceed $700 million dollars! Trading one B-2 bomber that will most likely never be used in a future conflict for flexible, all-weather, day or night, "near real-time" global intelligence by SR-71s makes eminent sense.

With the demise of the Soviet Empire, the world is so unstable that it's now impossible to predict which third-world country we'll need to gather intelligence on tomorrow. In the "New World Order" scheme of things, the SR-71's capabilities are needed more today than they were five years ago!

Finally, through a lot of hard work and persuasion, Larry Kettlewell had Congressional language put into a senate bill that directed the Air Force to fund the SR-71 program at a reduced level of $155 million. The SR-71's opponents in the Pentagon knew there was a push on the Hill to add money to continue flying the aircraft. They drafted a letter for the Secretary of Defense to sign and sent it to Senator Danniel K. Inouye (D. HI), Chairman, Subcommittee on Defense, Committee on Appropriations, in an effort to thwart Larry's efforts. The letter reads as follows.

> As part of scheduled floor action on the FY 90 Defense Appropriation Act, I understand the Senate will consider reinstating funding for the SR-71 reconnaissance aircraft program. I strongly urge the Congress to adhere to the President's position not to seek funding for the SR-71 in FY 90.
>
> As you know, the Administration was forced to make some very tough budget decisions this year. On the airborne reconnaissance program, I had to balance the cost and capabilities of the SR-71 against other resource requirements. In deciding not to proceed with the SR-71, I did not ignore the need for an airborne reconnaissance capability. You may be assured the Department will continue to provide an airborne reconnaissance complement to our other collection systems for use in peacetime and crisis. The SR-71 is simply not a cost effective solution to our needs at this time.
>
> In legislative decisions made over the last several weeks, the Armed Services and Intelligence Committees of both House and Senate have refused to support the continuation of the SR-71 program. I urge you and your colleagues to remain consistent with this approach and defeat any efforts to sustain the SR-71.

Even over the objections of the Pentagon, a bill was passed directing the Air Force to fund the SR-71 program at a reduced level. However, the Air Force totally ignored the provisions in the defense bill and never put a penny into the SR-71's operating budget.

Around this time also, SAC Headquarters had just come out with their Operational Plan (OPS PLAN) for the phase-out of the SR-71 at both Dets and at Beale. The plan had lots of guidance, but offered little help in its execution. Throughout 1987 and 1988, Habu emotions were running extremely high, as no one wanted to move a muscle to help close down the program. Weekly we heard new rumors that the program might still survive in some capacity, and the last thing any Habu wanted to do was to go too far into terminating the program, such that it couldn't be revived. Every Habu knew that at some point during the shutdown process we would eventually reach that final point of no return—collectively, we referred to it as, "putting the final nail in the coffin." Consequently, every step we took in closing down the program we delayed until the last possible moment.

A Need for the SR-71

"What enables an intelligent General and a wise military leadership to overrun others and achieve extraordinary accomplishments is foreknowledge"—San Tzu—Circa 500 B.C.

I am absolutely convinced that had Desert Storm kicked off in early 1987, the SR-71 program would never have been retired. During an interview with *Aviation Week and Space Technology*, Lt. Gen. Charles A. Horner, Central Command's air component commander said there is a "big BDA (Bomb Damage Assessment) flap within the defense community which would indicate we may have been overly entranced with some forms of intelligence collection." This was an apparent reference to the Air Force decision to abandon the SR-71 and rely instead on satellites.

General Norman Schwarzkopf and DIA Deputy Director for Intelligence, Capt. Robert Brown (USN), openly criticized intelligence handling during the Persian Gulf crisis. After the war, Captain Brown told a Senate Armed Services Committee that, "fast, accurate BDA will save lives." Too many pilots had to restrike targets that couldn't be verified as destroyed the first time. General Schwarzkopf asked the Senate Committee for, "a new military reconnaissance system that can deliver a real-time product to a theater commander when he requests it. Current intelligence focuses too much on national systems—meaning satellites—that respond mainly to Washington."

Iraq was covered in clouds for nearly half of the Gulf war. Captain Brown complained that existing systems, including the newest Lacrosse radar satellites, "did not provide enough definition for accurate battle damage assessment." The Lacrosse radar imaging satellite, launched in December 1988 is the only spacecraft aloft with the ability to image through clouds. Apparently, the all-weather satellite coverage was not continuous enough to spot small unit movements with sufficient accuracy, nor rapid enough to supply battlefield commanders with timely information. Captain Brown asked the Senate Committee for broad-area, synoptic coverage (a general view of a whole, characterized by comprehensiveness) that could be used at night and through clouds. Desert Storm pilots were sent into combat with target photographs over 24 hours old—we did better than that during Vietnam!

It turned out that the Air Force had to purchase France's Spot satellite imagery (10 meter resolution) in order to rehearse key missions in Operation Desert Storm. Major General William K. James, Director of the Defense Mapping Agency, told the House Intelligence Committee that the extensive use and dependence on foreign satellites for intelligence should, "cause all of us some concern." Many Air Force officials believe the SR-71's presence could have played an important role prior to the outbreak of hostilities because of its ability to rapidly cover large areas of land in a high threat environment.

The SR-71 could have flown unimpeded, daily reconnaissance sorties directly over Baghdad gathering intelligence, further frustrating Saddam Hussein's efforts. I often wonder whether Saddam Hussein would have even invaded Kuwait if the SR-71 had been flying routine reconnaissance sorties over Iraq months before? We'll never know the answer to that question, but do know that he might have thought twice about the act he was about to take if he knew he was being watched. An example of how US resolve from the SR-71 gets translated into action involved the German government. US Intelligence reports indicated that a West German firm was building a ballistic missile site in the Libyan desert. SR-71 flights confirmed the sites being built, and our government politely told the West German government to get their people out of there. They had no choice but to comply.

The synoptic coverage provided by the SR-71 is far superior to satellite reconnaissance. Broad area coverage from different approach angles, in a relatively short time span, produces considerably better intelligence than a predictable single satellite pass every 90 minutes. The SR-71 flew two missions into the Persian Gulf to image the entire Iranian coast at one time and provided a benchmark for forces location, all because the overhead community simply did not have the capability to provide the coverage. The synoptic intelligence gathered on those two missions provided the baseline for all subsequent follow-on "recce" sorties by tactical and overhead reconnaissance assets, as the Iranians moved their Silkworm missile sites, patrol craft, ground forces, aircraft, etc., to other locations.

The unique ability of the SR-71 to acquire the Electronic Order of Battle (EOB) simultaneously with the imagery (either optical or radar) and make random passes over the area of interest can not be accomplished by the most sophisticated satellites. Synoptic coverage is something satellites cannot provide. A very astute follower of the SR-71 wrote in the December 1990/January 1991 issue of the Smithsonian's *Air & Space* magazine:

> . . . *The real tragedy, however, is the loss of important intelligence gathering capabilities. Had the SR-71 been available last August, the Bush administration might have had notice of the impending Iraqi attack against Kuwait. ABC News reported in September that US spy satellites lost track of eight divisions of Iraqi Republican Guard as they were supposedly "pulling back" from the Kuwait border shortly before the invasion. Other sources have said that Secretary of Defense Richard Cheney turned down an urgent request by senior military leaders in the region to reactivate the SR-71 fleet in order to provide crucial intelligence when other overhead coverage was unavailable.*

Satellites are ideal for checking fixed targets (such as military test sites or manufacturing plants) at regular intervals. Changing a satellite's orbit, either to bring it over a specific point on short notice or to make it less predictable, eats into its precious fuel supply, and when that supply is gone the satellite is junk. Reconnaissance satellites must be replaced every five years or so while aircraft can last at least 30 years. The SR-71 by contrast, can be sent over any point on the globe, any time surveillance is required.

The value of the SR-71 for reconnaissance stems from a very extraordinary and unique capability, its capability to sustain extremely high-speed, high-altitude flight for long periods of time. And, what makes the airplane extremely valuable is its unpredictable high-speed flight path, that permits it to arrive at a target area unannounced and collect high-resolution intelligence data without allowing those targets time to cover up or move assets. Of all the currently operating reconnaissance platforms, satellites as well as aircraft, the SR-71 is the only one that has all of the following capabilities: survivability, wide-area synoptic coverage, unpredictable flight paths, and global range. Accordingly, the SR-71 can collect intelligence data that is otherwise unobtainable.

The Bitter End

In the end, funds never materialized for continuing the SR-71 program, and we finally had to plan for the future. At Beale, Det 1, and Det 4, talk began to revolve around reassignments for SR-71 military personnel and what to do with the aircraft's assets and facilities. Confusion reigned. Everyday, some office at SAC Headquarters phoned to ask me why certain steps of the OPS PLAN were not being taken at Beale or the Dets. Lieutenant Colonel John Manzi, discusses the deep emotion during the final days.

Even as we celebrated SR-71 milestones and anniversaries, the Blackbird program was dying a slow and painful death. From 1988 through 1990, the squadron suffered budget cuts which grounded aircraft, the crews, and severely restricted flying hours. Through two complete budget cycles our hopes of saving the program were alternately raised and dashed by rumors from Washington. The final blow came late one evening when Congress sacrificed the program in the name of budgetary compromise. Numbed from the constant cycling of emotion, I actually felt relief when the axe finally fell on the program.

Even as the program was approaching its scheduled closing day, 30 September 1989 (end of the Fiscal Year), there was still hope among ardent SR-71 supporters that the program would remain alive in some fashion. During the summer the SR-71 participated in the Paris Air Show (7-12 Jun 1989) and the Oshkosh Air Show (28-31 July 1989). While awaiting a final decision, Habus continued to fly proficiency sorties between 1 October 1989 and 22 January 1990. Operational sorties were flown right up to the bitter end, the last one occurring on 7 November 1989, with pilot Lt. Col. Tom McCleary and RSO Lt. Col. Stan Gudmundson. The final SR-71 operational sortie was exactly 21 years, 7 months, and 17 days after the first operational sortie.

After months of turmoil and agonizing speculation, filled with constant rumors, SAC established a date for the final SR-71 flight—26 January 1990. It was only fitting that the last 1st SRS Commander, Lt. Col. Rod Dyckman, and his RSO, Lt. Col. Tom Bergam, flew aircraft 960 on the last SR-71 sortie. Although retired from the Air Force at the time, I was there for the highly emotional and somber event. Rod flew beautiful passes over the field that day. As I stood among the crowd to watch the aircraft fly by, I found it hard to believe that the skies over Beale would never be graced by its presence again. For so many years our SR-71s were part of Beale's landscape, and suddenly it felt uncanny that this was to be the last flight. Finally, Rod brought 960 to a halt in front of the crowd, and the reality of the occasion set in once again. While it seems incongruous that one of the prime architects of the dissolution of the SR-71 program would attend, General Chain (CINC-SAC) made an appearance at the final ceremonies.

That evening, a dinner ceremony, honoring the final flight of the SR-71 was held in the Beale Officers' Club. The dining room was overflowing with people who had supported and flown the aircraft over the years, including local community leaders who were close to the SR-71 program. All the former 9th SRW Commanders in attendance were introduced by Col. Jim Savarda, the 9th SRW Commander. Each received a warm round of applause, and probably the proudest moment of my entire military career occurred when my wife and I were introduced. Everyone in the entire room suddenly got up from their chairs and stood there clapping, cheering, and hollering as we acknowledged the introduction. The standing ovation went on for what seemed like several minutes.

The applause and cheering for my wife and I that night were totally spontaneous. What most people don't know, is that I was removed from command of the 9th SRW by General Chain in November of 1988 because the SR-71 program phase-out was proceeding too slowly and met resistance to SAC Headquarters plans in every step of the way. Politics demanded someone in command who didn't have SR-71 roots, so that the termination could proceed on schedule and without adverse publicity. The heartfelt emotional response from Habus that evening told me that my efforts to confront the termination of the SR-71 program were appreciated by those I cared for the most.

My wife and I were extremely proud to be among Habu company that evening. After dinner, one of the SAC General officers present said to my wife and I, "I think we just heard a political statement by way of that applause." General Chain was also present that evening, and some of the Habus still on active duty may have "paid the price" because only one of the ten Majors up for promotion to Lieutenant Colonel that year made the list. These were all first class officers, and this was the first time the SR-71 crew force had such a high passover rate. Surely this could not be a coincidence, but a fallout of the political execution of the SR-71 program!

Mr. Ben Rich, representing the Lockheed "Skunk Works," was the keynote speaker that evening. Ben had worked side-by-side with "Kelly" Johnson in designing the SR-71 and was a close friend of all the Habus. His speech compared the SR-71 to Lockheed's F-117 "stealth" fighter, the B-2 "stealth" bomber, and other current technological advances in aviation. In every comparison he spoke of that night, the SR-71 was unparalleled for purpose and design. His speech was perfect for the occasion and received a standing ovation.

The last 1st SRS Squadron Commander, Lt. Col. Rod Dyckman, had plenty to cope with during those final days. Besides having his crews passed over for promotion, they were getting jerked around on TDYs and finding it difficult in their search for other Air Force jobs. Rod recalls the turmoil during those final days.

> My tenure began in November 1988 and ended when I retired, and the squadron was disbanded in July 1990. This was the best of times and the worst of times for me. As you can imagine, to be the squadron commander of the Blackbird unit was the greatest thrill of my life. To see the politics used against the mission and the airplane, which resulted in a slow painful death of the unit, was very disheartening. Nonetheless, in the waning moments of the program's history, the airplane and the crews continued to set records and perform at the sustained unmatched level noted throughout the history of the program.
>
> From the beginning of my tenure as commander, we were under the gun to cut the program. SAC (and Congress) had reduced our appropriation to around $200 million for the Fiscal Year. SAC, trying to run our operational business, demanded that we cut the crew force. Instead, my Operations Officer, Lt. Col. Mike Smith, and I along with the support of the Wing Commander and Deputy Commander for Operations, resisted. We submitted changes to decrease sortie length while increasing the productivity of each mission. SAC didn't buy it, but we resisted change and eventually won a minor battle. We kept our operational crew strength at 1988 levels.
>
> We knew that our days were numbered. In fact, one and one half years earlier, I was told by Brig. Gen. Al Rogers, the SAC/DO and a long-time friend of mine, that Air Force support for the SR-71 program was non-existent and that it was just a matter of time before the aircraft and mission were put to bed.
>
> The threat to close Kadena (Det 1) became stronger in early 1989. We had not acquired any significant new missions, and the Korean DMZ was saturated with coverage from the U-2 and other reconnaissance platforms. We fought to keep two crews and two airplanes at Kadena and were successful until we lost 974 in March 1989. After that unfortunate occurrence, we did not know from month to month if we were going to need to send TDY crews to the island. As with

all uncertainty, this wore on the crew members and created frustration in scheduling. Mildenhall continued to operate per status quo, but uncertainty about our future at Det 4 was mounting. This also caused frustration for crews and their families.

Nineteen eighty-nine was a tough year for all of the Air Force (and the military in general). The Soviets had thrown in the towel, and peace supposedly broke out all over. Many in Congress sided with the Air Force's position that the SR-71 was no longer needed, but many felt that there was still a need for the reconnaissance provided by the Blackbird. Therefore, we were either called or visited several times by Congressional staffers asking questions concerning the mission and our position on the matter. The fact that Congress was reaching to the lowest level of command (1st SRS and the 9th SRW) for answers concerning the vitality and viability of the program did not sit well with the Chief of Staff of the Air Force. My crew members and I did our best to answer questions honestly and objectively without stepping directly on the toes of the Air Force hierarchy (even though you can only imagine how bad we wanted to!). Staffers gave us positive vibrations and assured us that the war was not over. Unfortunately, the Charles Keating scandal allegedly involved some of our strongest supporters. Another strike against the program and more tension for my squadron.

Congress and their staff support were not the only agencies asking about the future of the SR-71. Many news sources from the Discovery Channel (Wings) to local news stations to ABC national news interviewed crew members from my squadron. Again, my crew members couched their remarks, being objective, but cautiously supporting the Air Force position. Again, these interviews frustrated the Air Force senior staff. As 1989 proceeded, uncertainty continued to mount. Then came the biggest disappointment in my tenure as squadron commander.

A total of ten of my officers were up for promotion to Lieutenant Colonel—eight in the primary zone and two previous passovers. Only one of these officers was promoted! Only the most skilled airmen and the highest caliber officers are chosen for the SR-71 program. The reason for hiring skilled aviators goes without saying, but the need for outstanding officers was equally important. We were very critical of our crew members official personnel records when we chose them. The bottom line—most all SR-71 crew members were exceptional officers who deserved to be promoted. The low promotion rate gave us the feeling that possible discrimination against the SR-71 crew force was used during the promotion cycle. An Inspector General (IG) inquiry was started, but action was delayed until the program was terminated, and the crew members dispersed.

At the end of the fiscal year it was all over but the shouting, and even though we continued to fly into the next fiscal year, the SR-71 program as we knew it was over. Eventually, we brought the overseas aircraft home and began to set up a schedule for dispersing SR-71s for permanent static display. The crew members shared the wealth of their last *flights. Everyone got a final Blackbird "hot" flight that was considered their last sortie. Most got one or two more subsonic flights when they ferried airplanes to the SR's new static display home.*

During the final days, the squadron existed on paper only. The airplanes were gone, most of the crew members were reassigned, and the only work to be done was to relocate the memorabilia that had been collected around the world during the 25 year history of the aircraft. My final task while on active duty was to construct a memorial to the 1st SRS at the Beale museum. A small sized heritage room was recreated at the museum and outfitted to resemble the 1st SRS. The heritage room, the scrap books, the static SR-71, the friends, and the memories of the crew members are about all that is left of this great airplane and squadron.

This may all sound like "doom and gloom" but nothing could be further from the truth. These were the best of times for me. Even though our days were numbered and there were disappointments, this was the best job, working with the best people of my Air Force career. I have never enjoyed a job as much as I liked being the 1st SRS Commander, and I believe that I never will have a better job. Flying the SR was the thrill of a lifetime and commanding the unit was the greatest opportunity of my military career.

Once the official word was out that the SR-71 program was going to be terminated, requests for using the SR-71 as a static display poured into the Air Force Museum Headquarters at Wright-Patterson AFB, Ohio, which had a major vote in where the aircraft would be sent. Between 12 February 1990 and 27 March 1990, ten SR-71 aircraft were ferried by Habus to their final resting places throughout the United States. The good news is, the SR-71 was so heavily requested for static displays and museums around the country that the majority of Blackbirds will be available for the rest of the world, as well as my grandchildren, to enjoy. They will be able to look back in awe of a "unique" aircraft that was built well ahead of its time. Appendix A contains a disposition list of all the aircraft.

Closing up and Preserving History

During the final days of the 1st SRS, Lt. Col. Dyckman had no SR-71 crew members to command (although they continued to fly the T-38 until reassigned), only assets to manage. The SAC and Air Force personnel systems were not "beating down the bushes" to help SR-71 crews find their next job, many of which were passed over for promotion to Lieutenant Colonel. You learn quickly in the Air Force that no organization wants take on a passed over Major into their ranks. Consequently, most of the crews had to search for their next assignment on their own.

Over the years, the squadron had amassed tons of classified documents and historical records that had to be disposed of properly. Rod and the few remaining crews worked closely with the Beale museum to preserve as much of the Blackbird and Habu legend as possible. Some of the 1st SRS memorabilia is stored and displayed at the museum.

A room on the upper level of the Beale museum has been used to recreate the 1st SRS crew lounge. Our crew lounge was the one place where Habus could gather in late afternoon and into the night to trade "war stories" and talk openly about their classified missions while having a beer and eating peanuts. The recreated room contains all the SR-71 crew photographs, the large bar, the Mach 3 floor patch, our first operational sortie crew ties, a Habu snake, historical albums, and a picture board of the final squadron crew members. The room contains other significant historical plaques and momentos that have a profound meaning to this special group of aviators. Habus owe Rod a deep debt of gratitude for preserving a small, but highly significant piece of Blackbird history. The museum also displays a J-58 engine, a "Buick" start cart, pressure suits, and various sensors carried on the SR-71.

At the request of the 9th SRW, the Air Force approved the U-2's 5th Strategic Reconnaissance Training Squadron (5th SRTS) to be redesignated as the 1st SRS. On 30 June 1990, the 5th SRTS became the 1st SRS, as the 22 year marriage between the 1st SRS and the SR-71 was officially terminated. With the demise of SAC in 1992, the 1st SRS was shortened to the 1st Reconnaissance Squadron (1st RS) and continues its proud heritage with the 9th RW at Beale AFB today.

Over the years, many flying records were set by SR-71 crews. Those who were fortunate enough to set the official records, we owe a debt of gratitude. However, there's not a speed or altitude record on the books that most Habus have not surpassed at one time or another. Some of those unofficial records will remain with each and every Habu forever. The following list of lifetime achievements includes all of the Blackbird family (YF-12, A-12, and SR-71):

Total Operational Sorties: 3551
Total Hours: 53,490 Total, 11,008 Operational
Mach 3+ Time: 11,675 Total, 2752 Operational
Total Sorties: 17,300
Total Persons to Mach 3: 389 (284 crew members and 105 VIPs)
Crew members over 300 hours: 163
Crew members over 600 hours: 69
Crew members over 900 hours: 18
Crew members over 1000 hours: 8
Total number of operational SR-71 pilots: 93
Total number of operational SR-71 RSOs: 89
Most SR-71 flying time: Lt. Col. Joseph T. "JT" Vida with 1,492.7 hours

One Last Record

On 6 March 1990, nearly two months after the SR-71 was officially retired from the Air Force, an SR-71 (972) set four international speed records while being delivered to the Smithsonian National Air and Space Museum at Dulles International Airport, Washington, D.C.

The record flight had been canceled at least once by General Welch, presumably he didn't want *any* favorable publicity concerning the SR-71. The flight was finally pushed through by certain Lockheed executives, politicians supporting the SR-71, and a small cadre of lower ranking but influential Air Force officers. Had it not been for the initiative of these Air Force officers, the media would not have been informed about the record breaking event, much to the wishes of those who wanted no more publicity for the SR-71.

Just to show how wide the rift was between senior Air Force commanders and supporters of the SR-71 program, no senior Air Force officers attended the event. Dignitaries greeting the SR-71's arrival at Dulles were Ben Rich (Lockheed ADP), Dr. Martin Harwit (Director, National Air and Space Museum), the Honorable John Warner (Virginia Senator), and Lynn Helms (former CIA Director).

The aircraft was flown by Lt. Col. Ed Yeilding (pilot) and Lt. Col. Joseph T. "JT" Vida (RSO) who were assigned to the Palmdale, Plant 42, Flight Test Facility. I was fortunate to attend the record-breaking ceremony at Dulles and get together with Habus once again. The next day, Senator John Glenn closed the final chapter on the SR-71 by making a speech on the floor the Senate. His words were profound and to the point. He chastised the Department of Defense for lacking the moral leadership to utilize the aircraft at its full potential.

> While it is undoubtedly true that the SR-71 fleet was not being utilized to its fullest potential, I believe that this shortcoming could have easily been redressed by the Department of Defense and by no means warranted program termination. In view of the high costs of other Air Force programs, the costs of this program and its benefits were both affordable and reasonable.... The SR-71 provides coverage on demand with little or no warning to the reconnaissance target—it is a highly flexible system ... the SR-71 is able to penetrate hostile territory with comparatively little vulnerability to attack unlike other reconnaissance platforms.
>
> While opponents of the SR-71 have argued that national technical means are capable of performing the same mission, these systems are less flexible and survivable than the SR-71. ... In retiring the SR-71, the United States has essentially removed itself from the strategic aerial reconnaissance business. Intelligence systems such as the SR-71 are the eyes and ears for our Nation's defense and are therefore true force-multipliers.
>
> Mr. President, the termination of the SR-71 was a grave mistake and could place our nation at a serious disadvantage in the event of a future crisis. Yesterday's historic transcontinental flight was a sad memorial to our short-sighted policy in strategic aerial reconnaissance.

NASA Takes Over

Throughout 1989 and 1990, as the rumors of terminating the SR-71 program were getting stronger, NASA began to take interest in the potential use of the aircraft. Having flown three YF-12s during the

70s as a high-altitude/high-speed test aircraft for NASA engineers, they saw the retiring SR-71s as an excellent platform to work on the development of the X-30, National Aerospace Plane (NASP). The X-30 is envisioned for speeds up to Mach 25, and the SR-71 would provide an excellent platform for testing equipment and new materials in a 500-1,000°F environment.

Prior to the time of uncertainty surrounding the SR-71 program, Det 6 had already contracted with Singer-Link for $22 million to upgrade the SR-71 simulator. Over the years our simulator had become increasingly unreliable and difficult to maintain and no longer closely "simulated" the aircraft. Unfortunately, the SR-71 program closed down while the simulator overhaul was in progress.

Singer-Link finished the simulator in late 1990 and had to have it certified as acceptable and meeting Det-6's contract specifications. There were no experienced crews remaining at Beale to certify the simulator, so logically Lt. Col. Rod Dyckman and Col. Don "Snake" Emmons crewed up together and flew to New York to evaluate the new simulator. It performed beyond expectations and paralleled aircraft performance perfectly. When NASA made a proposal for the use of three of Beale's SR-71s it also included the new simulator, which was then shipped to Edwards AFB.

Besides the two "A" models, NASA also received the "B" model trainer, 956. The "B" model was already at Palmdale receiving a major overhaul before the SR-71 program ended. After the SR-71 program was "financially terminated," funds to complete the "B" model overhaul were sought and found. Lieutenant Colonel Rod Dyckman (Ret) took a leave of absence from American Airlines in June 1991 to fly the Functional Check Flight (FCF) on 956. Originally, NASA wanted Rod to fly the FCF as a subsonic sortie until he convinced them otherwise. Instinctively, every Habu knows that you don't learn a thing about how well the SR-71 will perform unless it gets up to Mach 3 speeds.

Since NASA didn't have anyone current in the SR-71, Rod flew two more sorties in 956 to check out one of the NASA pilots, Steve Ishmael, who in turn, would check out their other NASA pilot, Rogers Smith. Flying under civilian registry, NASA redesignated 956, 971, and 980 to tail numbers 831, 832, and 844, respectively. NASA developed a talented flight and maintenance crew for operating their trio of Blackbirds. Many Habus have offered NASA free assistance and technical advice to keep their SR-71 program up to speed and the birds in the air.

CHAPTER FIFTEEN

THE HABU RETURNS!

During Desert Storm, the question was raised about bringing back the three SR-71s to gather intelligence lacking from other sources. More recently (March/April 1994), as tensions increased between the United States and North Korea over inspection of their nuclear sites, the questions of reactivating three SR-71s was asked once again. The 23 May 1994 issue of *Aviation Week & Space Technology* reports;

> *A recent Lockheed study concluded that reactivating three SR-71s and operating them for one year would cost $79.8 million. Requested by Pentagon policy analysts, the study said three to six months would be needed to reactivate the aircraft, in storage at Palmdale, Calif. Interest was piqued while North Korea was a hot topic in February, when Clinton Administration officials learned that an SR-71 could take off from Palmdale, gather photographs and radar imagery of all Korean nuclear sites and land at Kadena AB five hours later. Lockheed studied reactivation several times in the past, usually to a hostile Pentagon reception, but the February exercise went into greater detail, including locating all the sensors to equip three aircraft. Emotions for and against the SR-71 still run strong in the Pentagon, and an official stressed that the Lockheed study was "hip-pocket" only—to weigh options available with low budgets and to facilitate rapid decisions if a crisis occurred.*

The *New York Times* reported in July of 1994 that Senator Byrd (D. WV) and other members of the Armed Services and Intelligence Committees were led to believe by the Pentagon back in 1990 that a successor to the SR-71 was in the works, and that's the reason it was being retired. I remember well, all the rumors going around about a successor to the SR-71 being developed—faster, higher, and more capable. It was all part of a disinformation campaign that began in 1987 by those who wanted to see the SR-71s retired. Senator Byrd and others have now discovered there is no successor and are attempting to revive three SR-71s.

On 29 August 1994, *ABC World News Tonight* profiled the possible reactivation of the three SR-71s in a very unfavorable manner. They obtained their information on the SR-71 program from the Center for Strategic and International Studies (CSIS) in Washington, D.C., and it was riddled with outrageous errors of fact. On the program, they stated that the cost of operating the SR-71 was $700 million per year! During the last year of the program there were thirteen aircraft flying, nine of them operationally, at a cost of only $220 million. The program went on to state that the newest version of the U-2 (with an improved engine) can fly the same mission as the SR-71. The U-2 aircraft, however improved, will never be able to fly over a high-threat area because of its slow speed and vulnerability to both air-to-air and surface-to-air missiles.

The last issue raised on *ABC World News Tonight* is whether it's better to spend money on new systems aimed at the future rather than spend it on SR-71s. This argument falls precisely in line with an article I wrote for the *Air University Review* in 1984, concerning the military-industrial procurement process and titled it, "Better Than is the Enemy of Good Enough." I borrowed the phrase from an anonymous Soviet General officer who was trying to make a point about the inherent dangers of buying new military hardware. It's common knowledge that a large portion of the Pentagon's budget and manpower, as well as that of major defense contractor's, is devoted to always searching for something "better than" what already exists.

No one disputes the fact that research and development is necessary. However, while the search goes on for something "better than," the existing system is placed at a high risk of obsolescence. General officers and others in Congress who believe they have the "big picture" or "the reconnaissance road map of the future" tend to push aside funding for current systems while patiently waiting for "better than" to come along. As Senator Byrd and others pointed out about the SR-71's successor, sometimes "better than" never becomes developed, and the entire process is at the expense of "good enough." To design, build, and test a system with capabilities similar to the SR-71 in an era of a constrained defense budgets would be impossible.

Even today there are painful reminders of how the SR-71 was left behind in a world of rapidly increasing technological sophistication. In an *Aviation Week* report on airborne intelligence sensors, Congress had been prodding the Pentagon for an integrated reconnaissance strategy for the post-Soviet world. In November 1993, authorization conferees stated that the multi-spectral imaging sensor under development for U-2 aircraft was on the Pentagon's chopping block and argued it should be retained. They went on to state that their "experience with the SR-71 serves as a reminder of the pitfalls of failing to keep existing systems up-to-date and capable in the hope of acquiring other capabilities."

With the SR-71's demise, defense contractors as well as the Pentagon saw a reconnaissance void that needed to be filled. It had to be an aircraft that was cheap to operate, could "dwell" over the area of interest for long periods of time, and was able to fly in a high threat environment. The obvious answer to fill all three of these requirements were unmanned aircraft, better known today as Unmanned Aerial Vehicles, or "UAVs" for short.

Two of the current UAVs in competition have been labeled the "Tier 2 plus" and the "Tier 3 minus." The stealthier Lockheed/Boeing Tier 3 minus UAV(Darkstar) is an offshoot of the secret Tier 3 project that was canceled because of high costs (thus the new "minus" label). The Tier 3 minus UAV is expected to cost around $10-12 million each and be able to dwell undetected over a target area for a minimum of 8 hours. To keep costs down on the Tier 3 minus UAV, it was designed to be a Very Low Observable (VLO) flying wing, rather than incorporating the more costly stealth technology.

The non-stealthy Tier 2 plus UAV(Global Hawk) is expected to loiter for 24 hours over a target area and have a range of 3,000 miles at 65,000 feet. Both UAVs are expected to share the same Synthetic Aperture Radar (SAR) and electro-optical camera sensor systems; however, the Tier 3 minus can only carry one sensor at a time. Supporters of UAVs were naturally concerned over competition from the SR-71s possible return. Bringing back the SR-71 had many quarters of the Pentagon, as well as certain defense contractors, in a state of panic. Many were worried about their programs being on the "chopping block" to fund the SR-71's return. Others were worried about the competition from the aircraft and the impact it may have on their own programs. To stave off concern about competition with the SR-71, "Conferees also agreed to add about $100 million to bring three SR-71s back to operational status but emphasized that would not prejudice support for long-endurance UAVs."

On 29 September 1994, Congress passed the $244 billion defense authorization bill for Fiscal Year 1995. Congressional language, adding $100 million to bring three SR-71s out of storage, was included in the defense bill. In mid-April 1995, Congress rescinded $27.5 million leaving the program with $72.5 million. The Air Force wants nothing to do with the return of the SR-71s and consequently has not budgeted for the aircraft. It will be up to congress to fund the program each year, making it extremely difficult to plan for the future. Former Habu and Det 4 Commander, Col. Jay Murphy (Ret), now working for Lockheed, was chosen to be the Program Manager for Lockheed's participation in reactivating the aircraft. Former RSOs, Colonels Don Emmons (Ret) and Barry MacKean (Ret), working under a government contract, were brought back to pull the logistics and support structure for the aircraft together.

The Air Force asked former SR-71 pilots and RSOs still on active duty if they would like to volunteer to fly the reactivated aircraft. On 29 January 1994, three crews were selected to fly the aircraft. The pilots are Gil Luloff, Tom McCleary, and Don Watkins. The RSOs selected were Blair Bozek, Mike Finan, and Jim Greenwood. The crews and aircraft will be under the command and control of the 9th RW at Beale and remain at Edwards AFB as Det 2 of the parent wing. They are flying two SR-71s (971 and 967) and share the "B" model and simulator with NASA.

On 26 April 1995, aircraft 971 flew its first sortie with NASA crews at the controls. Since then, all three crews have completed their recurrency training and are now mission ready. Aircraft 967 was modified with a data link to provide "near real-time" transmission of ASARS imagery to ground sites; 971 should be modified early in 1996. It should be noted that an exceptional effort by the NASA crews has made the reactivation a "seamless" process. The smooth transition for the Habu's simulator training and "B" model training was exemplary in every respect. In January the entire Det 2, 9th Reconnaissance Wing moved into a renovated hangar at Edwards AFB. The hangar houses the two aircraft, as well as maintenance, logistics, and operations personnel. The sole person on active duty with the Air Force who has put in more sweat and toil to make the reactivation work is Capt. Mike "Z-Man" Zimmerman. The entire Habu community owes him a debt of gratitude for all of his efforts.

Participating in a recent Red Flag Exercise over the Nellis AFB, Nevada range, an SR-71 acquired 70 of 84 targets assigned in only four minutes, using TEOC cameras only. The 14 targets were missed due to weather and the resolution on the rest was considered outstanding. The following reactivation numbers are current as of 13 March 1996.

Sorties flown: 56
Flying hours: 134.5
Air Force crew sorties: 26
Air Force/NASA sorties: 16
NASA sorties: 14
Single loop sorties: 51
Double loop sorties: 5
First A-model flight: 26 April 1995
First Air Force B-model flight: 27 June 1995
First Air Force A-model flight: 25 July 1995
Max speed to date: Mach 3.23
Max altitude to date: 81,400 feet
Three OBCs validated
Six ASARS validated
Six TEOCs validated
All DEF systems operational

The Habu Spirit Lives Forever

Regardless of what future is in store for the Blackbirds, the Habu community will continue to perpetuate its legacy. It's difficult for those who didn't belong to imagine the closeness of this small group of aviators and their associates. Those of you who belonged to a fraternity or sorority may be able to partially understand this special relationship. And those of you who have shared a combat experience, i.e., lived and died together, can understand the higher level of brotherhood reached among Habus. As one who has experienced combat, I must tell you that there is no higher level of comradeship, brotherhood, or fellowship than that experienced among Habus. In a very special way they are closer than brothers, more faithful than an old dog, and more dependable than a beating heart. I know of no military relationship that is all-encompassing as the respect, admiration, and friendship that each has for his fellow Habu!

Despite all the efforts to terminate the SR-71 program, the people who built it, equipped it, maintained it, and flew it, have a unique relationship with each other that will never die. Every two years in Reno, Nevada, our "Blackbird Reunion" brings together all the people who have a common bond and fondness for the Blackbird family of aircraft. The very first reunion was held in 1975 and was strictly a A-12, YF-12, and SR-71 reunion. Subsequently, the U-2s at Davis-Monthan AFB, in Tucson, Arizona, were assigned to Beale and were included in all future reunions after 1975. Hence, the "SR-71 Reunion" transitioned into the "Blackbird Reunion" as we know it today. Even after the SR-71 was retired, the "11th Blackbird Reunion", held on 1-4 June 1995, brought over 630 people together to trade "war stories" and reminisce over the past.

The most accurate accounting of operational SR-71 aircrews lists 93 pilots and 89 RSOs who have flown the aircraft. Several Habus and close friends of the program have passed away over the years. After a long illness, the SR-71 designer, Clarence L. "Kelly" Johnson, died in December 1990. Ben Rich, the number two man under Kelly Johnson and designer of the SR-71's inlets, died on 5 January 1995.

Lieutenant Colonel Joseph T. "JT" Vida (Ret) was the first of my contemporaries to pass away. He arrived at Beale AFB in August of 1974, where he crewed up with Tom Alison and flew the SR-71 operational for the next six years. When he saw his days of flying the SR getting slimmer and slimmer, his love and devotion drove him to volunteer for a flight test position at Palmdale. In August of 1980, he began flying SR-71 flight-test missions and eventually became Chief of the SR-71 Flight Test Division. On 6 March 1990, JT and Ed Yielding flew 972 across the United States setting four world speed records before turning the aircraft over to the Smithsonian Air and Space Museum at Dulles International Airport. They set the coast-to-coast (2,404 miles at 2,124 mph) world speed record in 67 minutes and 54 seconds. JT had more flying time in the SR-71 than anyone in the world—1,392.7 hours! In giving 16 continuous years to flying the SR-71, JT knowingly sacrificed promotion, placing the program above his own personal gain. He was one of our most highly respected crew members, who believed very much in the SR-71 program and gave it his all. This book is dedicated to the deep devotion and Habu spirit JT gave to the program.

He was laid to rest after a long, courageous bout with cancer. Habus from all over the United States were present. After a 21-gun salute and taps, an Air Force Captain presented JT's flag to his wife, Sherry. A NASA F/A-18 provided a final tribute, a high speed fly-by, in full afterburner on the deck, pulling up smartly out of sight. As the aircraft passed directly over the grave-side ceremony, its high speed and treetop-level pass created an overpressure, causing dozens of car alarms in the area to be activated. It was a perfect fly-by for someone who deserved so much more. A group of Habus surrounded his casket, and Col. Tom Alison (his SR-71 pilot) gently placed a HABU patch on top of it before it was lowered. One final Habu salute to JT as Tom called out, "PRESENT, ARMS! . . . ORDER, ARMS!" There wasn't a dry eye among us as we turned and slowly walked away.

On 20 December 1989, Palmdale's SR-71 made a final pass down the Burbank runway to honor all those who worked in producing the greatest aircraft of the 20th Century. Ben Rich, head of Lockheed's Skunk Works, planned the fly-by and had Kelly Johnson there to watch. Although too sick to get out of the limousine or say anything, Kelly had tears in his eyes as he heard the SR-71 roar past the crowd. Lockheed employee, Jim Norris stood there that day and watched the Blackbird pull up and disappear out of sight from the Burbank airport. As Jim watched the aircraft drift out of sight, he recalled the first flight of the SR-71. On that cold December day back in 1964, as the SR-71 pulled up out of sight and became no more than a dark pinpoint, a crew chief standing next to Jim Norris murmured in awe of her beauty and grace, "Her enemies will never be natural." How difficult it must have been back in 1964, to predict that the Blackbird's only real enemies in the end, were as natural as you and I.

Appendix A
Current Aircraft Status Roster

A-12924 Blackbird Airpark, Palmdale, CA
A-12925 USS Intrepid Museum, New York City, N.Y.
A-12926 Lost
A-12927 California Museum of Science, L.A.
A-12928 Lost
A-12929 Lost
A-12930 Huntsville Space and Rocket Museum, AL
A-12931 Minnesota ANG, St. Paul, MN
A-12932 Lost
A-12933 San Diego Aerospace Museum, CA
YF-12934 Aft section used to make SR-71C
YF-12935 Wright-Patterson AFB Museum, OH
YF-12936 Lost
A-12937 Palmdale, CA
A-12938 USS Alabama, Mobile, AL
A-12939 Lost
A-12940 Museum of Flight, Seattle, WA
A-12941 Lost
SR-71950 Lost
SR-71951 Pima Museum, Tucson, AZ
SR-71952 Lost
SR-71953 Lost
SR-71 954 Lost
SR-71955 Edwards AFB Museum, CA
SR-71B956 Edwards AFB, NASA (renumbered NASA 831)
SR-71B957 Lost
SR-71958 Warner-Robbins AFB, GA
SR-71959 Eglin AFB, FL
SR-71960 Castle AFB, CA
SR-71961 Hutchinson, KS
SR-71962 Palmdale, CA, storage (USAF)
SR-71963 Beale AFB, CA
SR-71964 Offutt AFB, NE
SR-71965 Lost
SR-71966 Lost
SR-71967 Edwards AFB, CA, USAF
SR-71968 Palmdale, CA, storage (USAF)
SR-71969 Lost
SR-71970 Lost
SR-71971 Edwards AFB, CA, USAF
SR-71972 Smithsonian Museum, Dulles Annex, VA
SR-71973 Blackbird Airpark, Palmdale, CA
SR-71974 Lost
SR-71975 March AFB, CA
SR-71976 Wright-Patterson AFB, OH
SR-71977 Lost
SR-71978 Lost
SR-71979 Lackland AFB, TX
SR-71980 Edwards AFB, CA, NASA (renumbered NASA 844)
SR-71981 Hill AFB, UT

Appendix B
Abbreviations

AB Afterburner
AC Alternating Current
ACC Air Combat Command
AD Aerodynamic Disturbance
ADF Automatic Direction Finding
ADI Attitude Directional Indicator
ADP Advanced Development Projects
ADS Accessory Drive System
AFB Air Force Base
AFCS Automatic Flight Control System (autopilot)
ALCM Air Launched Cruise Missile
AIC Air Inlet Computer
AIM Air Intercept Missile
AMRAAM Advanced Medium Range Air to Air Missile
AMS Avionics Maintenance Squadron
ANS Astro-inertial Navigation System
AOA Angle of Attack
APW Automatic Pitch Warning
ARCP Air Refueling Control Point
ARCT Air Refueling Control Time
ASARS Advanced Synthetic Aperture Radar System
AWACS Airborne Warning And Control System
BDA Bomb Damage Assessment
BOQ Bachelor Officers' Quarters
CAPRE Capability Reconnaissance
CG Center of Gravity
CIA Central Intelligence Agency
CINCLANT Commander In Chief Atlantic
CINCSAC Commander In Chief SAC
CIT Compressor Inlet Temperature
CPA Closest Point of Approach
CR Combat Ready
CRM Cockpit Resource Management
CSD Constant Speed Drive
CSIS Center for Strategic and International Studies
DAFICS Digital Automatic Flight and Inlet Control System
DC Direct Current

DCI Director of Central Intelligence
DEF Defensive (systems)
DIA Director of Intelligence Agency
DME Distance Measuring Equipment
DMZ Demilitarized Zone
DPM Drips Per Minute
DPR Duct Pressure Ratio
DV Distinguished Visitor
EAR End Air Refueling (point)
ECM Electronic Counter Measures
EEG Electroencephalogram
EGT Exhaust Gas Temperature
EIP EMR Improvement Program
ELINT Electronic Intelligence
EMR Electro Magnetic Recorder
ENP Engine Nozzle Position
EOB Electronic Order of Battle
EPT Effective Performance Time
FAI Federation Aeronautique Internationale
FCF Functional Check Flight
FCS Fire Control System
FRS Flight Reference System
FTD Foreign Technology Division
FYDP Five Year Defense Plan (budget)
GAO General Accounting Office
GCA Ground Controlled Approach
GCI Ground Controlled Intercept
GIB Guy-In-the-Back
GMT Greenwich Mean Time (Zulu)
HF High Frequency
HSI Horizontal Situation Indicator
I & W Indications & Warning
ICBM Inter Continental Ballistic Missile
IGV Inlet Guide Vane
IFF/SIF Identification Friend or Foe/Selective Identification Feature
IG Inspector General
ILS Instrument Landing System
INS Inertial Navigation System
IP Instructor Pilot, or in navigation usage, the Initial Point
IPIR Initial Photographic Interpretation Report

JRC Joint Reconnaissance Center
KEAS Knot Equivalent Air Speed
KIAS Knot Indicated Air Speed
KOOM Kadena Officers' Open Mess
MOA Military Operating Area
MRS Mission Recording System
KTAS Knots True Air Speed
NASA National Aeronautics & Space Administration
NASP National Aerospace Plane
NATO North Atlantic Treaty Organization
NCA National Command Authority
NOFORN No Foreign (dissemination)
NOTAM Notice To Airmen
NRO National Reconnaissance Office
NSA National Security Agency
NWS Nose Wheel Steering
OBC Optical Bar Camera
OER Officer Efficiency Report
OL 8 Operating Location 8
OL KA Operating Location Kadena
OL RK Operating Location Ryukyu
OPSPLAN Operational Plan
PACAF Pacific Air Force
PAR Precision Approach Radar
PARPRO Peacetime Aerial Reconnaissance Program
PCS Permanent Change of Station
PEM Program Element Monitor
PSD Physiological Support Division
PVD Peripheral Vision Device
RAF Royal Air Force (British)
RAM Radar Absorbing Material
RCD Recorder Correlator Display
RCR Runway Condition Reading
RD Rapid Decompression
RSO Reconnaissance Systems Officer
RW Reconnaissance Wing
SAC Strategic Air Command
SAC/DOSAC Director of Operations
SAC/INSAC Director of Intelligence
SAM Surface to Air Missile
SAS Stability Augmentation System
SECDEF Secretary of Defense
SES Shock Expulsion Sensor
SIOP Single Integrated Operational Plan

SLR Side Looking Radar
SRC Strategic Reconnaissance Center
SRS Strategic Reconnaissance Squadron
SRW Strategic Reconnaissance Wing
STAN/EVAL Standardization/Evaluation
TAC Tactical Air Command
TACAN Tactical Air Navigation
TAS True Air Speed
TDI Triple Display Indicator
TDY Temporary Duty
TEB Triethylborane
TEOC Technical Objective Camera
TR Transformer Rectifier
TS Top Secret
UAV Unmanned Aerial Vehicle
UCD Urine Collection Device
USN United States Navy
UHF Ultra High Frequency
VHF Very High Frequency
VLO Very Low Observable

INDEX